Study Guide

for use with

International Economics
Tenth Edition

Peter H. Lindert
Thomas A. Pugel

Prepared by

Kerry Odell
Scripps College, Claremont

IRWIN
Chicago • Bogotá • Boston • Buenos Aires • Caracas
London • Madrid • Mexico City • Sydney • Toronto

© Richard D. Irwin, Inc., 1996

All rights reserved. No part of this publication may be reproduced, stored in a retrieval system, or transmitted, in any form or by any means, electronic, mechanical, photocopying, recording, or otherwise, without the prior written permission of the publisher.

Printed in the United States of America.

ISBN 0-256-14027-8

1 2 3 4 5 6 7 8 9 0 P 3 2 1 0 9 8 7 6

CONTENTS

Preface v

1. International Economics Is Different 1

The Theory of International Trade

2. The Basic Theory of International Trade 3
3. Why Everybody Trades 11
4. Who Gains and Who Loses from Trade? 19
5. Growth and Trade 29
6. Alternative Theories of Modern Trade 37

Trade Policy

7. The Basic Analysis of a Tariff 43
8. Nontariff Barriers to Imports 53
9. Arguments for and against Protection 61
10. Pushing Exports 67
11. Trade Blocs and Trade Blocks 77
12. Trade and the Environment 97
13. Trade Policies for Developing Countries 105
14. The Political Economy of Trade and Agriculture 117

Understanding Foreign Exchange

15. Payments among Nations 123
16. The Foreign Exchange Market 133
17. Forward Exchange 141
18. What Determines Exchange Rates in the Long Run? 151
19. What Determines Exchange Rates in the Short Run? 159
20. Government Policies toward the Foreign Exchange Market 167

Macro Policies for Open Economies

21. How Does the Open Macroeconomy Work? 179
22. Internal and External Balance with Fixed Exchange Rates 189
23. Floating Exchange Rates and Internal Balance 199
24. National and Global Choices 207

Factor Movements

25. The International Movement of Labor 217
26. International Lending and the World Debt Crisis 225
27. Direct Foreign Investment and the Multinationals 235

Answers 245

PREFACE

The purpose of this study guide is *not* to make you shell out more of your hard-earned (or hard-won) money. Really. There is a lot to know in International Economics, and the study guide is intended to help you focus on the big picture. After all, your professors want you to be able to apply what you learn here to the ultimate "big picture" — the real world.

Each chapter in the guide corresponds to a chapter in the text. Your best bet is to read the text chapter first, then look at the Objectives and Key Terms sections in the study guide. Run through the text again, and take a stab at the Warm-up Questions. When you feel you have mastered those, go on to the Problems. They are designed to see how well you can integrate and apply the information from each text chapter; they do not have answers that you can "parrot" back. Since many of the problems come from my exam files, success with them is a pretty good sign that you are on the right track.

A final bit of advice with no sales pitch attached: A terrific, low-cost way to find out if you know something is to try to explain it to someone else. I urge you to form study groups with other people in the class. Go over the material together. Think up test questions and map out the answers. Debate the topics for discussion. And, whenever possible, *have fun*. Really.

Kerry Odell
Claremont, California

CHAPTER 1
International Economics Is Different

Objectives of the Chapter

While it is true that international economics is different, your other courses in economics were not wasted! Both the microeconomic and macroeconomic theories that you have learned in the past will be useful in analyzing the different predicaments faced when dealing with interactions of economic actors *across* national borders. You will be able to discuss issues ranging from rumors and currency speculation to political lobbyists and trade wars.

If you want to keep abreast of international economic developments in "the real world," you should regularly read the business section of a major daily paper. *The Wall Street Journal*, the weekly magazine *The Economist*, and the London daily *Financial Times* provide the most thorough coverage and look really impressive sitting on your desk. Most offer students discounted subscription rates.

At the end of your course of study, you should be able to understand current issues related to foreign trade and international finance and to critically evaluate the debate around the policy options available to your country's government. While we can't guarantee that this will make you a better person, it will make you a better informed person.

Final Thought

> *The theory of economics does not furnish a body of settled conclusions immediately applicable to policy. It is a method rather than a doctrine, an apparatus of the mind, a technique of thinking which helps its possessor to draw correct conclusions.*
>
> — John Maynard Keynes, 1923

CHAPTER 2
The Basic Theory of International Trade

Objectives of the Chapter

Chapter 2 sets up supply and demand for our basic trade model. It enables us to determine precisely the equilibrium relative price and equilibrium quantities traded, and the distribution of the gains from trade.

After studying Chapter 2, you should understand

1. the basic theory of supply and demand and the concept of market equilibrium
2. construction of the demand for imports curve and the supply of exports curve
3. the determination of the equilibrium world price with trade
4. consumer surplus and producer surplus, and how they reflect the gains from trade
5. the concept of "one-dollar, one-vote"
6. the relationship between price elasticities and gains from trade

Key Terms

Arbitrage   buying something at a low price in one market and reselling it at a higher price in another market.

Consumer surplus   measures what it is worth to consumers to be able to buy a product at a price lower than the prices some of them would be willing and able to pay. It is the area below the demand curve and above the price level.

Producer surplus   measures what it is worth to producers to be able to sell their products at a price higher than the prices some of them would be willing to sell for. It is the area above the supply curve and below the price level.

Part I: The Theory of International Trade

Warm-up Questions

True or False? Explain.

1. T / F   When trade opens up, all consumers are made better off.

2. T / F   In the simple trade model, countries with identical pre-trade prices for a good have no incentive to trade in that good.

3. T / F   If one producer is made better off by trade, then all producers in a country must be made better off by trade.

4. T / F   At the equilibrium trade price between two countries, the excess supply of the good in one country must equal the excess demand for the good in the other country.

5. T / F   There ain't no such thing as a free lunch, but there is such a thing as free trade.

Multiple Choice

1. After trade has opened up, the gains that trade brings to consumers of the imported good are, in absolute value,
   a. larger than the losses to domestic producers of that good
   b. smaller than the losses to domestic producers of that good
   c. exactly equal to the losses to domestic producers of that good
   d. immeasurable

2. All but *one* of the following are likely to promote free trade in lumber between countries:
   a. pre-trade lumber prices that are equal across countries
   b. profit-seeking lumber arbitrageurs
   c. lumber supply differences across countries
   d. lumber demand differences across countries.

3. Consumer surplus is
   a. what consumers must pay the government to produce goods
   b. what consumers can get below the market price
   c. what it is worth to consumers to be able to buy the product at a price lower than the price some of them would be willing and able to pay
   d. what they can get at all prices

4. After trade, the distribution of income in a country changes as
   a. import-competing producers lose while producers of the exportable good gain
   b. the nation as a whole gains while individuals lose
   c. consumers lose while producers gain
   d. income flows from consumers to producers

5. If export supply is less price elastic than import demand
   a. the importing country will not want to trade
   b. the exporting country will not want to trade
   c. the exporting country will receive the largest share of the gains to trade
   d. the importing country will receive the largest share of the gains from trade

Problems

1. Consider the graphs of the domestic markets for bread in the hypothetical countries of Leinster and Saxony:

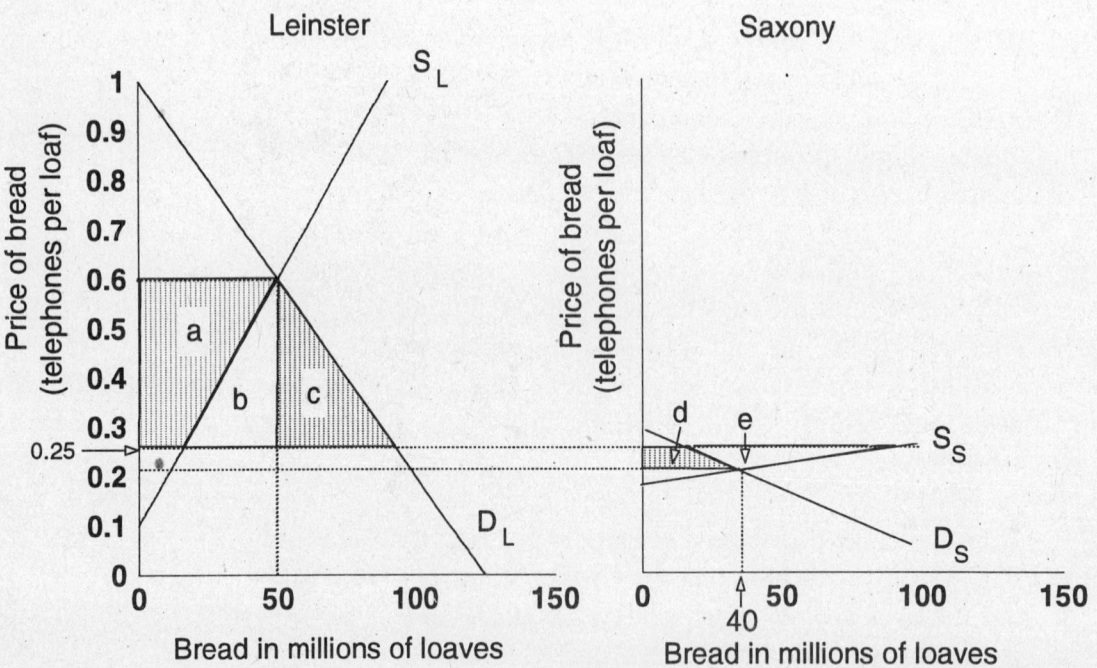

Figure 2.1

a. What is the pre-trade equilibrium price of bread in each country?

b. Is there a reason for trade in bread between Leinster and Saxony?

c. Construct the appropriate import demand and export supply curves, assuming that "the world" consists of only these two countries.

d. What is the equilibrium trade price of bread in Leinster? in Saxony?

e. On the domestic market graphs, show that, at the equilibrium trade price, the quantity of bread exported from Saxony equals the quantity of bread imported into Leinster.

f. On the domestic market graphs, indicate the changes in consumer and producer welfare which result from trade opening in each country.

g. Which groups in the two countries would be happy with free trade in bread between the countries? Which groups would wish that free trade would be banned?

h. On your "international" graph with the export and import curves, indicate the net gains from trade for each country.

i. Which country gains the larger share from trade? Why? (Hint: Look at the elasticities of the trade curves you derived.)

j. Indicate the losses that each country would incur if trade in bread were eliminated.

2. Assume that, for an unknown reason, both the domestic supply of and the domestic demand for bread in Leinster become very elastic, while the curves for Saxony are unchanged. What impact would this have on the international price, the quantities traded, and the net gains from trade for Leinster and Saxony?

3. U.S. lumber companies make 52 billion board-feet of lumber each year, of which 10 billion board-feet are exported and 42 billion are sold in the United States. The average price is $0.30 per board-foot. If lumber exports were banned by law, production (now for the domestic market only) would be 48 billion board-feet, and the price would drop to $0.25 per board-foot. How much revenue would U.S. lumber producers lose each year as a result of the export ban?

4. Suppose that opening up trade would make our nation export beans and import jeans. Let's say that it raises the price of beans from 0.20 jeans/bushel to 0.25 jeans/bushel (so that jeans drop in price from 5 bushels of beans to 4 bushels).

   a. What are the welfare effects of trade on bean consumers, bean producers, jeans consumers, and jeans producers?

   b. Will the opening of trade bring a net national gain? How do you know?

c. Describe how to measure the net national gain or loss (measured in units of real goods) from the opening of trade.

Discussion Topics

1. What ways of measuring welfare can you think of besides the "one-dollar, one-vote" yardstick?

2. Is profiting from arbitrage in commodities a good or a bad thing?

3. What might motivate trade between two countries other than price differentials?

4. Using the ideas of consumer and producer surplus, try to formulate an argument for avoiding a (trade) war between two countries.

Final Thought

Economics is a subject that does not greatly respect one's wishes.

— Nikita Khrushchev, 1965

CHAPTER 3
Why Everybody Trades

Objectives of the Chapter

Chapter 3 looks at trade in a hypothetical world of two countries and two commodities. This simple trade model is based on barter, where countries exchange only goods without any money being paid. The price of each good is, therefore, in terms of what each unit of the good is worth in units of the other good. Countries trade because their prices would differ if something prevented international trade. In this chapter we focus on production-side differences between countries as a source of price differentials. Each country has a comparative advantage in producing some good for which it has more resources or higher productivity than other countries.

To understand this chapter, you should be able to

1. explain production-possibilities curves and community indifference curves
2. relate opportunity cost and price
3. understand trade and arbitrage profits
4. show how countries can gain from trade on the basis of absolute advantage
5. explain the development of the theory of comparative advantage through:
   a. Ricardo's basic comparative advantage using the labor theory of value
   b. the measurement of opportunity cost theory under constant and under increasing costs
   c. the Heckscher-Ohlin (H-O) theory—or the modern factor-proportions theory of trade

Key Terms

Absolute advantage   a nation has an absolute advantage in a commodity it produces more efficiently (with higher productivity) than the rest of the world.

Barter trade   a method of exchanging goods and services directly for other goods and services without using a separate unit of account or medium of exchange.

Basis for trade (Why do countries trade?)
the mechanism that explains differences in (relative) prices in different countries, which in turn give rise to trade between countries.

Community indifference curves
an illustration of the different combinations of commodity quantities that would bring the whole community (here, the nation) the same level of satisfaction.

Comparative advantage
a nation has a comparative advantage in the production of those goods which (compared to other goods and countries in the world) it produces less inefficiently than other commodities. A country will have a comparative advantage in one or more commodities, whether or not it has absolute advantages.

Factor abundance and scarcity
a country is relatively abundant (scarce) in some factor if the ratio of the amount of that factor to other factors in that country is higher (lower) than in the rest of the world.

Factor intensity   a product is intensive in some factor if the cost of that factor is a greater share of the product's value than it is of the value of other products.

Heckscher-Ohlin (H-O) theory
a country will export that good which intensively uses the country's abundant (cheap) factor, and import the good which intensively uses its scarce (expensive) factor.

Mercantilism   a school of thought which was dominant in Europe (roughly in the 16th century through the 18th century). Mercantilism advocates trade restrictions through restriction of imports and expansion of exports so as to accumulate gold and foreign exchange.

Terms of trade   the ratio of the price of exports to the price of imports.

Warm-up Questions

True or False? Explain.

1. T / F A country can have a comparative advantage in a good even if it is at an absolute disadvantage in producing that same good.

2. T / F David Ricardo was the husband in "I Love Lucy."

3. T / F Under the H-O theory, a country is considered "land-abundant" if it has more acres of land than another country.

4. T / F Under increasing costs, countries will not necessarily specialize completely in one good.

5. T / F The Heckscher-Ohlin theory assumes each country has the same tastes for goods.

Multiple Choice

1. The economist credited with the first systematic expression of the principle of comparative advantage was
   a. Bertil Ohlin
   b. Eli Heckscher
   c. John Maynard Keynes
   d. David Ricardo
   e. Adam Smith

2. The Heckscher-Ohlin theorem indicates that
   a. nations with much labor relative to other resources do not have a comparative advantage
   b. a nation with a high ratio of labor to nonlabor resources should minimize participation in international trade
   c. a nation relatively rich in nonlabor resources will not gain from international trade
   d. nations will be led by international market forces to specialize in production and export of goods that heavily use their relatively abundant factors

3. If with one hour of labor time nation A can produce either 3x or 3y, while nation B can produce either 1x or 1y with an hour of labor, and if labor is the only input
   a. nation A has an absolute advantage in both goods
   b. nation B has an absolute advantage in both goods
   c. nation A has a comparative disadvantage in both goods
   d. nation A has a comparative advantage in both goods

4. For Heckscher-Ohlin, the most important cause of the difference in relative commodity prices is the difference between countries in
   a. factor endowments
   b. national income
   c. technology
   d. tastes

5. In the absence of trade, the consumption points available to a nation
   a. are above the production possibilities curve
   b. are on or inside the production possibilities curve
   c. lie on the production possibilities curve
   d. cannot be identified

Chapter 3: Why Everybody Trades

Problems

1. Consider the following hypothetical data on labor requirements in Leinster and Saxony, the only two countries in "the world":

	In Leinster	In Saxony
Labor required to make:		
one loaf of bread	3 hours	4 hours
one telephone	5 hours	20 hours

   a. Which country, if any, has an absolute advantage in bread? in telephones?

   b. Which country has a comparative advantage in bread? in telephones?

   c. What price ratios (telephones per loaf) are possible with free trade?

   d. What price ratios are likely in the two countries if trade is stopped?

2. Let's try an application of the Heckscher-Ohlin model to the countries of Leinster and Saxony. Assume that the only two factors of production in the countries are labor and land.

   a. If Leinster has 8 million acres of land and 2 million laborers while Saxony has 2 million acres of land and 400,000 laborers, which of the countries is "labor abundant?" Which is "land abundant?" Explain.

   b. If labor accounts for 80% of the total cost of producing telephones but only 20% of the total cost of producing bread, which country is more likely to export telephones? bread? Why?

3. Consider two countries that have exactly the same increasing-cost production possibilities curves. Show how a difference in the tastes of the two countries can then determine the pattern of trade between the countries.

4. Assume that Chile has 600 units of labor and Brazil has 1000 units of labor. Both countries produce cloth and wheat. In Chile, the labor requirement for a yard of cloth is 3 units, while for a bushel of wheat it is 2 units. In Brazil, the labor requirement for a yard of cloth is 5 units, while for a bushel of wheat it is 2 units. In both countries, there are constant costs of production.

   a. Draw the production possibilities curves for each country, and calculate the pre-trade price of wheat in each country.

   b. When these two countries engage in free trade, which country would export cloth? Why? Is it possible for the cloth-exporting country to charge 5 bushels/yard for its cloth?

   c. Suppose that the labor endowment in Chile increases to 1200 units. How could this affect the pattern of trade?

   d. Suppose instead that the unit labor requirement in Brazil's cloth industry drops to 2. What will happen to the pattern of trade?

Discussion Topics

1. Can a country do anything to change its relative factor abundances?

2. Are there reasons for a country to want relative abundance in one factor rather than another?

Final Thought

My principles, sir, in these things are, to take as much as I can get, and to pay no more than I can help. These are everyman's principles, whether they be the right principles or not. There, sir, is political economy in a nutshell.
— Thomas Love Peacock, 1831

CHAPTER 4
Who Gains and Who Loses from Trade?

Objectives of the Chapter

In this chapter we see how trade patterns predicted by the Heckscher-Ohlin model may lead to a change in income distribution. International trade divides society into gainers from trade and losers from trade as a result of changes in relative commodity prices. The Stolper-Samuelson theorem explains that in the short run, factors employed to produce the rising-price good gain, while the factors employed to produce the falling-price good lose. In the long run when factors are mobile between industries, the factor used intensively in producing the rising-price good gains whether or not it is actually employed in that industry. Similarly, the factor used intensively in producing the falling-price good loses.

The factor price equalization theorem uses both the H-O model and the Stolper-Samuelson theorem. It assumes that the more abundant factor works more in the export industry while the more scarce factor is bound to work more in the import-competing industry; furthermore, it assumes that factors producing the rising-price good have rising incomes in the long run As a result, scarce labor in one country sees its wage fall, while abundant labor in another country sees its wage rise. Consequently, wages in the two countries converge.

Because the Heckscher-Ohlin model is central to these other theorems, economists have tested the validity of the H-O theory using the trade patterns of different countries. Using data from the United States, Leontief came up with the paradoxical observation that Americans imported capital-intensive goods. Other tests indicate some trade follows the Heckscher-Ohlin predictions, but some tests do not.

After studying Chapter 4, you should know

1. how income distribution relates to international trade through the Stolper-Samuelson theorem
2. the assumptions and conclusions of the factor price equalization theorem
3. the Leontief Paradox

Key Terms

Factor price equalization theorem
under certain assumptions free trade will equalize not only commodity prices between countries but also *factor* prices so that all laborers will earn the same wage rate and all units of land will earn the same rental return in both countries regardless of the factor supplies or the demand patterns in the two countries.

Factor specialization refers to the degree of concentration of a factor in the production of a commodity or group of commodities.

Neutral factor takes the same share of the value of output in all commodity lines.

Magnification effect refers to the greater percentage change in the ratio of factor rewards than the change in the commodity price ratio that caused it.

Stolper-Samuelson theorem
under certain assumptions, moving from no trade to free trade unambiguously raises the returns to the factor used intensively in the rising-price industry and lowers the returns to the factor used intensively in the falling-price industry, regardless of which goods the owners of the factors prefer to consume.

Warm-up Questions

True or False? Explain.

1. T / F The Leontief Paradox may be resolved by using more disaggregated definitions of factors of production.

2. T / F The Stolper Samuelson theorem says that trade will cause the owners of the abundant factor to receive lower real incomes while the real incomes received by owners of the scarce factor will rise.

Chapter 4: Who Gains and Who Loses From Trade?

3. T / F Nobel prizes are not given to dead economists.

4. T / F Factor prices will not be equalized by trade if technologies are not the same in different countries.

5. T / F Unskilled workers in the United States should be more opposed to free trade than skilled workers in the United States.

Multiple Choice

1. Studies of U.S. trade and its effects on employment of U.S. labor show that, on average,
   a. trade has no effect on total employment
   b. replacing imports (e.g. through protection from foreign competition) saved (or created) more jobs than an equivalent expansion of exports
   c. expanding exports creates more jobs than an equivalent amount of import substitution
   d. foreign competition has clearly raised the unemployment rate, particularly in the 1980s

2. After trade opens up, in the short run
   a. all groups tied to the declining sectors lose
   b. only factors more intensively used in the declining sectors lose
   c. only factors less intensively used in the declining sectors lose
   d. only the most abundant factor in the country loses

3. Mexico is an unskilled-labor abundant country, while the United States is a skilled-labor abundant country. With the opening of trade you would expect that in the long run wages for unskilled workers
   a. decline in both countries
   b. decline in the United States and rise in Mexico
   c. rise in the United States and decline in Mexico
   d. rise in both countries

4. Which of the following statements is *false*?
   a. Consumption patterns do not matter for the welfare gains or losses of neutral factors.
   b. Consumption patterns do affect the size of the gains or losses to all factors.
   c. Consumption patterns do not affect the direction of gains or losses for the most specialized factors.
   d. Consumption patterns do not matter for the welfare gains or losses of a nation as a whole.

5. Factor price equalization will not hold if
   a. factors are immobile between sectors of the economy
   b. factors have different productivities in different countries
   c. countries put up barriers to free trade
   d. all of the above

Problems

1. Recall our hypothetical trade model: Leinster is a labor-abundant country and Saxony is a land-abundant country; telephones are labor-intensive goods and bread is a land-intensive good. Assume that free trade prevails between the two countries.

   a. What happens to wages earned by workers in Leinster in the short run? in the long run? Explain.

   b. What happens to wages earned by workers in Saxony in the short run? in the long run? Explain.

   c. According to the factor price equalization theorem, will labor wages in Leinster equal land rents in Leinster, or will Leinster wages equal Saxony wages?

2. Given the implications of trade models for factor prices, how would you explain an observation that, in the late 1980s, the hourly manufacturing wage in West Germany was $13.44 while the wage was only $7.46 in the United Kingdom?

3. Consider an economy producing capital-intensive computers and land-intensive wheat. Labor is employed to produce both goods. If free trade raises the price of computers relative to wheat, who would gain and who would lose in each of the following two cases:

   a. factors are perfectly immobile between the two sectors

   b. factors are perfectly mobile between the two sectors

Part I: The Theory of International Trade

4. a. Have America's existing import barriers raised or lowered the demand for U.S. labor? Explain.

   b. Would a uniform percentage cut in U.S. imports raise or lower the demand for U.S. labor? Explain.

5. You are given the following cost data for France, where they have nothing but capital and labor and make nothing but bread and wine:

	To make a loaf of bread	To make a bottle of wine
capital input cost	5 francs	20 francs
labor input cost	4 francs	10 francs
total cost	9 francs	30 francs

   a. Is bread-making more capital-intensive than wine-making, or vice versa? Explain.

b. Suppose trade opens and the price of wine rises while the price of bread falls.

If capital and labor were completely immobile between bread-making and wine making, who, in France, would gain from the shift in prices? Who would lose? (Consider the four groups of bread capitalists, bread laborers, wine capitalists, and wine laborers.)

Which group of consumers will rejoice with the winemakers? Which group of consumers will commiserate with the breadmakers?

6. Suppose that a new isolationist government in Pakistan decides to shut off the country's imports of land-intensive food, preferring to grow its own food instead of making labor-intensive manufactures for export. After trade is shut off, food becomes 14 percent more expensive relative to manufactures (i.e., manufactures become 14 percent cheaper relative to food). Over the long run how greatly, and in what direction, will the isolation change

   a. Pakistani laborers' real wage incomes?

   b. Pakistani landlords' real rental incomes?

Discussion Topics

1. What do you think would happen to factor prices internationally if another OPEC crisis tripled the cost of shipping goods around the globe?

2. Policymakers today are concerned about retraining unemployed workers. Try to make a case for such programs as a means of increasing public support for free trade.

Final Thought

> *Of all the quacks that ever quacked, political economists are the loudest. Instead of telling us what is meant by one's country, by what causes men are happy, moral, religious, or the contrary, they tell us how flannel jackets are exchanged for pork hams, and speak much of the land last taken into cultivation.*
>
> —Thomas Carlyle, 1881

THE WALL STREET JOURNAL
February 7, 1992

America's Growing Economic Lead

By Lawrence B. Lindsey

Two leading Japanese politicians, Prime Minister Kiichi Miyazawa and Speaker of the House Yoshio Sakurauchi have caused a firestorm by questioning the quality and work ethic of America's workers and this country's ability to compete in the world. But doubts about America are not confined to foreigners. Not too long ago, some American leaders warned that the country is at risk of a future of flipping hamburgers and sweeping up around Japanese computers.

Fortunately, the evidence is strong that those who are bearish about America's future are wrong about both the past and the future. But the pessimism about America is so widespread that talk of protectionism and a retreat from active involvement in international economic and political affairs is again fashionable. The facts suggest that those seeking a truly effective industrial policy should actually favor active American promotion of rapid world-wide economic growth in the context of free trade.

Research by Andrew Warner of Harvard University and the Federal Reserve shows that, contrary to popular belief, America's advantage is in the production of high-technology capital goods, and that this advantage has been growing. A key reason for the recent boom in exports has been the rapid rise of world-wide spending on capital goods.

Back in the late 1960s, when by all accounts the U.S. was the world's industrial giant, manufacturing amounted to about 22% of real gross domestic product. Much of this manufacturing went into defense and the production of consumer goods from shirts to automobiles. Only 28% of the manufacturing base was devoted to capital goods such as computers, aircraft and industrial machinery, and only 20% of American capital-goods were exported. The total value of U.S. capital goods exports was just 1.4% of GDP.

Today, when some assert that the U.S. has lost its manufacturing base, manufacturing output has risen to 23% of real GDP. The share of the manufacturing base devoted to capital goods has risen to 38%. This capital-goods boom has been made possible by exports: About 45% of capital goods output is now sold abroad, more than double the proportion of the late 1960s. Capital-goods exports now amount to 4% of GDP.

Contrary to the pessimists' view, a major part of this improvement occurred during the 1980s, and particularly the late 1980s. During the 1980s, the growth in real exports amounted to one-fifth of the real growth of the economy. Inflation-adjusted growth in exports of capital goods outpaced overall growth by better than two to one. Since 1986, the story is even more striking. Nearly half of America's real economic growth over the past five years has been in exports.

Also contrary to the pessimists' claims, U.S. exports have become less based on farm and other primary goods and more focused on high technology. Capital equipment has risen to 41% of U.S. exports from 30% in the late 1960s, largely as a result of the world-wide investment boom: As other countries develop their economies, they purchase increasing amounts of American-made machines, computers and airplanes.

During the past two decades, the investment share of world product has risen to 26% from 22%. In dollar terms, gross world investment outside the U.S. in 1992 will be roughly $5 trillion.

We should hope that this process continues, not only for humanitarian reasons, but also to benefit the American economy. Each 1% in world investment spending produces a 1.5% increase in exports of capital goods, and almost a full point increase in total merchandise exports. Strikingly, not only does the relationship between world-wide investment and U.S. exports pass traditional statistical tests easily, the relationship stands up to a wide variety of mathematical and statistical specifications. In fact, the link between U.S. exports and world-wide investment shows some signs of having strengthened in recent years.

It is interesting to contrast the U.S. performance with that of Japan. There is no evidence of a statistical relationship between Japanese exports and world investment spending over the past quarter century. There does appear to be some improvement over time for Japan, although this improving trend does not pass statistical muster. Further, even at its highest, the sensitivity of Japanese exports to world-wide investment spending remained below America's.

One reason for the popularity of the pessimists' view is that America's strengths are not apparent in goods that consumers normally buy. To see them, one has to visit factories, construction sites and airport hangars — not your usual tourist stops.

The regional composition of investment also appears to be shifting in America's favor. Latin America as a whole and Mexico in particular are increasing their pace of investment. During 1989, the U.S. exported twice as many capital goods to Latin America as did Japan. The other area of potential investment in the years ahead is the former communist bloc, which could become a staggering source of future growth of U.S. capital goods exports.

The most urgent message of this analysis is that encouraging faster worldwide economic development might be the single most effective policy for promoting the growth of exports. The export-promotion policy that many suggest as an alternative to freer trade is a reduction in the exchange value of the dollar. This has three potential drawbacks. First, it's not clear that a country's monetary authorities can control the value of their currency. Second, if foreign-exchange markets perceive that devaluation is an intended policy of the U.S. government, interest rates in assets denominated in dollars might rise to offset the exchange-rate loss. Third, devaluation would reduce Americans' purchasing power and standard of living.

Recent history provides a good test of the relative efficacy of world-wide investment and exchange-rate depreciation. The late 1980s were a period not only of rapidly growing world-wide investment spending, but also of real dollar depreciation. During the five years following the Plaza Accord of 1985, the dollar fell 38% on a tradeweighted basis. World-wide investment spending rose 38% over the same period.

Over those five years, total U.S. merchandise exports rose $192 billion in inflation-adjusted terms. $106 billion of the additional merchandise exports, or 55%, was statistically associated with the rise of global investment.

Let there be no mistake: Neither America nor any other country can expect to enjoy an economic free ride. Americans should continue their efforts to reform the nation's schools, increase the investment rate, encourage the natural entrepreneurship of the population and subject government spending and regulation to rigorous cost-benefit tests. But these are commonsense ideas that we would be well advised to undertake regardless of the international trading situation.

There may be some advantage in having Mr. Miyazawa and his countrymen think that America is in decline. It probably pays to be underestimated. But we would be foolish to underestimate ourselves. World economic trends are moving our way and we do not need to be protected from them. If anything, we need to reinforce them and to increase our exposure to them. The best industrial policy for America to pursue is active involvement in the world's affairs to promote global economic development and free trade.

―――――

Mr. Lindsey is a governor of the Federal Reserve, in Washington, D.C.

Source: *The Wall Street Journal*, February 7, 1992. Reprinted with permission of THE WALL STREET JOURNAL, 1992 Dow Jones & Company, Inc. All rights reserved worldwide.

CHAPTER 5
Growth and Trade

Objectives of the Chapter

In this chapter, the Heckscher-Ohlin model of international trade is extended to include growth in a country's endowment of factors of production and in its technological sophistication. The impact of economic growth on international trade will depend on whether the growth is balanced or biased, and on whether the country experiencing growth is large or small.

After reading Chapter 5 you should be able to

1. show how trade patterns are influenced by the source of economic growth
2. show how economic growth can change the sectoral patterns of a country
3. discuss how growth can affect the terms of trade and the welfare of the country experiencing growth
4. relate theories of growth to trade between developing, developed, and newly industrializing countries (NICs)

Key Terms

Dutch disease   a famous example of the phenomenon described by the Rybczynski theorem. The term was used to describe a problem experienced by the Netherlands, where the discovery of new natural gas fields was thought to have led to a decline in the production of manufactured goods.

Immiserizing growth   in a large trading country which is export-biased, growth in the export sector may lead to a deterioration in its terms of trade large enough to reduce the country's welfare.

Knowledge-intensive sectors
    sectors of the economy making the heaviest use of knowledge and of the scientists and technicians that create and supply knowledge.

Product cycle hypothesis
predicts that as the technology of a product becomes more standardized and static, labor costs become a more important basis for comparative advantage than do research and development.

Rybczynski theorem in a two-good world with constant product prices, the growth of one factor of production results in a decrease in the output of the good that does not use this factor intensively.

Small country/large country assumption
a small country has no impact on international prices; a large country can have an impact on prices.

Warm-up Questions

True or False? Explain.

1. T / F   A country which is "large" may improve its terms of trade by investing in import-competing growth rather than in the export sector.

2. T / F   Growth in a small country, by definition, will leave the terms of trade unchanged.

3. T / F   Adolescence is an example of "immiserizing growth."

4. T / F   Growth in a country's factors of production always makes the country more self-sufficient and less reliant on international trade.

5. T / F   Comparative advantage in knowledge-intensive products is dynamic.

Multiple Choice

1. "Rapid accumulation of new capital in a fast-growing trading country can make the country import more natural resources." This statement is implied by
   a. the Heckscher-Ohlin theorem
   b. the Stolper-Samuelson theorem
   c. the Rybczynski theorem
   d. the factor price equalization theorem

2. If a nation has a comparative advantage in a capital-intensively produced good, and the rate of growth of capital is greater than the rate of growth of other inputs (e.g., labor), according to trade theory, the pattern of growth which will result
   a. will be import-replacing
   b. will be neutral as between capital-intensive and other internationally traded goods
   c. will be export-expanding
   d. none of the above

3. A necessary condition for immiserizing growth is that
   a. the country's growth is biased toward the export sector
   b. the foreign demand for the country's export is price elastic
   c. the country's consumption preferences are heavily biased in favor of the export good
   d. trade is not a significant part of the country's economy

4. The Heckscher-Ohlin theory successfully explains
   a. the product-innovation process and the location of industries in countries other than the United States
   b. the rising importance of a country both exporting and importing the same product
   c. the rising trade between the United States and Canada because both are similar in factor endowments
   d. the trade patterns between industrialized countries and the developing countries which differ in factor endowments

5. Which of the following is most likely to undergo a product cycle?
   a. rice
   b. TV sets
   c. crude oil
   d. minerals

Problems

1. Back to our countries of Leinster and Saxony. PPCs for each of the countries are drawn below with the free trade price of 0.25 telephones/loaf indicated. (*From this question forward, you should consider Leinster a "large country" and Saxony a "small country."*)

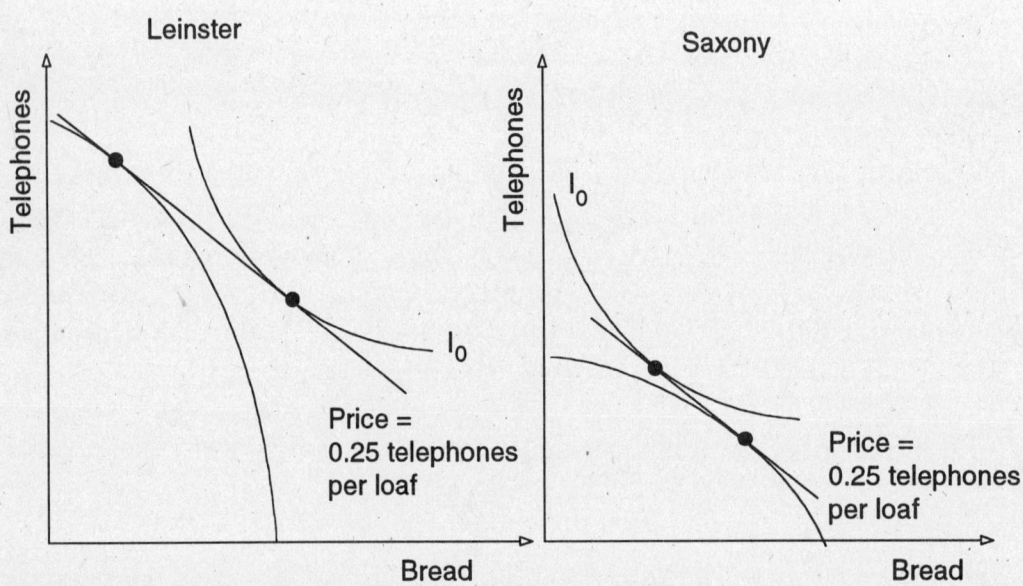

Figure 5.1

Suppose that Saxony discovers a way of irrigating previously arid land.

a. What would you expect to happen to the volume of trade between Leinster and Saxony?

b. What would happen to the level of economic welfare in Saxony as a result of the growth it experienced?

Suppose *instead* that a plague wipes out 20 percent of Leinster's labor force.

c. What would you expect to happen to the volume of trade between Leinster and Saxony?

d. What would happen to the level of economic welfare in Leinster?

2. Assume that Canada exports land-intensive wheat and imports cloth that uses unskilled labor intensively, even though Canada does make some cloth at home. If a major discovery in biotechnology doubles Canada's ability to grow wheat, and if the extra wheat supply lowers the world price of wheat (in yards of cloth per bushel of wheat):

a. Will this set of events make Canada better off or worse off as a nation?

b. Will this set of events make the rest of the world better off or worse off?

c. Will this set of events raise or lower the real wage rate of unskilled laborers in Canada?

If, *instead*, the rest of the world's labor supply doubles while its land supply remains the same:

d. Will this event and its effects make Canada better off or worse off as a nation?

3. Suppose that Peru is abundant in land and unskilled labor, and scarce in capital and skilled labor.

   a. According to the Heckscher-Ohlin model, what type of goods will Peru export, and what type will it import?

   b. Suppose that Peru wants to achieve "import-replacing" growth. What change in its endowments would achieve this growth? If Peru were large, what would be the effect on its terms of trade?

4. Some oil executives are urging Congress to open up the wildlife preserves in the Arctic region of Alaska to exploration for oil. If, indeed, huge new oil reserves are discovered there,

   a. what is likely to be the impact on American imports of oil?

   b. what is likely to be the impact on national welfare?

   c. could the United States ultimately suffer from "the Dutch Disease?"

   d. what other costs might we face? (Think broadly here.)

Chapter 5: Growth and Trade

Discussion Topics

1. If growth can make a country worse off, why is it allowed to happen?

2. Are the developed countries or the developing countries more prone to experience immiserizing growth?

3. What "new" goods in the United States do you foresee going through the product cycle in the near future? What countries do you think will ultimately end up producing these goods?

Final Thought

Economic growth is not only unnecessary, it is ruinous.

— Aleksandr Solzhenitsyn, 1973

CHAPTER 6
Alternative Theories of Modern Trade

Objectives of the Chapter

This chapter updates and puts into perspective the various theories examined in the previous chapters. The discussion highlights the rise of intra-industry trade between nations that have similar factor endowments. Product differentiation, monopolistic competition, and global oligopoly all play a role in explaining how a country can both import and export the same basic product. Economies of scale—both internal and external—also help determine why industries locate in some countries and not in others.

After studying Chapter 6, you should be able to identify

1. intra-industry trade (IIT)
2. the apparent contradiction between Heckscher-Ohlin theory and IIT
3. how demand theory and income elasticities can be used to explain the rise of IIT
4. how internal economies of scale relate to monopolistic competition and oligopoly

Key Terms

Economies of scale the percent reduction in average costs achieved by expanding all inputs by a given percentage.

External economies productivity gains and cost reductions that an individual firm reaps from the expansion of other firms in the same location.

Income elasticity of demand
  the percentage change in the demand for a good resulting from a one percent change in the income of consumers of the good.

Internal economies these exist if expanding the firm's own scale of production raises its productivity and cuts its average cost.

Intra-industry trade two-way trade in similar products between countries.

Luxuries goods that take a rising share of expenditures as income increases. For luxuries, in other words, income elasticity is greater than one.

Monopolistic competition
a market structure with many firms selling a differentiated product, with low barriers to entry and exit in the industry. It is like monopoly in that the firm has some control over the price it charges since products are differentiated. Yet, since there are many sellers, it is like perfect competition in that the free entry and exit of other firms in the industry pushes each firm toward having zero net profit.

Oligopoly a market structure with a few firms supplying most of the output. Firms know that their actions affect each other.

Staples goods that take a declining share of expenditures as income increases. For staples, in other words, income elasticity is less than one.

Warm-up Questions

True or False? Explain.

1. T / F Luxury goods are income-elastic.

2. T / F IIT is significantly more prevalent in perfectly competitive industries.

3. T / F Economies of scale are said to exist whenever a balanced growth of resources causes a rise in average costs.

4. T / F Explanations for IIT include product differentiation, economies of scale, and income distribution.

5. T / F The motto for developed countries is "Just Do IIT."

Multiple-Choice

1. Intra-industry trade is more likely to occur between
   a. rich and poor countries
   b. countries with high and similar income levels
   c. developing countries
   d. developed and developing countries

2. Which of the following statements is most true?
   a. Economies of scale determine each country's comparative advantage.
   b. Economies of scale do not determine each country's comparative advantage, but rather translate any given comparative advantage into lower prices and greater expansion of output and trade.
   c. Comparative advantage can be explained better through external economies than internal economies, since external economies imply an expansion in output of other competing firms.
   d. Comparative advantage can best be explained by internal economies because of the resultant higher productivity and lower costs of the firm.

3. Economies of scale are more likely to occur in
   a. a small-scale textile industry
   b. the aircraft industry
   c. the footwear industry
   d. small business

4. In a monopolistic competition model of trade
   a. if two countries have the same overall capital-labor ratio there is no trade
   b. there are gains from trade from an increased variety of goods and large firm scale
   c. firms earn positive economic profits in the long run
   d. factor endowments do not play any role in determining inter-industry trade

5. In the Heckscher-Ohlin model, international trade is based mostly on a difference in
   a. technology
   b. factor endowments
   c. economies of scale
   d. product differentiation

Problems

1. Could two countries with identical abilities to produce (same production possibilities curves) and identical tastes (same indifference curves) gain from trading with each other? Explain how or why not, making assumptions clear.

2. Under which of the following cost conditions is a nation *least* likely to specialize completely, (i.e., to import goods it does not produce at all):

   a. increasing returns to scale (economies of scale)

   b. Ricardian constant returns to scale

   c. decreasing returns to scale (increasing costs)

   Compare and explain.

3. Until now, the United States has not been allowed to export many computer products to Eastern Europe. If free trade in computer products is legalized, could this benefit U.S. buyers (consumers) of computer products? If not, explain why that is impossible. If so, explain what conditions could make U.S. computer buyers better off.

4. Suppose the automobile industries in the United States and in Japan are characterized by monopolistic competition. What happens when trade is opened up between these countries? How do countries gain from trade in this case?

5. Consider a hypothetical example of trade between the United States, Japan (a developed country), and Sudan (a developing country):

	Exports ($b) of U.S. to		Imports ($b) of U.S. to	
	Japan	Sudan	Japan	Sudan
Product Category:				
Primary Products	75	50	60	55
Manufactures	70	65	150	0

a. Compare the IIT trade share of the United States with Japan and with Sudan.

b. Is the IIT trade higher with Japan or with Sudan? Why?

Discussion Topics

1. How does the theory of intra-industry trade explain why Canada is the largest trading partner of the United States?

2. How does the theory of intra-industry trade explain why Mexico is *not* the largest trading partner of the United States?

Final Thought

> *The comparative importance of a small number of great corporations in the American economy cannot be denied except by those who have a singular immunity to statistical evidence or striking capacity to manipulate it.*
>
> — John Kenneth Galbraith, 1952

CHAPTER 7
The Basic Analysis of a Tariff

Objectives of the Chapter

This chapter explicitly explains the advantages and disadvantages of a tariff imposition. Except for some recognized exceptional cases, there is a rare consensus among economists that freer trade is better than protectionism. As illustrated in this chapter, economic analysis has consistently demonstrated that there are usually net gains from freer trade for the nation as well as for the world. A tariff helps import-substituting producers, and the government collects some tariff revenue (import taxes). However, this can only be attained at the expense of a net loss to the whole nation, and particularly to consumers.

After studying Chapter 7, you should be able to identify

1. the advantages and disadvantages of a tariff
2. how a tariff lowers the welfare of the world as a whole
3. *ad valorem* tariff and *specific* tariff
4. effective rate of protection
5. how demand-supply analysis can be used to assess the gains and losses of a tariff, using both graphical and tabular expositions
6. who gains and who loses from a tariff imposition

Key Terms

Ad valorem tariff   a tariff that is set as a percentage of the value of the goods when they reach the importing country.

Consumption effect   the welfare loss to consumers in the importing nation that corresponds to their being forced to cut their total consumption as a result of the tariff.

Deadweight loss   the parts of what consumers lose as a result of a tariff, but that neither the government nor producers gain.

Part II: Trade Policy

Effective rate of protection
the percentage by which the entire set of a nation's trade barriers raises the industry's value added per unit of output. (Abbreviated e.r.p.)

Nationally optimal tariff
a tariff set at the rate which maximizes the gains for a *large* country (at the expense of foreign countries). Technically, the optimal rate, as a fraction of the price paid to foreigners, equals the reciprocal of the elasticity of import supply.

Price-taking countries ("small" countries)
countries that cannot affect the outside world price of the goods and services they trade. In these countries, the import supply curve is infinitely elastic.

Production effect the cost of shifting to more expensive home production in the import-competing sector, which is protected by the tariff on foreign goods.

Prohibitive tariff a tariff which is set so high that it makes all imports unprofitable.

Specific tariff a tariff stipulated as a money amount per physical unit of import.

Warm-up Questions

True or False? Explain.

1. T / F Free trade is always a better policy than a tariff.

2. T / F An advantage of a specific tariff is that its protective value keeps pace with increases in the price of the imported good.

3. T / F While a tariff may be nationally optimal, it is not globally optimal.

4. T / F *Ad valorem* is just another way of saying *ad nauseam*.

5. T / F A tariff results in losses to consumers that are in excess of the gains to producers.

Multiple Choice

1. The optimal tariff for a small (price-taking) country
   a. is zero
   b. is a prohibitive tariff
   c. is unambiguously positive
   d. increases as that country's elasticity of demand increases

2. An optimal tariff, which yields a net national welfare gain, requires that
   a. the nation be a "price taker"
   b. there be no loss of consumer surplus
   c. trading partner nations not be injured by the tariff
   d. the nation have monopsony power in the international market

3. The imposition of a tariff
   a. generates revenue which is paid entirely by foreigners
   b. always increases the domestic price in the exporting country
   c. reduces the welfare of a "small" importing country relative to free trade
   d. is always welfare-increasing

4. The effective rate of protection of an industry is
   a. always more than the optimal tariff
   b. a measure of the jobs gained by the economy imposing a tariff
   c. more or less than the nominal tariff rate depending on the domestic output's share in GDP
   d. more or less than the nominal tariff rate depending on the tariffs on inputs

5. The imposition of an import tariff by a large nation
   a. increases the nation's welfare
   b. reduces the nation's welfare
   c. leaves the nation's welfare unchanged
   d. any of the above is possible

Problems

1. Consider a case in which the large country, Leinster, imposes a tariff on Saxon bread. This tariff reduces the volume of trade in bread from 80 million loaves to 40 million loaves, and causes the price to fall to 0.23 telephones per loaf of bread.

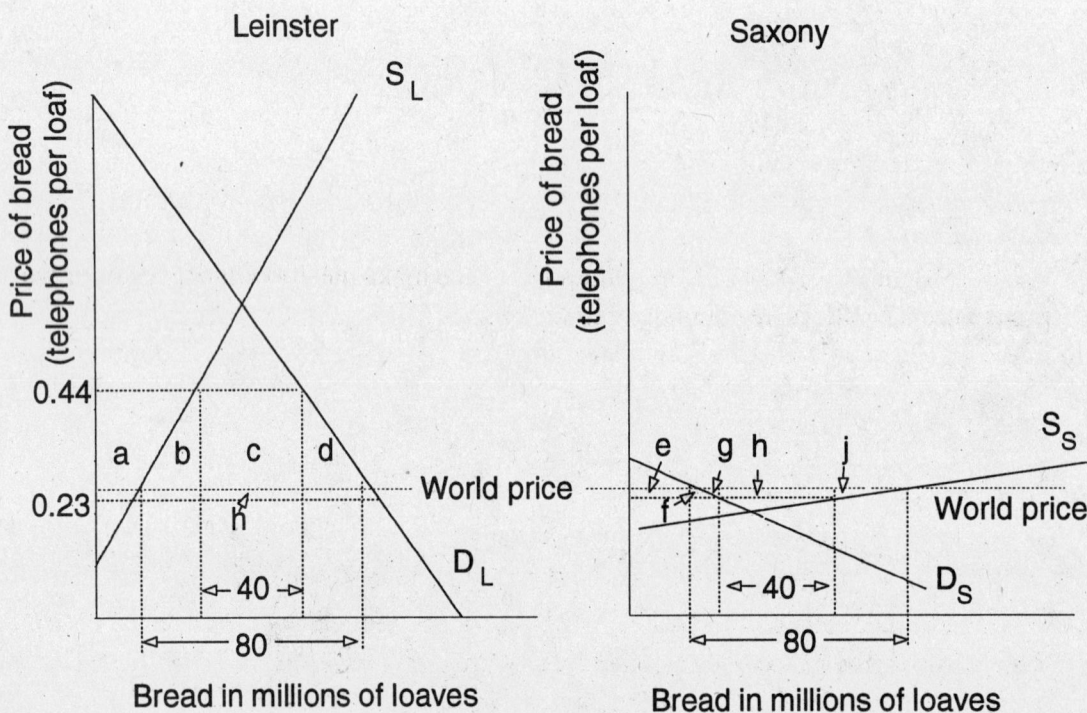

Figure 7.1

Using the domestic market graphs, illustrate the impact of this tariff on

a. bread consumer surplus in Leinster and in Saxony

b. bread producer surplus in Leinster and in Saxony

c. national welfare in Leinster and in Saxony

d. "world" welfare

2. Suppose that the United States puts a 200% tariff on all imported wines. You have been asked to estimate the net national gain (or loss) from the tariff. Consider how your measure of net national gain (or loss) is affected by the different elasticities of demand and supply:

   a. Would a higher elasticity of U.S. demand for wine make the 200% tariff better or worse if we were a small, price-taking country?

   b. Would a higher elasticity of U.S. wine supply make the 200% tariff better or worse for the U.S. as a whole if we were a small, price-taking country?

   c. Would a higher elasticity of foreign wine supply make a 200% tariff better or worse for the United States as a whole?

Part II: Trade Policy

3. Assume that the United States has imposed a $1.50 tariff on each sixpack of imported beer. (All beers are of the same quality and all are sold in sixpacks.) Careful studies have shown that the tariff has these effects:

	Without tariff (free trade)	With tariff of $1.50
Domestic price (dollars per sixpack)	$3.00	$4.00
World price (c.i.f. Oakland)	$3.00	$2.50
Domestic demand (millions of sixpacks per year)	3,200	2,800
Domestic supply (millions of sixpacks per year)	2,000	2,500
Imports (millions of sixpacks per year)	1,200	300

   a. Calculate the net national U.S. gain (or loss) from the tariff, assuming the "one-dollar, one-vote" standard.

   b. Suppose that $2.00 of purchased inputs go into each sixpack of domestic beer, with or without the tariff; the rest of the price is the industry's value added. What is the effective rate of protection given to the beer industry? (There are no tariffs on barley, hops, mascots for advertising, or other purchased inputs.)

4. The United States currently imports baseball bats without tariff, with the results shown in the first column of numbers below. Suppose that Congress is thinking of imposing a tariff of $35 per bat, and has asked you to estimate the gains and losses to different groups. You find that the $35 tariff would yield the prices and quantities shown in the right-hand column.

	Free-trade situation (no tariff)	Situation with $35 tariff on bats
Domestic U.S. price of bats	$80	$100
Tariff	$0	$35
World price of bats	$80	$65
U.S. production of bats per year	160,000	220,000
U.S. imports of bats per year	200,000	100,000
U.S. consumption of bats per year	360,000	320,000

Chapter 7: The Basic Analysis of a Tariff

In the following questions, explain your answers and give numerical results if possible.

a. What is the gain or loss to U.S. bat consumers from the tariff?

b. What is the gain or loss to U.S. bat producers from the tariff?

c. What is the government revenue from the tariff?

d. What is the net gain or loss for the United States as a whole?

e. What is the net gain or loss for other countries?

f. What is the gain or loss for the world as a whole?

5. The World Bank calculates that the effective rate of protection for Pakistani clothing producers is −30%. You are asked to advise the Pakistani government on their trade policy towards the clothing industry. Interpret the meaning of the −30% effective rate of protection and suggest the tariff changes that would most benefit the Pakistani clothing industry.

6. The production of heating devices requires the use of copper wire. Suppose that 10 percent of the total value of a heating device is comprised of the value of copper wire. German firms that are producing heating devices import the copper wire that is used in production. If the German tariff on imported heating devices is 12% and the German tariff on imported copper wire is 10%, what is the effective rate of protection for the German heating device industry?

Discussion Topics

1. For a small country, economic theory says that the imposition of a tariff will reduce the country's welfare. Why is it, then, that so many small countries do impose tariffs?

2. A tariff increases producer welfare at the expense of consumer welfare, and is never economically "efficient." Is a tariff ever "equitable?"

Final Thought

Free-trade, they concede, is very well as a principle, but it is never quite time for its adoption.

— Ralph Waldo Emerson, 1876

THE WALL STREET JOURNAL
March 24, 1988

U.S. Says Car, Japanese Auto Makers Say Truck, Customs Isn't About to Call the Whole Thing Off

By Melinda Grenier Guiles
Staff Reporter of The Wall Street Journal

It sounds like a joke from a comedy skit about pointy-headed bureaucrats: Government officials are trying to discern the difference between a truck and a car.

But the question is no joke to federal agencies currently wrestling with the problem. It's also no laughing matter to several Japanese auto makers whose shipments to the U.S. are restricted by Japan's export quota.

Government and industry sources say the U.S. Customs Service could shed some light on the controversy as early as today. The agency is expected to respond to Japanese manufacturers who complained when customs proposed reclassifying as cars the Jeeplike sport utility vehicles they have been exporting as trucks.

This latest round in U.S.-Japan trade tensions began last fall when Rep. John D. Dingell (D., Mich.), chairman of the House Energy and Commerce Committee, decided some Japanese auto makers were trying to circumvent the auto export quota by classifying their sport utility models as trucks. Besides alerting customs of his concerns, Mr. Dingell also recently asked the General Accounting Office to look into the matter.

A change in the classification would be more than just academic. It could create serious problems for such companies as Suzuki Motor Co. and Isuzu Motors Ltd., who aren't allowed to export many cars here and who depend on sport utility vehicles in the U.S.

"These things represent a significant part of our sales, no question," says a spokesman for Isuzu's U.S. unit.

The roots of the conflict go back seven years. When Japan adopted its 1,680,000-car quota (now 2.3 million) in 1981, the question of how to classify sport utility vehicles wasn't a major issue. Most of the domestic and foreign-made models were spartan, truck-based, off-road buggies with no back seats and few amenities. Only one Japanese manufacturer, Toyota Motor Corp., exported them to the U.S. anyway.

So Japan set up a small, separate quota of about 82,000 vehicles (now 100,000) to cover station wagons and the few sport utility "cars" shipped here with back seats. The sport utility models that entered the U.S. without back seats were classified as trucks. Truck exports haven't been restricted but face a 25% U.S. tariff, compared with the 2.5% tariff levied on cars.

Then sales of sport utility vehicles took off, as companies gussied them up to broaden their appeal. Sales of Japanese-made models nearly reached 200,000 here in 1987 — stealing some sales from their U.S.-made cousins. Many of the Japanese vehicles, like their domestic counterparts, offer such carlike features as cut-pile carpeting and AM-FM stereo radio. Most also have back seats — installed at the U.S. port or the dealership after the vehicles clear customs as trucks.

"In a recent survey of Suzuki Samurai buyers, the majority of new owners who were replacing a vehicle were replacing a car, not a truck," crowed a Suzuki of America Automotive Corp. press release issued about a year after Samurai's November 1985 debut. "The fact that so many subcompact buyers are turning to the Samurai is evidence of the vehicle's appeal in that category."

That's precisely Mr. Dingell's point. If people use sport utility vehicles as substitutes for cars, the vehicles should be considered cars for tariff and quota purposes. At his urging, the Customs Service last year ordered its field offices to take a closer look at the situation. "Absence

Japanese-made Sport Utility Vehicles

	IMPORTED IN 1987 AS		
	Cars	Trucks	Total
Suzuki Samurai	3,000	78,349	81,349
Isuzu Trooper	2,100	40,212	42,312
Toyota 4 Runner	3,635	31,423	35,058
Dodge Raider*	0	19,539	19,539
Mitsubishi Montero	2,013	8,912	10,925
Nissan Pathfinder	5,314	0	5,314
Total	16,062	178,435	194,497

* Raider made by Mitsubishi for Chrysler Corp.

of rear passenger seating is not conclusive evidence of classification," the department said in a message that ordered its agents to be on the lookout for such "passenger amenities" in the rear compartment as carpeting, insulation, "windows that open," ventilation ducts, audio speakers, ashtrays, armrests and "similar features typical of a vehicle designed for transport of persons rather than cargo."

The department's Los Angeles district office promptly proposed reclassifying a number of sport utility vehicles. The U.S. sales arms of Mitsubishi Motors Corp., Suzuki, Isuzu, and Toyota separately protested. The companies insist that they comply with customs regulations, which assign a classification based on the vehicle's condition "as imported." Still, Mitsubishi and Toyota stopped most shipments of their sport utility "trucks."

Mitsubishi now plans to resume shipments April 1, says Richard D. Recchia, executive vice president and chief operating officer of Mitsubishi Motor Sales of America Inc. Toyota is "contemplating" a similar move, says a Toyota Motor Sales, U.S.A. spokeswoman, who didn't indicate a target date. Both companies say they are changing their position because they expect customs to affirm the truck classification of the affected vehicles already shipped here. What they don't know is what customs "is going to say about the future," says Mr. Recchia.

Customs could decide to change the criteria for classification, a process that would likely take at least a few months. Customs also has to respond to the protests filed last year.

Suzuki and Isuzu, both partly owned by General Motors Corp., would be hurt the most if a reclassification is ultimately approved. Both have tiny car quotas with little hope of expansion given Japan's recent decision to hold the restraints at the current level. About 96% of the vehicles Suzuki sold in the U.S. in 1987 were brought into the U.S. as trucks. About a third of all Isuzu models sold here were sport utility "trucks."

The continuing slowdown in sales of Japanese cars could help untie the knot. Higher prices caused by the strength of the Japanese yen have made it difficult, if not impossible, for most of the Japanese companies to sell their car-quota allocations. Thus, some companies say it won't hurt as much now to call their sport utility vehicles cars. It also might be possible for Isuzu and Suzuki to get a bit of their competitors' "leftover" allocations.

Some news indicating what will finally happen should come "pretty quickly," says a Customs Service spokesman. He and a spokesman for Rep. Dingell confirmed that the congressman and Customs Commissioner William von Rabb met late yesterday to discuss the classification issue, although neither would say exactly what the discussion covered.

The customs spokesman said the problem is particularly difficult because it involves "a significant revenue issue." One U.S. official estimated that the government takes in about $200 million a year from the 25% tariff on the sport utility "trucks." Reclassifying these models as cars, with the 2.5% tariff, would sharply cut that total. The lower tariff could mean lower prices as well, although the companies could choose to pocket the difference.

"But you also have to look at it in the spirit of the law and good trade relations," he added. "There's a lot of strong arguments here."

Source: *The Wall Street Journal*, March 24, 1988. Reprinted with permission of THE WALL STREET JOURNAL, 1988 Dow Jones & Company, Inc. All rights reserved worldwide.

CHAPTER 8
Nontariff Barriers to Imports

Objectives of the Chapter

This chapter notes numerous other ways to restrict foreign trade without using a tariff. Nontariff barriers have gained importance since World War II as a result of continuous multilateral negotiations to cut tariffs. Many of these barriers decrease imports to a fixed amount by either setting an import quota or coercing the exporting country to limit its exported quantity. Others restrict the quantity of imports through discrimination by quality or content.

After studying Chapter 8, you should know

1. the rationale behind imposing nontariff trade barriers
2. the import quota and reasons for using it
3. how a tariff and a quota can be equivalent
4. the ways to allocate import licenses
5. comparisons between import quotas and VERs
6. other ways to limit the quantity of imports

Key Terms

Domestic content requirements
these stipulate that the importer must buy a certain percentage of the final product locally.

Fixed favoritism a way of allocating import licenses in which the government simply assigns fixed shares to firms, often based on the shares of imports the firms had before the quota was imposed.

General Agreement on Tariffs and Trade (GATT)
an international organization set up in 1947 and devoted to the dismantling of trade barriers. It is headquartered in Geneva, Switzerland. Under the auspices of GATT, tariff barriers have been substantially reduced in the postwar period, but nontariff barriers have relatively increased.

Import license a legal right to import goods subject to quotas or other nontariff barriers. Import licenses can be allocated by governments on a competitive auctions basis, fixed favoritism, or resource-using application procedures.

Import quota a limit on the total quantity of imports allowed into a country each year. It is the most prevalent nontariff trade barrier.

Section 301 part of the United States Trade Act of 1974. It gives the president power to impose barriers against imports from a country using "unfair trade practices" to shut out imports from the United States and other countries.

Voluntary export restraints (VERs)
nontariff barriers to trade, equivalent to quotas. Exporting countries are coerced into allocating a limited quota of exports. VERs are not legislated and can be imposed with or without formal international negotiations.

World Trade Organization
new name for GATT (since 1994).

Warm-up Questions

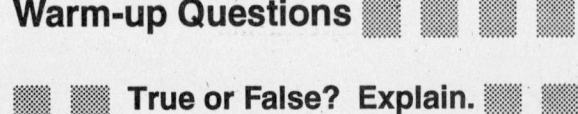

True or False? Explain.

1. T / F Quotas give government officials greater administrative flexibility than tariffs do.

2. T / F The welfare effects of a quota are equivalent to the welfare effects of a tariff under monopoly conditions.

3. T / F If a government has a small tax base, it might prefer tariffs to quotas.

Chapter 8: Nontariff Barriers to Imports

4. T / F   A VER is worse for the country which imposes it than a quota would be.

5. T / F   There is very little that is voluntary about a Voluntary Export Restraint.

Multiple Choice

1. Which of the following is most correct?
   a. Import quotas usually create monopoly rents.
   b. The quota system is more efficient than a tariff system.
   c. An import quota is more suitable for urgent emergency applications by government officials than a comparable tariff.
   d. Under competitive conditions an import quota allows import-competing producers to reap more profits than a tariff.

2. Quotas are often preferred to tariffs because
   a. quotas are a richer source of government revenues
   b. tariff changes are strictly controlled by international trade agreements
   c. quotas do not hinder competition in the domestic market
   d. quotas create a less fertile environment for corrupted government officials

3. Under a VER regime, the tariff equivalent revenue accrues to
   a. the importing-country government
   b. the importing-country consumers
   c. the exporting country
   d. the import-competing industries

4. A domestic monopolist facing import competition
   a. prefers a tariff to its equivalent quota
   b. prefers a quota to its equivalent tariff
   c. is indifferent between a tariff and an equivalent quota
   d. loves free trade

5. Which is the most efficient method of allocating import licenses?
   a. competitive auctions
   b. fixed favoritism toward domestic importers
   c. resource-using application procedures
   d. fixed favoritism toward foreign exporters

Problems

1. Leinster bakers have petitioned their government officials for protection from competition from imported Saxon bread. You have been hired by the government to discuss the options available. The minister of trade wants to know about the ease of implementation and the welfare effects of the following:

   a. an import quota of 40 million loaves

   b. a VER of 40 million loaves

2. In response to information received from a "mole" (spy) in Leinster's Ministry of Trade, the Prime Minister of Saxony wants a retaliatory reduction in imports of telephones. He is especially interested in tariffs and quotas. Keep in mind that Saxony is a "small country" when you provide the following:

   a. Illustrate how a tariff and a quota can have equivalent effects on the price and quantity of imported telephones.

   b. Describe two different ways that the quota licenses can be allocated, and explain who would get the quota rents in each case.

c. Suppose that the Saxon Telephone Factory acts as a monopolist. Illustrate how the equivalence between tariffs and quotas in (a) no longer holds.

3. You are given the following data comparing the effects of free trade, a U.S. import quota, and a Voluntary Export Restraint on the American market for compact disks (CDs):

	With free trade	With an import quota of 8 million	With a VER of 8 million
Price of CDs in the U.S.	$12	$15	$15
Foreign price per CD (at U.S. ports)	$12	$10	$10
Imports of CDs into US (millions/yr)	10	8	8

a. Quantify the welfare gains for the United States from the import quota and from the VER, both relative to free trade. Which of the two import-reducing policies is better for the United States?

b. Quantify the welfare gains for countries that export CDs to the United States from the import quota and the VER, both relative to free trade. Which of the two trade-reducing policies is better for those exporting countries?

Part II: Trade Policy

4. The diagram below depicts an import quota of 100,000 cameras imposed by a small country. The quota raises the domestic price from the free trade level of $100 to a level of $150.

Figure 8.4

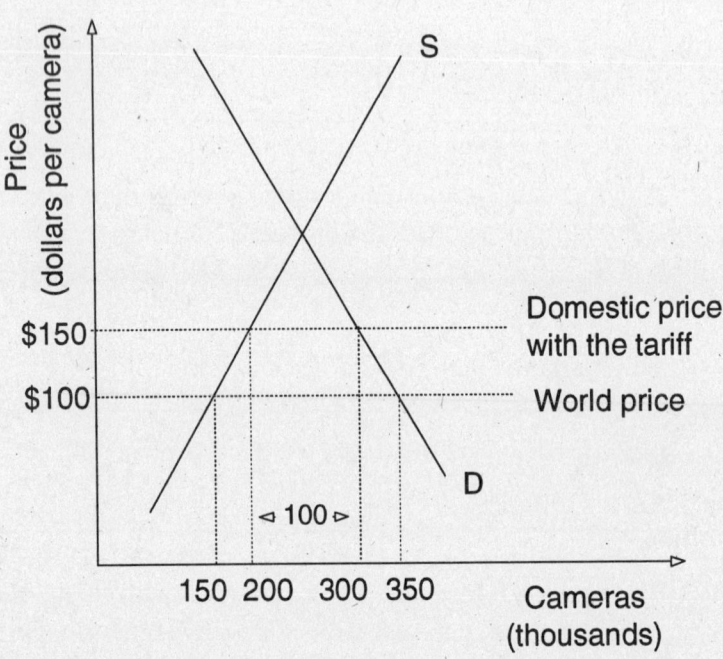

Using the information from this diagram, quantify the following:

a. the gains from international trade before the imposition of the quota

b. the revenue gained by the government by auctioning licenses at $50 each

c. the tariff-equivalent revenue of the quota

d. the value of the increase in producer surplus associated with the imposition of the quota

e. the value of the decrease in consumer surplus associated with the imposition of the quota

f. the net effect on the country's welfare from the imposition of the quota

Discussion Topics

1. Do you think replacing all import quotas with Voluntary Export Restraints would improve or worsen relations between the United States and Japan?

2. Some people think that the United States' "free trade" stance is hypocritical. Do you agree with them?

Final Thought

What has been the effect of coercion? To make one half the world fools, and the other half hypocrites.

—Thomas Jefferson, 1781–1785

THE WALL STREET JOURNAL

January 5, 1995

Russia Imposes Tax on Oil Exports But Won't Require Sales Quotas

By Steve Liesman and
Neela Banerjee
Staff Reporters of The Wall Street Journal

MOSCOW — Splitting the difference between reformers and conservatives, the Russian government imposed a steep tax on petroleum exports but won't, as earlier feared, require oil companies to sell a set percentage of their production on the domestic market. Russia's new oil-export regulations appear, at least on the surface, to meet International Monetary Fund and World Bank demands to free oil exports in return for about $7 billion in loans. "On face value, it looks like an improvement, but there are lots of ambiguities that we would want qualified," said one World Bank official in Washington who was broadly familiar with the decree.

The new regulations don't affect Western joint ventures pumping Russian oil. These exporters remain covered by regulations allowing them to export 100% of their production, said one oil analyst who had seen the decree. Joint ventures with tax exemptions will retain them. "This is better than it could have been," said Alexander Malkov, vice president of Sidanco, one of Russia's largest oil companies. Under earlier drafts, the law would have required Russian companies to sell 65% of their production in the domestic market. But the decree seeks to control exports through a tax of 23 European currency units ($28) per ton of crude. While this represents a decline from the previous tax of 30 ECUs per ton, most Russian oil companies didn't pay the levy because they had received exemptions. One oil analyst said the new system would "just allow Russian companies to survive, not to rehabilitate existing wells." According to Mr. Malkov, big companies such as his that own refineries and wells will weather the new decree better than smaller companies, which will have difficulty paying the tax. "For some smaller companies this could be a mortal blow," he said. The decree, signed Dec. 31 by Prime Minister Viktor Chernomyrdin, is a product of a pitched battle between conservatives and liberals within the Russian cabinet. Conservatives had feared that opening the spigot on Russian oil exports would leave nothing for the domestic market, where prices are 20% to 30% of world levels, and would lead to sharply higher prices within Russia. But reformers argued that export liberalization was vital to boost investment in the dilapidated Russian oil sector. Increased oil exports would also give a boost to the treasury. They also argued that exports would be limited naturally by the capacity of Russian pipelines, which is about 100 million tons a year. Both the IMF and the World Bank threatened to withhold loans if Russia implemented the domestic sales-quota system. Mr. Chernomyrdin fudged the issue and tried to strike a compromise. For example, the new tax will be imposed only in the first quarter and, the decree said, will be reviewed before Feb. 1. Access to Russia's crowded oil pipelines now will be distributed according to each company's level of production, the document said. "They wanted money from the IMF," said one Western oil executive. "Unless they came up with a system like this which guarantees equal access to pipelines and ports, they weren't going to get it." Yet, in a bow to conservative forces, several sections in the decree appear to allow for quota systems or other administrative measures in the future.

Source: *The Wall Street Journal*, January 5, 1995. Reprinted with permission of THE WALL STREET JOURNAL, 1995 Dow Jones & Company, Inc. All rights reserved worldwide.

CHAPTER 9
Arguments for and against Protection

Objectives of the Chapter

This chapter extends and qualifies the arguments presented in Chapters 7 and 8. The arguments for and against a tariff are more varied than those presented earlier. Specifically, the chapter puts into perspective the limits for the case of free trade by identifying the conditions under which imposing a tariff is beneficial. There are valid arguments for the "optimal tariff" and "second-best" cases. A tariff is particularly desirable (up to a limit) when the defect in the economy relates to international trade.

After studying Chapter 9, you should be able to identify

1. where the limits to the case of free trade lie
2. when imposing a tariff is sometimes better than doing nothing
3. how some other policy is usually better than the tariff in the "second-best" cases
4. the limits within which the infant industry argument is valid
5. the dying industry, infant-government, national pride, and national defense arguments for import protection

Key Terms

Adjustment assistance
: government financial assistance to relocate and retrain workers (and firms) for re-employment in expanding sectors and away from sectors that are declining as a result of import competition.

Distortions
: restrictions that prevent the market from equating social benefits and costs of an economic activity. For example, the market price of cigarettes does not reflect the indirect effect (externally) on third parties (other than the producer and the smoker), resulting in too many cigarettes being produced and consumed. The total social cost of smoking is higher than the private cost.

Infant government argument
the notion that in poor countries taxes cannot be effectively collected and, hence, tariffs are an important source of public revenues.

Infant industry argument
the argument that a new industry (especially in less developed countries) needs protection until it attains a competitive level of cost (and output) in world markets.

Second-best world a world that contains market distortions.

Specificity rule this guideline states that it is more efficient to use those policy tools that are closest to the sources of the distortions separating private and social benefits or costs.

Warm-up Questions

True or False? Explain.

1. T / F The specificity rule says that tariffs are usually not the best way of curing distortions in a country's economy.

2. T / F National defense and national pride arguments for protection are basically second-best.

3. T / F If "learning by doing" means that more production now translates into lower costs later, the best policy is a protective tariff.

4. T / F "Learning by doing" is what study guides in international economics are for.

5. T / F Some "infant industries" never grow up.

Multiple Choice

1. Imposing a tariff aimed at counteracting the undesirable effects of domestic distortions
   a. always reduces net national welfare
   b. is the optimal policy response
   c. is ineffective in achieving its stated goal
   d. can be better than doing nothing

2. In which case is the national defense argument a valid one for tariff protection?
   a. when the crucial goods are depletable mineral resources
   b. when stocks of the crucial goods can be cheaply stored
   c. when production subsidies or stockpiling are prohibitively expensive
   d. when a war with a neighboring country is feared

3. Which of these arguments in favor of a tariff is most likely to be valid for poor countries?
   a. protection of domestic labor against cheap foreign labor
   b. correction of the balance of payments problem
   c. increase in domestic employment
   d. a poorly developed system for collecting domestic taxes

4. In which of the following cases does economic analysis (using the "one-dollar, one-vote" yardstick) justify the use of tariffs as better than adopting other policies?
   a. the infant government case
   b. the infant industry case
   c. the dying industry case
   d. low "country esteem"

5. Compared with a tariff, a subsidy for import-competing producers
   a. is of no concern to foreign exporters
   b. avoids the consumer surplus loss
   c. brings a larger net welfare loss because the consumers have to pay for it, rather than taking in revenues as with a tariff
   d. is better than a tariff when the importing nation has some monopoly power

Problems

1. Because it is a small country, if Saxony placed a tariff on telephones imported from Leinster, it would cause a net reduction in Saxon welfare. What, then, could be the second-best arguments for the imposition of such a tariff? Can you think of methods other than a tariff to achieve the country's goals?

2. If an infant industry tariff is removed in the future, is society made better off or worse off? Why?

3. Studies have shown that practice makes perfect in building airplanes. For new firms, there is an early "learning by doing" period in which the costs are high, but the production experience itself is guaranteed to reduce later costs. Japan cannot yet produce airplanes as efficiently as Boeing or Airbus, but could ultimately produce at lower cost if given the chance to survive against competition from cheaper imported airplanes.

    Should Japan use a tariff on imported airplanes, forcing Japan Air Lines and others to pay more until Japan's airplane industry "gets off the ground?" Discuss carefully.

4. Trade barriers which protect the income of a scarce factor of production (such as unskilled labor in the United States) are really income redistribution tools. What are the costs associated with using tariffs to meet this goal? What are more economically efficient means of accomplishing this goal?

Discussion Topics

1. Is "adjustment assistance" a logical response to a non-Stolper-Samuelson world in which laborers are somehow not freely mobile between sectors?

2. What goods do you think are justified in receiving a national defense tariff?

3. Think about the international trade consequences of balancing the federal budget by reducing subsidies to American manufacturers and farmers.

Final Thought

No nation was ever ruined by trade.

— Benjamin Franklin, 1779

CHAPTER 10 Pushing Exports

Objectives of the Chapter

In contrast to limiting the number of imports into a country, governments may actively promote exports of goods from the country. While this sounds like a policy of encouraging free trade, in practice it is implemented to gain some "unfair" advantage over a trading partner.

After studying Chapter 10, you should understand

1. the economic meaning of "dumping"
2. the difference between predatory dumping and persistent dumping
3. export subsidies and countervailing import duties
4. the welfare effects of subsidies and duties
5. examples of export promotion such as in steel, autos, and televisions

Key Terms

Antidumping duty tariffs sanctioned under the International Anti-Dumping Code (signed by most parties to GATT) to counteract or prevent dumping.

Countervailing import duties
 retaliatory duties against a foreign government subsidizing exports into your national market.

Dumping a form of international price discrimination in which an exporting firm sells at a lower price in a foreign market than it charges in other markets (usually its domestic market), or sells its exports at a price that is below its costs.

Export subsidy government policy to encourage export of goods and discourage sale of goods on the domestic market.

Industrial targeting having government and industry agree in advance on which industrial products need encouragement and subsidy, in anticipation of being able to export them in the future.

Persistent dumping dumping that goes on indefinitely, as opposed to "distress dumping" which occurs only during periods of economic downturn, or predatory dumping.

Predatory dumping this type of dumping occurs when the firm temporarily discriminates in favor of some foreign buyers with the intent of eliminating competitors and later raising its price after the competition is dead.

Strategic trade policy
a government campaign to develop export advantage and cut imports in targeted sectors, to gain world market shares in global oligopoly industries.

Warm-up Questions

True or False? Explain.

1. T / F   An export subsidy is more common than an export duty.

2. T / F   Although it discourages most tariffs, GATT allows an importing country to levy antidumping tariffs.

3. T / F   Strategic trade policy and predatory dumping are weapons of economic warfare.

4. T / F   Japan is the world's leading steel exporter.

5. T / F   If a country levies a countervailing duty against a subsidized exporter, trade volumes and prices end up being about the same as those that would exist without the subsidy and duty.

Multiple Choice

1. Which of the following is a correct statement?
   a. Dumping is a money-losing venture for any firm. Therefore, it can only be a temporary phenomenon.
   b. Firms engage in dumping for the sole purpose of driving competition out of the market to later raise prices.
   c. Dumping is only possible when a firm can discriminate between markets. Otherwise, the dumpee can re-export the dumped goods at a profit.
   d. Dumping is always a profitable venture. Otherwise, no one would engage in dumping at all.

2. In 1970, one major dumping case was brought against Sony of Japan. Sony was selling televisions made in Japan to U.S. consumers for $180 while charging Japanese consumers $333 for the same model. In response to the threat issued by the U.S. government, Sony shifted its supply for the U.S. market to a plant built in California, but did not change prices of televisions in either country. This case best describes
   a. protection by the U.S. government of Japanese producers and consumers
   b. persistent dumping
   c. predatory dumping
   d. trade retaliation

3. If a foreign government is subsidizing exports into your national market, what should you do to maximize the net welfare effect on your nation (assuming no monoposony power)?
   a. enjoy the bargain prices for imports
   b. retaliate by imposing a countervailing duty to protect the domestic industry
   c. subsidize your own exports to foreign markets
   d. retaliate by imposing an import quota

4. For profitable dumping to take place,
   a. the demand elasticities in both markets must be the same
   b. the demands in both markets must be inelastic
   c. the demands in both markets must be elastic
   d. the demand in the foreign market must be more elastic than the demand in the home market

5. Governments have frequently used export-promoting policies in
   a. steel
   b. autos
   c. aircraft
   d. all of the above
   e. none of the above

Problems

1. Suppose that Leinster subsidizes exports of telephones to Saxony. How would that affect the level of welfare in Leinster and in Saxony? (Hint: Recall that Saxony is a small country and Leinster is a large country.)

2. Describe how each of the following policies could plausibly bring a net gain to the world as a whole.

   a. the United States levies an anti-dumping duty against Canadian beer

   b. the United States levies a countervailing duty against subsidized steel imports from Brazil

c. the United States forces foreign suppliers of pocket calculators to reach a voluntary export restraining agreement

3. Which of the following television-exporting countries is guilty of dumping in the Saudi Arabian market?

	Phillips (Holland)	Sharp (Japan)	RCA (USA)
Average unit cost	$250	$300	$295
Domestic price in exporting country	$250	$325	$300
Export price from factory	$200	$310	$300
Price in Saudi Arabia	$260	$350	$350

4. Suppose that a European steel manufacturing firm is acting as a discriminating monopolist when selling at home and exporting to the United States.

   a. Illustrate whether the firm will "dump" on the U.S. market, and show how this result depends on the demand curves.

b. Assume that the United States responds with a tariff (countervailing duty) which *does* influence the price of steel imports. Illustrate the effect of the tariff on U.S. consumers, producers, and net national welfare.

Discussion Topics

1. Try to formulate arguments for export subsidies in terms of the national defense and the infant industry models.

2. What sectors (if any) do you think are likely to receive future export promotion from the U.S. government?

Final Thought

The holder of a monopoly is a sinner and offender.

— Mohammed, c. 610

THE WALL STREET JOURNAL
October 21, 1994

The Americas: U.S. Protectionists Prick Colombian Rose Growers

By Eduardo Urdaneta

BOGOTA — Recently, while sitting in my office preparing for my next trip to the Miami office of the U.S Department of Commerce, I realized that it has been six months since I've had the chance to check up on the performance of my rose production company. During that time, I have not visited clients, planned production, assisted in technical seminars, or arranged and promoted the international trade shows that are so critical to my industry. Instead, I've been forced to spend all my time dealing with the thousands of pages of reports and support documentation necessary to respond to antidumping questionnaires initiated by my U.S. competitors.

For the ninth time in the last 13 years, U.S. flower producers have decided to go after their counterparts in Colombia, relying on governmental protection to offset their comparative disadvantages in production. We've survived past assaults. But this time, I must personally bring close to three tons of sales and cost records to Miami, because the U.S. regulators won't travel to Bogota for safety reasons. And besides transporting all these documents, I have to bring my entire administrative staff to answer specific questions about our industry. Since there won't be anyone in Colombia to run my company while we're in the U.S., I'm deeply concerned that I may not have a successful business to come back to.

The most recent antidumping petition by U.S. rose producers against imports of fresh-cut roses from Colombia and Ecuador was filed in February. Only one of the eight other antidumping petitions resulted in the imposition of an antidumping order. But despite the lack of success in these actions, millions of dollars in legal fees and expenses have been spent pursuing and defending the various actions brought by U.S. producers against Colombian producers.

In a recent presentation made in Israel about future developments in the global floriculture market, the chairman of the executive board of the Holland-based Cebeco group talked about the driving forces behind the industry. He included demographic development, communication and biotechnology, market globalization, consumer behavior, and more international competition. Protectionism was not among the forces recommended for expanding the industry. However, it's beginning to look as though U.S. producers believe that the best way of improving their competitive position is by pulling their competitors down to their own production levels. Perhaps this sounds petulant. But consider our burden. People in the U.S. may have grown accustomed to frivolous lawsuits, but the specifics of what we have to go through to comply with the most recent complaint are outrageous even by U.S. standards. Commerce has issued at least 10 questionnaires to my company, as well as to the 15 other companies included in the sample group, requesting detailed information about sales and incurred costs in 1993. These questionnaires include many questions — some times more than 200 — most of which have been already properly answered in previous questionnaires.

Information on sales has to be provided for each rose variety — segregated by stem length, channel of distribution, term of sale and packing style. That request was overwhelming since there are nearly 100 rose varieties, five standard stem lengths, four different kinds of distribution, two terms of sales and several packing modalities. We had to hire consultants to develop computer software to gather all the possible permutations.

We were also requested to go through every selling invoice for every sale made in 1993. Although the information requested monthly prices, it was necessary to check every single transaction. Deadlines to provide the above information were ludicrous. The antidumping statute has strict deadlines that may not be modified by interested parties or the administering authority. Therefore we had no other choice but to dedicate all our administrative personnel to the preparation of responses. The whole staff has been working around the clock, and general managers have been directly involved in the preparation of these responses. Simply put, no one is taking care of the business. And now we're required to pack up all this paper work, ship it to Miami, and bring our entire support staff to explain it all to U.S. regulators.

Well, the goals of U.S. domestic producers may have been achieved: For different reasons, both Colombian and U.S. producers are at this time producing roses at the same inefficient cost levels — the U.S. producers, because of high land and labor costs, with lower quality products; and Colombian producers, because of the time and money wasted attending to the dictates of an absurd lawsuit.

In addition to this external burden, Colombian flower producers have had to absorb the enormous costs placed on us by the illegal drug market. Since 1991, the Colombian peso has artificially gained value against the dollar, primarily because of the huge influx of drug dollars. And an overvalued currency kills exporters. In addition, we have had to provide 24-hour surveillance to ensure that our shipments to foreign markets contain flowers and only flowers. There is a high cost involved in safety seals and round-the-clock security inspections. Working under these circumstances, we have the firm conviction that Colombian flower growers have not taken their success in the world flower business for granted.

As one who has closely followed the liberalization of trading policies over the past decade, I think the position of the U.S. vis-a-vis Colombian flower growers is particularly untenable. Antidumping laws should be applied when and where unfair trading practices are in place. But they should not be used as an excuse for protectionism, particularly by a government trying to play the role of leader in the movement toward open markets in this hemisphere and elsewhere.

And last but not least, one cannot forget that by penalizing the Colombian growers, a burden is placed on U.S. consumers: They will have to pay a higher price for the product. I wonder how this age-old practice of political favoritism at the expense of the majority will play during an election year when politics-as-usual has become the prime target of candidates on both sides.

— *Mr. Urdaneta is manager of the Bogota-based Grupo Prisma.*

Source: *The Wall Street Journal*, October 21, 1994. Reprinted with permission of THE WALL STREET JOURNAL, 1994 Dow Jones & Company, Inc. All rights reserved worldwide.

THE WALL STREET JOURNAL
March 17, 1995

Mexico's Mantra for Salvation: Export, Export, Export — Some Doubt the Economic Foundation Has Been Laid for the Nation to Compete

By Craig Torres and
Paul B. Carroll
Staff Reporters of The Wall Street Journal

MEXICO CITY — Can Mexico become an export powerhouse virtually overnight? That's the $52 billion question hovering over the Mexican government's bold new plan to rescue the country from its deepest financial crisis in more than a decade. Wall Street has focused mainly on arcane economic targets contained in the recovery plan released last week. But senior Mexican officials make clear that it boils down to a simple imperative: export or else.

"This year we should have a huge trade surplus," says Finance Minister Guillermo Ortiz. "We must keep exports competitive."

It's a colossal challenge, and it isn't at all clear Mexico will succeed. The problem is time, and the country hasn't had enough of it. Despite huge inflows of foreign investment during the past six years, when Mexico seemed to be a model for emerging economies everywhere, surprisingly little money found its way into the infrastructure projects and machinery that make companies globally competitive.

The country's telephone system is a mess, highways are expensive to use and railroads are creaky remnants from the turn of the century. Worse, most Mexican companies, accustomed to an overvalued peso, have geared their products to less-demanding domestic consumers rather than investing in plant improvements to penetrate foreign markets. Now they are playing catch-up during a crippling recession.

The Mexican government's chief tool in engineering an export turnaround is the peso devaluation announced Dec. 20. The peso has been falling steadily since then, closing yesterday at 7.15 pesos to the dollar. That represents a drop of 52% in the peso's value since the devaluation, and makes Mexican goods cheaper overseas.

But it's a move fraught with danger. Because they raise the price of foreign imports, devaluations can lead to destabilizing inflation. And studies show a declining currency in and of itself won't quickly boost exports. "You need quality products, service, good packaging and logistics," says Victor Almeida, chief executive of Chihuahua-based tile maker Internacional de Ceramica SA. "Most importantly, you have to convince the customer to try your product. It takes years to open a market."

The problem is, Mexico doesn't have years. The government's recovery plan, backed up by $52 billion in loan guarantees by the U.S. and international agencies, calls for Mexico to lower its appetite for foreign capital by cutting its current-account deficit to $2 billion this year from a whopping $29 billion in 1994. The current account deficit is a broad measure of trade in goods and services plus certain financial transfers. Part of the deficit reduction will come from fewer imports, because Mexicans won't be able to afford them. But officials say export growth must accelerate as well. They're expecting foreign sales to grow 27% this year, nearly double 1994's 16% pace.

Finance Minister Ortiz insists the target can be hit, and says the government is preparing plans to help exporters. He wants to cut red tape such as removing what he calls "ancient" labor taxes. He's even talking about revamping the country's bankruptcy laws so troubled exporters can emerge more quickly from reorganization proceedings.

Early signs are encouraging. In February, the country recorded its first trade surplus in four years, driven partly by a 24% jump in exports of goods other than oil. Some big companies that already have a good export track record are reporting a quick boost from the devaluation.

But big manufacturing exporters represent just 14% of the Mexican economy. And there's little to suggest that smaller companies will be able to crank up foreign sales, especially since they are being crushed by high financing costs. Partly to hold down inflation, the government has boosted interest rates to more than 80%.

Take Aluart, a small Mexico City-based company that exports pewter and aluminum gift items. Owner Cecilia Zavala says the peso devaluation has helped her business, and U.S. buyers are flocking to Mexico. Aluart's sales are up, but the company is suffering because buyers typically wait 70 days before paying. So Aluart, which can't get loans because interest rates are more than 90% today, must scrape together whatever cash it has to rebuild its inventories.

Things weren't supposed to turn out this way. The economic growth model of former President Carlos Salinas de Gortari called for Mexico to go through a long incubation period before emerging as a big exporter. In the meantime, officials counted on attracting billions of dollars a year in foreign investment to plow into infrastructure and factories to prepare itself.

Although the plan meant running a current-account deficit equivalent to 7% or 8% of gross domestic product, Pedro Aspe, Mr. Salinas's finance minister, used to say Singapore ran a 15% deficit for 15 years before becoming a modern economy.

For a long time, it worked. During the 1988-1994 term of Mr. Salinas, foreign investors poured more than $100 billion into the economy, so confident were they that Mexico was an excellent long-term bet.

Some of the money helped improve the infrastructure, as planned. Foreign and domestic investors built 3,000 miles of roads during the Salinas years, and in many cases helped pay for new technology systems inside banks, or new assembly lines inside bottling plants. Mr. Salinas also denationalized banks and engineered Mexico's entry into the North American Free Trade Agreement, potentially opening vast new export markets.

Of course, a good portion of the investment turned out to be "hot money" in stocks and bonds that could vanish virtually overnight. Last year it happened. The rising current-account deficit and political unrest, punctuated by two assassinations and a peasant uprising, led to a virtual run on the peso that depleted the country's foreign reserves. The new administration of President Ernesto Zedillo decided it had no choice but to devalue the currency as investors turned in their pesos for dollars and left the country.

And with that, the incubation period was over. Since foreign money wasn't going to flood back anytime soon, officials concluded that the country would have to finance its own foreign-exchange needs by competing in export markets immediately.

The big question is, does Mexico have the capacity?

A look at major foreign investments in Mexico shows how the strong peso distracted companies from any export opportunities and focused them on the domestic market. The high-profile investments during the Salinas years were mostly like the Bell Atlantic Corp. announcement in October 1993 that it would spend $1.04 billion to buy a 42% stake in Mexican cellular company Iusacell. That was hardly an export opportunity.

Also, much of the investment went toward satisfying Mexico's new consumer culture, because executives didn't understand that the economy was living on both borrowed money and on borrowed time. Retailers such as Wal-Mart Stores Inc. began huge expansion projects in Mexico, to take advantage of the enormous pent-up demand for everything from boom-box radios to silk ties, as the strong peso reduced inflation and gave a big boost to disposable income in Mexico. Now they have had to slow their plans because the bottom has dropped out of the domestic market after the devaluation made imported goods too expensive for many Mexicans to buy.

Infrastructure development, too, has been less than many thought. Take those beautiful highways, for example. Cost overruns in the construction of toll roads made tolls so high that the roads are little used. A transportation executive jokes that when he uses the Mexico City-Acapulco road, which has a toll of $80, he doubles the traffic.

Railroads are also old and poorly maintained. As a result, while Mexico's Sinaloa valley is perfect for growing nice, fat tomatoes during times of the year when the U.S. can't supply its own needs, it's hard for them to find their way north. Companies wanting to ship tomatoes to the U.S. have to contend with a sprawling bureaucracy and then negotiate a handoff to a U.S. carrier at the border. Trains move very slowly over many sections of track because repairs that take about two weeks in the U.S. may require six or seven years in Mexico.

With so much working against Mexican exports, trade data show that Mexico's export economy has been running mainly on its advantage in crude oil and cheap labor. Auto parts, crude oil and chemicals accounted for 53% of Mexican exports in 1993.

Analysts say there's huge wasted potential. For instance, despite millions of acres of fertile land and nearly year-round growing seasons, fresh vegetables accounted for only 2.2% of all exports in 1993, and fresh fruit only 1.4%.

Goods with greater value, such as computer chips, have little representation in the trade numbers, even though they're the type of skilled-labor products Mexico needs to produce eventually if it is to get away from commodities and labor-intensive goods and become a mature export economy.

Source: *The Wall Street Journal*, March 17, 1995. Reprinted with permission of THE WALL STREET JOURNAL, 1995 Dow Jones & Company, Inc. All rights reserved worldwide.

CHAPTER 11
Trade Blocs and Trade Blocks

Objectives of the Chapter

Previous chapters emphasized import barriers that are mainly imposed to restrict all imports. This chapter, however, examines import barriers meant to discriminate between countries, taxing goods and services (and assets) from some countries more than others. Some export barriers may also be imposed to direct the flow of merchandise and assets' trade to some countries more than to others.

Chapter 11 discusses the different forms of economic integration (including trade blocs) and their economic ramifications. Trade blocs have become increasingly important in recent years. Specifically, the European Union and the North American Free Trade Area have revived interest in the study of economic integration and trade blocs.

After studying this chapter, you should be able to identify

1. the different forms of economic integration
2. the economic implications of trade blocs and full unions
3. how trade blocs can lead to trade creation or trade diversion
4. the conditions under which trade blocs and full unions are likely to succeed or fail
5. how economic integration tends to be more successful among developed countries than developing countries

Key Terms

Common market an international union going beyond a customs union by also allowing for the free movement of labor and capital (factor flows) among member nations.

Customs union one in which members remove all barriers to trade among themselves and adopt a common set of external barriers, thereby eliminating the need for customs inspection at internal borders (e.g., EEC from 1957 – 1992).

Economic sanctions discriminatory restrictions or complete bans on economic exchange, designed to punish the target country or countries.

Economic union one which extends a common market by harmonizing the monetary and fiscal policies of the member nations as well.

Embargoes (boycotts)
complete bans on economic exchange.

Free trade area an area in which members remove trade barriers among themselves but keep their separate national barriers against trade with the outside world.

Most favored nation (MFN) principle
stipulates that any concession given to one foreign nation must be given to all foreign nations that have MFN status. GATT states that all contracting parties are entitled to MFN status.

Trade blocs forms of economic integration whereby members remove explicit trade barriers among themselves, but keep their national barriers to the flow of labor and capital and their national fiscal and monetary autonomy. Trade blocs are exemplified mainly by free-trade areas and custom unions.

Trade creation the increase in trade volume caused by union with a lower cost (more efficient) supplier within the trade bloc.

Trade diversion the volume of trade shifted from a lower-cost (more efficient) supplier outside the trade bloc to a higher-cost (less efficient) supplier within the union.

Warm-up Questions

True or False? Explain.

1. T / F Trade discrimination is bad in the sense that separate deals with separate nations may destroy much of the gains from global markets.

2. T / F The formation of a customs union will definitely raise welfare.

3. T / F The less elastic is the import demand curve, the greater the gains from a customs union.

4. T / F Customs unions are more likely to be successful among developed countries than among less developed countries.

5. T / F An export embargo will backfire if the embargoing country has an inelastic export supply curve while the target country has an elastic import demand curve.

Multiple Choice

1. If all member nations of a customs union are fully employed before and after the formation of the union, then (assuming that trade diversion does not dominate)
   a. the welfare of the member nations will decrease
   b. the welfare of the member nations will increase but world welfare will decrease
   c. the welfare of the member nations and the world will increase
   d. no member nations will have time to organize good soccer matches

2. Trade sanctions
   a. are usually successful as long as the imposing countries are developed countries
   b. are more likely to be successful when the sanctioning countries have high trade elasticities
   c. are more likely to be successful when the sanctioning countries have low trade elasticities
   d. are successful mostly due to world cooperation, not trade elasticities

3. Which of the following is *not* correct?
   a. The formation of a common market allows the free movement of factors of production between member nations.
   b. The 1992 EC common market overturned Italian Pasta Protection Laws which protected higher-cost producers.
   c. A common market coordinates monetary and fiscal policies of members.
   d. Common markets have been more successful among rich countries than among poor countries.

4. The United States was able to initiate most of the trade embargoes in the last four decades mainly because
   a. the United States is a superpower
   b. the United States has high demand and supply elasticities in a significant number of products and can, therefore, influence trade
   c. other countries cannot do without U.S. trade
   d. embargoes are usually successful

5. If, after the creation of the EU, the British have an incentive to purchase less-efficiently produced Irish cheese rather than importing inexpensive cheese from New Zealand, this probably shows
   a. trade creation
   b. trade diversion
   c. government interference in the marketplace
   d. common sense

Problems

1. If Saxony and Leinster currently have no barriers to free trade between them, are the two countries, in effect,

   a. a free trade area?

   b. a customs union?

   c. a common market?

   d. an economic union?

2. Assume that the United States currently imports 1000 pairs of shoes from South Korea at $20 per pair. With a 50% tariff, the consumer price in the United States is $30 per pair. The price of shoes in Mexico is $25 per pair. If the United States and Mexico were to reach a free trade agreement, the United States would import 1200 pairs of shoes from Mexico and none from South Korea.

Draw a graph to analyze possible welfare changes (in dollars) to American consumers, the U.S. government, and the nation as a whole.

3. Assume that China is a large country with elastic demand for foreign goods. Would U.S.-imposed economic sanctions (trade embargoes) on China be a successful policy to penalize the Chinese government?

4. Suppose that signing the North American Free Trade Agreement (NAFTA) changes U.S. import quantities as follows (you may assume there is no effect on U.S. imports from Canada):

	U.S. imports from Mexico	U.S. imports from outside North America
Before NAFTA	$30 billion	$300 billion
After ("afta") NAFTA	$50 billion	$295 billion

Does this evidence suggest a net world welfare gain or welfare loss from NAFTA?

5. Use the table below to calculate the benefits (or losses) from joining a customs union:

	Domestic price of wheat under free trade	Price to Britain when tariff on wheat = 50%	Price to Britain when tariff on wheat = 25%
Britain	100	100	100
EC	70	105	87.5
Canada	65	102.5	81.25

a. If Britain joins the EC in a customs union when the tariff on wheat imports is 50%, at what price will Britain import wheat from the EC? Is this a case of trade creation or trade diversion?

b. If Britain joins the EC in a customs union when the tariff on wheat imports is 25%, will this lead to trade creation or trade diversion?

c. Assume that Britain is not willing to join the EC union. If the tariff is 25%, should Britain import wheat (from whom?) or should Britain grow its own wheat?

Discussion Topics

1. If Japan were to join a free trade area with one other country, which country would you suggest it be?

2. Do you think the proliferation of trade blocs will increase or decrease tensions among the countries of the world?

3. Do you think the American embargo on Cuba has been an economic success? Has it been a political success?

4. When the Soviet Union invaded Afghanistan in 1979, the United States placed a grain embargo on the USSR. Discuss the economic and noneconomic implications of using food as a "weapon."

Final Thought

Peace is the natural effect of trade. Two nations who traffic with each other become reciprocally dependent; for if one has an interest in buying, the other has an interest in selling; and thus their union is founded on their natural necessities.

— C.S. Montesquieu, 1748

THE WALL STREET JOURNAL
November 14, 1994

Asia-Pacific Forum Finds Focus: Trade
Group's 18 Nations Move Toward Concrete Action

By Dan Biers and Craig Forman
Staff Reporters of The Wall Street Journal

JAKARTA — As 18 leaders of Asian-Pacific nations gather here for a summit starting tonight, it is APEC itself that appears to have arrived.

The two-day meeting seems likely to emerge as a turning point for the Asia-Pacific Economic Cooperation forum, which began only five years ago as a loose gathering of 12 nations without a clear goal.

That's no longer the case. After agreeing to a nonbinding set of principles to remove barriers to foreign investments, cabinet ministers this weekend wrestled with a draft plan for a more ambitious achievement: free trade, most likely by the year 2020, in an area that now covers a third of the world's people, 40% of its trade and half of its economic output.

Leaders will discuss the plans on Tuesday. "We in the United States hope and expect the vision and goal of free trade in the region by 2020 will be endorsed," U.S. Trade Secretary Mickey Kantor said Saturday after the ministerial meetings.

Some disagreements remain on the draft proposal's scope and pace, with Malaysia leading resistance to setting a deadline. But nobody is challenging the vision of removing economic barriers. That political commitment marks the continuing transformation of APEC from forum into substance.

The discussions thus far "have had a texture and breadth that suggest the evolution to a real community," said Walter Mondale, U.S. ambassador to Japan, in an interview.

Indonesia's Coordinating Minister for Industry and Trade Hartarto, who led the ministerial meeting, agreed that "we do believe we have taken significant steps."

Under the investment principles, for example, APEC members are to "minimize" use of performance requirements — such as demands for local content or export quotas or both — that limit growth in trade and investment. They also support equal treatment for foreign and domestic investors and transparency in investment laws, regulations and guidelines.

A flurry of bilateral meetings has formed a backdrop to the APEC summit. The U.S. and Japan agreed to try to restart stalled auto-trade negotiations, and the U.S. and China reviewed differences over conditions for Beijing's bid to join the General Agreement on Tariffs and Trade.

On auto trade, which accounts for much of America's huge trade imbalance with Japan, officials suggested that the two sides still remain far apart over steps the Japanese government might take to boost imports from the U.S.

On GATT, Mr. Kantor said the Chinese position was "not adequate" and specifically pointed to protection of intellectual-property rights as an area needing improvement. "I am not persuaded we can finish our negotiations by the end of the year, but we will make every effort," he said.

China would like quick agreement so it can be a founding member of the World Trade Organization, which is set to replace GATT in January. While Mr. Kantor stressed that "the pace of progress depends on China," his Chinese counterpart, Wu Yi, countered that the decision "isn't a one-way street."

Meanwhile, U.S. officials, led by Secretary of State Warren Christopher, spent much time informally and in the bilateral meetings assuring ministers that the electoral drubbing received by the Democratic Party last Tuesday won't affect U.S. trade policies, which Mr. Christopher stressed have bipartisan support.

The diplomatic activity will be capped today with bilateral meetings likely to focus on trade issues between President Clinton and Japanese Prime Minister Tomiichi Murayama, and between Mr. Clinton and Chinese President Jiang Zemin. They then will join the other leaders at the mountainside village of Bogor to consider the regional free-trade plan on Tuesday.

C. Fred Bergsten, chairman of the advisory panel that proposed 2020 as a deadline for free trade in the region, said failure to agree to a deadline "would not be fatal" but "would be less forceful to individual member countries as they try to implement the approach and less credible to private firms."

Malaysia's minister for international trade and industry, Datuk Rafidah Aziz, continues to publicly oppose the plan. Because the forum reaches agreement by consensus, a single member can block a proposal supported by all the others.

Datuk Rafidah has refused to say what stand Malaysian Prime Minister Mahathir Mohamad would take at the Tuesday summit. But she received strong applause from fellow ministers when she announced Malaysia's desire to host the APEC ministerial meeting in 1998, which was interpreted by some delegates as a sign that Malaysia would come on board.

Malaysia is wary of any attempt to institutionalize APEC, which it fears could be a forum for the U.S. to impose its will on the smaller, developing nations of Asia.

So far, the group's members have tried to allay such concerns by insisting that APEC won't be turned into a trade bloc, shying away from a fundamental debate over whether APEC may someday challenge other regional groups, such as the Association of Southeast Asian Nations, or Asean. At the moment, the remoteness of the free-trade goal is one explanation for why such diverse countries can even discuss these issues. There's a debate, too, over admitting new members, and over the conditions the group should use to extend its trade terms to outsiders.

Every nation participating seems to believe it can successfully negotiate tradeoffs for its benefit: For the U.S., APEC seems a good route to strengthen ties to the world's fastest growing countries, while pushing toward free trade. For Japan, APEC seems a way of hard-wiring the U.S. into Asia, and another route to keep Asia a stable landscape not dominated by any single nation. Developing nations see APEC as a way to keep the crucial U.S. market open.

Source: *The Wall Street Journal*, November 14, 1994. Reprinted with permission of THE WALL STREET JOURNAL, 1994 Dow Jones & Company, Inc. All rights reserved worldwide.

An Emerging Giant

APEC's role in the world economy

By Population
World population in 1992 was 5.48 billion;
    APEC accounts for 2.08 billion, or 38%

Others**	58%
China*	21%
ASEAN, NIEs*	7%
Americas*	7%
EC**	7%
Japan*	2%

GDP
World GDP in 1992 was $23.6 trillion;
    APEC accounts for $12.2 trillion, or 52%

Americas*	29%
EC**	28%
Others**	20%
Japan*	16%
ASEAN, NIEs*	4%
China*	2%
Oceania*	1%

Trade
World trade in 1992 was $7.5 trillion;
APEC accounts for $3.1 trillion, or 41%

EC**	40%
Others**	20%
Americas*	17%
ASEAN, NIEs*	12%
Japan*	2%
China*	1%
Oceania*	1%

*APEC
**Non-APEC
NIEs = Newly industrializing nations
Source: International Monetary Fund; Japanese government statistics

THE WALL STREET JOURNAL
November 25, 1994

Latin Trade Agreements Could Shut Out Nafta Members

By Jorge A. Vilches

BUENOS AIRES, Argentina— While the ruminations on how and when to expand the North American Free Trade Agreement southward linger on, the steady progress of a South American trade agreement deserves immediate attention from those interested in establishing a hemispheric trading union. It's time to stop the Nafta expansion debate long enough to consider the impact of "that other" trade agreement—one that may soon steal the limelight from, and possibly impede the further development of, Nafta's extension.

Many Wall Street Journal readers probably have heard about Mercosur. Incorrectly defined by some as a "free trade zone," Mercosur is a customs union linking Brazil, Argentina, Paraguay and Uruguay. After several delays, it is due to go into effect on Jan. 1.

But with just a few weeks to go before implementation, Argentine Finance Minister Domingo Cavallo reportedly expressed last-minute misgivings about the agreement to Brazilian President-elect Fernando Henrique Cardoso at a recent luncheon. It seems that few have considered the effect Mercosur could have on South American development, particularly since member states might not be able to participate in nontariff trade with countries outside the union. And fewer still have considered the presence of an even larger exclusionary agreement looming on the horizon: Alcsa, a Spanish acronym for "South American Area of Free Commerce."

Alcsa was designed by the Brazilian Ministry of Foreign Affairs to be the extension of Mercosur. It has been officially endorsed by current Brazilian President Itamar Franco and by President-elect Cardoso. Once again, at the core of this larger trade agreement would be Brazil, the most powerful country in the hemisphere next to the U.S., the world's ninth-largest economy and the fifth-largest weapons manufacturer. In a nutshell, there is a growing fear of many here that Alcsa and Mercosur embody Brazil's geopolitical scheme to keep most of Latin America under Brazil's sphere of influence.

Since it is a customs union and not a free trade zone, Mercosur's members will tax the rest of the world — including Nafta members — with an "External Common Tariff" of 15% to 20%, at least until 2006. This includes tariffs on everything our countries need to modernize: including telecommunications, computer technology and other capital goods. Not coincidentally, these are items that Brazil's economy produces in abundance.

Clearly many Brazilians don't really want to get into Nafta, believing that they are better off without U.S. competition and with a captive Alcsa market. When Brazilian Foreign Minister Celso Amorim predicted that "free trade should include all of South America within the next 10 years," he was referring to Alcsa, not Nafta. But no one in North America seems to have paid attention to this. Contrary to what many experts have been saying north of the equator, some of the 34 heads of state attending the Summit for the Americas next month in Miami are not focused on the creation of a free trade zone extending from pole to pole in the Americas.

But even some of those who want inclusion in Nafta are becoming frustrated. As Chile's fast-track negotiations on Nafta got derailed, leaders of that country began looking into associate membership in Mercosur. Bolivia, too, is beginning negotiations, and the concept of Alcsa is gaining power by the minute. Nafta members better work fast; otherwise Brazil will win this game. And unfortunately, South Americans will be left without a direct trade link to Uncle Sam and all the social benefits that arise from such a union (standardization of property rights issues, for example). Worse, we will have sealed ourselves within a tomb of underdevelopment.

As good as things may look for Brazil at the moment, no one should be fooled. Brazil remains a sick giant, with a horrendous bureaucracy, serious political disunity and a real potential for slipping right back into the grips of hyperinflation. It doesn't have the stability, the widely available advanced technologies, the capacity to make huge capital investments, or the middle-class markets to make it the "powerhouse" of any trading block. During the past 35 years, more than a dozen Latin American trade schemes have failed because of the glaring absence of a fully developed member country.

Perhaps five years from now, Brazil's slow evolution from a closed, highly taxed and regulated economy into one more driven by market forces will make it a desirable trading partner, both for Nafta members and for other nations of the Americas. But for the time being, the Brazilian miracle has been vastly overstated, and is certainly not reason enough to create a customs union that would limit the full participation of a truly developed giant like the U.S.

As U.S. Ambassador to Brazil Melvin Levitsky notes, "Either Mercosur or Nafta could be the grid upon which a hemispheric trade zone is developed." To which one could add: If Mercosur continues to beat Nafta in offering some kind of treaty more quickly, three quarters of the hemispheric trade zone will be blocked up and left to develop at a far slower pace led by not-so-developed Brazil instead of the U.S. In view of this, the need for Nafta (and especially the U.S.) to put its expansion act together is greater than ever.

The case for a genuine hemispheric free trade zone could take a dramatic and positive turn if Chile (the best and most experienced student in the free-market class) and Argentina (a new but quick learner) are grouped together for quick inclusion in Nafta, a move that could be pushed for at the Miami Summit. Together, the economies of Argentina and Chile add up to another Mexico, but without any of the Ross Perot objections — labor costs and social benefits are modest but comfortable; no migration problems; manageable environmental conflicts with development; no border problems with Nafta members; no major drug problems; stable and growing economies; relatively steady political structures, etc. And the inclusion of Argentina and Chile would just be the beginning. With the direct infusion of badly needed trade, technology and capital from the Nafta economy, Latin America would stand a real chance of finally emerging from its state of underdevelopment. The opportunity may not repeat itself again in the near future, because Brazil's Alcsa is just around the corner.

Mr. Vilches is an Argentine businessman and a columnist for El Cronista, an Argentine daily newspaper.

Source: *The Wall Street Journal*, November 25, 1994. Reprinted with permission of THE WALL STREET JOURNAL, 1994 Dow Jones & Company, Inc. All rights reserved worldwide.

THE WALL STREET JOURNAL
May 19, 1995

A Nafta for Europe

By Clayton K. Yeutter and Warren H. Maruyama

With strong leadership by President Clinton and bipartisan congressional support, the U.S. last year completed the Uruguay Round of GATT and began implementing the North American Free Trade Agreement. These initiatives, which were launched by Presidents Reagan and Bush, have shaped U.S. trade policy for nearly a decade. They represented a compelling vision, and by the turn of the century, their economic growth and job creation benefits to the U.S. will be substantial and universally recognized.

Today, however, U.S. trade policy lacks a comparable galvanizing vision. Last year, at the Asia Pacific Economic Conference and Miami's Summit of the Americas, President Clinton attempted to fill this void by looking to Asia and Latin America. Both are areas where the U.S. should foster trade, but neither is a likely candidate for a free-trade zone. Latin America has few countries aside from Chile that have a track record of political stability, open trade and sound macroeconomic policies. As for Asia, the prospects there took a nose-dive with the burgeoning trade war between Japan and the U.S. In both Asia and Latin America, it would probably take decades to set up a free-trade zone with the U.S.

The best area to replicate Nafta's success right away lies elsewhere: Europe. The European Union is already one of the largest overseas customers for U.S. goods and services. U.S. exports to Western Europe totaled $100 billion in 1994. A North Atlantic Free Trade Area would bring together three of the four largest export customers for U.S. goods and services — Canada, Western Europe and Mexico — creating a massive open-trade zone with a combined gross domestic product of more than $10 trillion and a total population of more than 770 million people.

Free trade agreements boil down to five core obligations: (1) phased elimination of tariffs on all goods, (2) liberalization of agricultural trade, (3) rules to protect investment and intellectual property rights, (4) services liberalization, particularly in the telecommunications, financial and audio-visual sectors, and (5) a dispute settlement system to arbitrate commercial disputes and interpret the agreement. All those elements would be achievable for a North Atlantic FTA.

With a few exceptions, U.S. and EU tariffs are not a big factor in trade flows. Indeed, most major U.S. and European companies regard such tariffs as a nuisance. Accordingly, there is unlikely to be strong resistance in either the U.S. or Europe to some form of phased tariff elimination, as long as it's structured properly.

The U.S. and Europe should also be able to agree on most of the new, emerging trade issues, such as intellectual property protection, financial services, investment, and competition policy. Both the U.S. and Europe have long championed strong legal protection for patents, trademarks, copyrights and computer software against Third World piracy. Cross-border investment by U.S. and European companies dates back to the early post-Cold War period. Today, most major U.S. corporations have European subsidiaries and many are so well established — e.g. Ford, IBM, and Xerox — they are regarded as essentially "European."

In addition, the U.S. and Europe share a strong tradition based on the rule of law and the use of courts and judges as neutral and objective decision-makers. If we entered into a free trade agreement, we would do so with confidence that the dispute settlement process would function effectively.

Of course, there would be plenty of disagreements to be resolved before a North Atlantic FTA becomes a reality. But none of these problems are deal-breakers.

One major obstacle is agriculture, which has been a source of endless bilateral friction dating back to the 1960s. But in recent years, the U.S. and European systems have converged dramatically. Sweeping reforms of the EU's Common Agricultural Policy, undertaken by then-Agriculture Commissioner Ray MacSharry, are gradually making European agriculture more free. In the U.S., Congress is starting to trim agriculture subsidies. So both the U.S. and the EU are moving toward a free market in food.

In the past, government subsidies in the aircraft and steel sectors generated nearly as much controversy between the U.S. and Western Europe as did agriculture. But Germany, the main driving force behind Europe's statist approach, can no longer afford to bankroll massive European-wide industrial subsidy programs. In the aircraft sector, Boeing, McDonnell-Douglas, and Airbus are all highly competitive worldwide and appear to be on the verge of a modus vivendi where all can survive.

We still have acrimonious disputes in steel trade, but these are dissipating somewhat. For two reasons: Increased U.S. competitiveness in steel overall reduces import pressures, and major U.S. investments in highly efficient mini-mills increases demand for steel slab imports from Europe.

Beyond that, the diminished political clout of the steel industry suggests that it could not block an FTA deemed to be in the best interests of the EU and the U.S.

Another obstacle to U.S.-EU accord is France's cultural protectionism. But the French government's insistence on quotas on foreign movies and television programs is doomed by advancing technology. Quotas may be viable on a state-run television system with three channels, but on a 500-channel cable TV system, cultural "protection" is impossible and irrelevant.

Finally, there's the question of conditioning free-trade agreements on wage harmonization, labor standards and environmental policies. This was a big issue with Nafta and GATT, but it won't loom as large for the North Atlantic FTA. Not only because Republicans now run Congress, but also because Europe is, if anything, "greener" and more regulatory than the U.S.

Besides the benefits to trade, a North Atlantic FTA would have important security ramifications. With the end of the Cold War, the glue which held NATO together and bound the U.S. and Europe in a security partnership has cracked. As a result, the U.S. and Europe have fallen into bickering over Bosnia and trade with Iraq and Iran. An FTA would provide a new bond that could hold Europe and the U.S. together in the 21st century.

It would also be good for the rest of the world. A North Atlantic trade alliance between the U.S. and Europe would provide a wake-up call for the developing country members of the World Trade Organization. Some of these developing countries still cling to statist, protectionist rhetoric and an abiding belief that the industrialized world owes them a hand-out. Once the U.S. and EU agree on new trade rules, uncooperative developing countries would face a rapidly diminishing set of choices — basically either to sign up or go it alone without attractive access to U.S. and EU markets. Most would fall into line behind a more open trade agenda.

U.S. trade policy is at an important crossroads. We are between major initiatives. This vacuum is dangerous. It creates openings for protectionist legislation and mischievous political posturing as the 1996 elections near. We should turn our backs on nativist sentiment and instead embrace our history of commercial ambitions. This restlessness drove wagon trains West, sent Yankee clipper ships on new routes to China, built the world's preeminent industrial power early in this century and sold the world on the idea of open trade and open markets. We need a bold new goal to galvanize Congress, U.S. business and the American people. A North Atlantic Free Trade Agreement is the right goal for the administration to pursue.

Mr. Yeutter is a former U.S. trade representative and agriculture secretary. He and Mr. Maruyama are lawyers in Washington.

Source: *The Wall Street Journal*, May 19, 1995. Reprinted with permission of THE WALL STREET JOURNAL, 1995 Dow Jones & Company, Inc. All rights reserved worldwide.

THE WALL STREET JOURNAL
May 26, 1995

Hemispheric Free Trade Is Still a National Priority

By Thomas F. McLarty III

The dream of Western Hemispheric integration, which brought together the 34 democratically elected hemispheric leaders last December in Miami, is alive and well, despite reservations voiced in the wake of the Mexico peso crisis. For the first time in history there exists a convergence of mutual trade interests and democratic values that unites every country in the hemisphere, except Cuba. In fact, the vibrancy of the free market and the promise of democracy, which were on display in Miami, were in marked contrast to the dreary model to which Castro still clings, throwing into relief Cuba's need for rapid democratic and economic change. The Clinton Administration has aggressively begun implementation of its Summit-related commitments. Leaders at the Summit called for completion of negotiations on the "Free Trade Area of the Americas" — a $12 trillion market of some 800 million consumers — by the year 2005. To this end, we already have been engaged in intensive consultations with key countries in preparation for the June 30 meeting of trade ministers in Denver. A follow-up Trade and Commerce Forum will be held in Denver July 1-2. Indeed, a second trade ministerial is already planned for March 1996. And the second meeting of the Summit Implementation Review Group met May 5 in San Salvador to prepare a report on Summit implementation for the upcoming meeting of OAS Foreign Ministers in Haiti next month.

Notwithstanding these positive developments, the Mexico peso crisis — as well as the short but bloody border conflict between Peru and Ecuador and rumors of problems elsewhere — has created jitters in some quarters about the path toward integration. But the message of the Summit was not that all of the hemisphere's problems have disappeared. Rather, it was that we are significantly better prepared now, and more fully committed, to deal with the problems that we face than we have been at any time in the past, and that

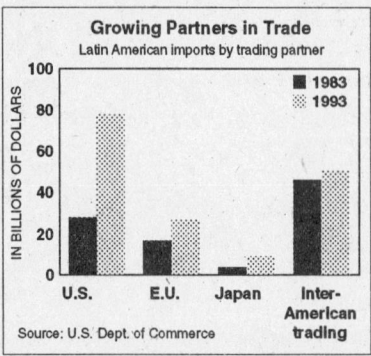

we have established a process of cooperative engagement to deal collectively with problems which arise. While there will be occasional setbacks, the trend for the region is clearly positive.

Some wonder why we should care so much about the rest of the hemisphere. The answer is simple: This hemisphere matters to the American people because our futures and our children's futures are inextricably linked with those of the rest of the hemisphere. Indeed, economic growth in the hemisphere enhances our own trade and investment opportunities.

— Latin America purchased $92 billion in U.S. goods last year. In comparison, the European Union purchased $103 billion.

— From 1987 through 1993, U.S. exports to Latin America grew at an average annual rate of 21%. That's twice the growth rate of our exports to the EU.

— We sell more to Chile, with 14 million people, than to India, with 920 million people. We sell about as much to Costa Rica as we do to all of Eastern Europe.

Yet our agenda is not just economic. Trade expansion and economic development will help us address other, more intractable problems. For example, one way to temper the impact of the narcotics plague, which threatens the entire fabric of the Western Hemisphere, is to create societies that provide viable alternatives to narcotics production and use. Almost invariably, people turn to drugs for profit and use only when they feel they have been marginalized by society. By making it easier for individuals to participate freely in truly competitive internal markets — within a large, open trading region — the destructive social and economic impact of drug cartels can be greatly marginalized. Our emphasis on trade during the Summit recognized this fact: increasing foreign trade breaks down traditional economic barriers and builds growing middle classes with a personal stake in democratic, drug-free societies.

Such societies also place a greater emphasis on stricter adherence to the rule of law, and measures designed to eradicate corruption will help U.S. businesses compete on a level playing field. Better cooperation to ensure a more measured flow of migrants throughout the hemisphere, and to reduce the numbers of illegal immigrants, is of obvious benefit. And there are others: environmental protection, tourism promotion, and cultural preservation, to name just a few. At bottom, we seek a closer relationship with our neighbors, based on shared values and mutual objectives, in order to promote what is unambiguously in the interests of our citizens.

Moreover, the rest of the hemisphere is moving ahead, with or without us. During his recent state visit, Brazilian President Fernando Henrique Cardoso reiterated his commitment to negotiate a hemispheric free trade agreement for implementation by 2005. And as Argentine President Carlos Menem's May 14 re-election shows, pro-democracy, pro-market leaders in the hemisphere enjoy crucial popular support. Now is not the time for the U.S. to question its commitment to greater cooperation and integration into this fast-growing region. Instead, we must reaffirm our commitment and demonstrate continued leadership.

Proceeding with negotiations to admit Chile into the North American Free Trade Agreement is the next critical test of our commitment to regional openness and shared prosperity. Failure to move ahead quickly would send the wrong signal to our hemispheric partners at a critical juncture and deal a blow to the vision of hemispheric integration to which we are so deeply committed. Former President Bush, who identified Chile as the likely next member of the Nafta back in 1992, recently acknowledged that hemispheric integration is in our vital national interest and should not be held hostage to partisan bickering. And Henry Kissinger recently wrote that if we do not seize the opportunities now facing us, there is a real danger the U.S. will become a bystander in our own hemisphere. Commercial integration among other countries of the hemisphere is moving ahead quickly. In short, the game is on, and we must compete.

Latin America is growing so fast that its infrastructure needs alone will require an estimated $500 billion in investment in the coming decade. But we must work cooperatively to sustain mutually beneficial progress. The opportunities presented by greater integration in the hemisphere are vast. Our legacy to our children demands we seize them.

Mr. McLarty is Counselor to the President and Special Representative of the President and the Secretary of State for the Summit of the Americas.

Source: *The Wall Street Journal*, May 26, 1995. Reprinted with permission of THE WALL STREET JOURNAL, 1995 Dow Jones & Company, Inc. All rights reserved worldwide.

THE WALL STREET JOURNAL
June 14, 1989

When Can Sanctions Succeed?

By John Train

The Chinese army mows down peaceful demonstrators. Besides deploring such goings on, what should the West do? Since in fact we cannot influence events, one answer would be, nothing. But the people, and their political representatives, want action. Sanctions! So President Bush suspends arms deliveries, hoping to preempt stronger congressional initiatives, and Her Majesty's Government, in a hammer-blow to the social standing of the bad guys, postpones a scheduled visit by Prince Charles and Lady Di. Take that! All this raises the perennial question of sanctions in general. Are they useful?

As the accompanying table shows, economic sanctions, like limited war, can be an effective instrument of policy under very particular circumstances. But while a country rarely starts a war without weighing the odds, it usually imposes sanctions without consulting the past to see if they are likely to work. The U.S.'s worst mistake was the embargo on oil and scrap steel against Japan that resulted in Pearl Harbor; there have been other failures, and there also have been a number of successes.

When can economic sanctions work? I recently chaired a conference of sanctions specialists, from diplomacy, economics, law and academia, held by Freedom House in New York. A number of conclusions emerged. First, sanctions, like wars, are most likely to succeed if your side holds overwhelming power. You usually are trying to asphyxiate the opponent, so for success all the major holes have to be plugged up. Significant leaks probably mean failure.

Then, the more limited your objectives, the better your chances. For instance, insisting that for most-favored-nation treatment a country must not send you goods made by convict labor is a simple idea to put across. But to demand that the target government do something that amounts to political suicide is not. If it yields, the electorate may repudiate it for bowing to foreign pressure.

At one time the U.S. had relatively more economic and other power than it does now, so it could singlehandedly push other countries around. Today it usually needs the help of its allies, who often do not agree with the U.S., particularly if U.S. actions are in response to internal political pressures they don't share. So America finds itself trying to push its reluctant allies into squeezing its enemies, a complicated undertaking.

Also, Congress has become rambunctious, particularly since Watergate, and sometimes conducts a different foreign policy from the administration's, as in Nicaragua. Many vehement congressional calls for sanctions arise from ethnic or ideological motives that an administration may feel are not in the national interest; if so, it won't enforce them with vigor.

So a good rule today is that the foreign policy and internal politics of both the U.S. and its allies must be in harmony if sanctions are to be comprehensive enough to have a chance of working. Sometimes this kind of inter-allied consensus can be assembled, as against Panama's Manuel Noriega. But more often it can't, particularly if export losses are involved, as in the grain and pipeline embargoes. Soviet grain imports rose after our embargo as Argentina, Australia and Canada rushed in, and the gas pipeline to Europe was finished ahead of schedule after Japan took over from us.

Sanctions, like war, should usually be applied, if at all, decisively and overwhelmingly. The idea that gradual escalation will make an opponent recognize the error of his ways is wishful thinking. As Nietzsche said, what does not kill me, fortifies me. If you want to bend an adversary to your will, you should crush his resistance, not stimulate him to greater efforts. Gradual sanctions may have that effect, as the victim reacts energetically and works out his responses.

The potential effectiveness of sanctions against the Soviets may be higher today than in the past, given their desperate economic straits. Against the South Africans, however, economic pressure holds decreasing promise. They have adapted to our oil and arms embargoes, and indeed have become substantial arms exporters (although the unavailability of the latest jets helped force an Angola-Namibian settlement).

There is little indication that what suffering the U.S. can inflict will produce useful political effects among the white South Africans. Most of the damage falls on the blacks, and black economic gains seem to be an important engine of political change there, as in the U.S.

Sanctions may go wrong because they are ill-considered expressions of political outrage rather than the result of careful calculation. But naive moral gestures often work in reverse, like Prohibition, the "experiment noble in motive" but disastrous in effect. For moral outrage, moral sanctions can be useful. Boycotting the Krugerrand does not reduce South African gold sales — the South Africans can market all they produce — but the sports boycott on South African athletes stings, since South Africans are sports-mad, like Australians.

Similarly, the Olympic boycott really did bother the Soviets.

Might an ineffective economic sanction then become a valid moral sanction? One can't help being impressed if an opponent puts his hand in the fire, even if that doesn't hurt you. However, great-power statecraft is too grave a matter, and the ultimate sanction, war, always too close, to permit silliness. The U.S. looks weak when it inverts Teddy Roosevelt's admonition to walk softly and carry a big stick. George Washington, for example, took particular care not to moralize publicly over abhorrent practices of foreign countries that America could do nothing about.

Then comes divestiture. It may have some moral significance, although it is economically counterpro-

A Partial U.S. Scorecard

DATE AND PURPOSE	RESULT
1940-41 End Japanese invasion of China	Costly failure (War)
1944-45 Reduce support of Argentina's Peron for Axis	Failure
1948-present COCOM: With Allies, deny strategic goods to Soviets	Moderate, declining
1948-49 Push Netherlands to grant independence to Indonesia	Success
1949-70 CHINCOM: With allies, deny strategic goods to China	Failure
1950-present U.S. and U.N.: Squeeze North Korea	Negligible
1951-53 Overthrow Iran's Mossadegh	Success (combined with covert action)
1956 Force Britain and France out of Suez	Success
1960-62 Force out Dominican Republic's Trujillo	Success (combined with covert action)
1960-present Weaken Castro and discourage Cuban Foreign adventures	Counterproductive (U.S.S.R. replaced U.S.)
1963-65 Push Egypt's Nasser to leave Yemen and reduce anti-U.S. propaganda	Success
1963-66 Moderate the aggressiveness of Indonesia's Sukarno	Some influence; internal factors decisive
1965-66 Roll back Chilean copper price increase	Success, with adverse side effects
1965-67 Encourage India to favor agriculture over industry	Success
1965-79 With Britain and U.N.: Black rule for Rhodesia	Counterproductive for 14 years; then, for other reasons, success
1974-78 Remove Turkish Troops from Cyprus	Failure
1975-present Facilitate Jewish emigration from U.S.S.R.	Failure, perhaps counterproductive
1975-79 Human rights in Cambodia	Failure
1976-present Human rights in Ethiopia	Failure (U.S.S.R. replaced U.S.)
1978-82 Improve situation of Soviet dissidents	Failure
1977-79 Remove Nicaragua's Somoza	Success (combined with covert action)
1979-present Bring democracy to Nicaragua	Failure (combined with covert action); (U.S.S.R. replaced U.S.)
1979 Recover Iranian hostages, settle claims	Helpful
1980-81 Impose grain embargo to end Soviet invasion of Afghanistan	Costly failure
1981-82 Prevent U.S.S.R.-Europe pipeline	Costly and humiliating failure

ductive. Suppose you push a university to sell stock in a company that is reluctant to leave South Africa (never the Soviet Union, even during Afghanistan). The new stockholder presumably likes management and its policies. So if you think a company should stay in South Africa you should join in urging your alma mater to sell the stock to, for example, the Japanese.

And of course when an American company does "get out" of South Africa, the business continues. The factory isn't destroyed or removed. It is sold to the local whites, or perhaps another foreign outfit, who may be less responsible owners. And the compensation is often inadequate. In other words, we are asking for expropriation, just what we once applied sanctions against Fidel Castro for doing. Except this time we're inflicting it on ourselves!

Maybe this procedure is a valid moral gesture, or a political safety valve, maybe not. But we should start by understanding what's happening.

Mr. Train, a New York-based investment counselor, writes for the Journal periodically on foreign and military affairs.

Source: *The Wall Street Journal*, June 14, 1989. Reprinted with permission of THE WALL STREET JOURNAL, 1989 Dow Jones & Company, Inc. All rights reserved worldwide.

THE WALL STREET JOURNAL
October 21, 1991

Talk of Trading Blocs May Exaggerate Risks

By Henry F. Myers

NEW YORK — With America's trade gap recently widening despite the deficit-reducing benefits of a weak dollar, many Americans are worried about the European Community's plans to further reduce its internal trade barriers after 1992.

Tony Riley, an economist at the consulting firm of A. Gary Shilling & Co., voices such fears: "The sheer size of the unified market, Europeans' desire to give themselves first shot at exploiting its advantages, and the associated shift away from Europe's traditional outward trading mentality toward a more inward orientation, will all undoubtedly shift the EC to a more self-sufficient and protectionist stance."

That worry has a familiar ring to it, of course. When the Common Market was being set up decades ago, some Americans said U.S. companies might be excluded from selling in Europe. As it turned out, they quickly became major beneficiaries.

But is the world now moving away from multilateral trade and toward a system of trading blocs? And if so, how protectionist will the new blocs be?

At a seminar held here recently by Oxford Economics USA, Nariman Behravesh, president of the consulting firm, commented: "A quick look at the data suggests that the development of blocs is happening only in Europe."

Talk of a Pacific Rim bloc led by Japan, Andrea Boltho of Magdalen College at Oxford University told the seminar, "doesn't make sense" because Asia is "too heterogeneous." He believes other Asian countries aren't eager for closer ties to Japan and don't want to endanger their U.S. trade.

And as for creation of a North American trade bloc, Carl Sonnen of Informetrica Ltd. of Ottawa said Canada favors multinational trade. It fears blocs and losing control of its industry. Mr. Sonnen noted that in the auto industry it's the U.S. Big Three, not Honda or Volkswagen, that causes concern.

Within all three regions, of course, neighboring countries already are major trading partners. European countries' trade relationships, Mr. Behravesh observed, have long been strengthened by cultural ties and transport networks. And between Canada and the U.S., Mr. Sonnen said, "Essentially, there is no economic border" right now.

Cornelis A. Los, chief U.S. economist at NMB Postbank Groep N.V., expects neighboring countries to grow even closer economically. He notes in an interview that despite political attitudes and emotional preferences, people tend to pursue economic self-interest. Whatever misgivings Southeast Asians have about Japan, for example, they nevertheless woo Japanese investment. And, he says, "Europe will be looking more eastward," attracted by the Soviet Union's plentiful natural resources.

Though the 1992 plan may not be protectionist by design, the world may get a bit more protectionist anyway. Mr. Riley notes that relatively free trade has flourished only when a single power favoring it dominated the world economy: For some decades prior to World War I, it was Britain, and after World War II, it was the U.S. "Now that the U.S. has lost its economic hegemony," he says, "the world economy may simply be reverting to the protectionist, bilaterally oriented trading relationships that characterize . . . leaderless epochs."

So far, however, the trend toward trading blocs hasn't significantly diverted trade flows even in Europe. Although intra-European trade increased substantially in the late 1960s and the 1970s, the percentage of total EC trade accounted for by members' trade with each other rose surprisingly little during the 1980s despite the elimination of internal tariffs. From 1979 to 1989, intra-EC trade rose from 54.3% to 58.5% of total trade. If exports and imports from OPEC nations are excluded, the share of intra-EC trade edged up from 59.9% to only 60.6%.

Even if many of the EC's internal nontariff barriers do fade away after 1992, intra-European trade probably will increase only gradually. Mr. Boltho noted that all EC regulations governing trade won't be revised overnight. European legislatures are moving slowly. Moreover, he said, national preferences — involving seemingly minor but costly differences such as whether washing machines are loaded from the top or the front — will linger on. Even apart from agriculture — "a sore point" — Mr. Boltho doesn't expect the liberalizing changes to be completed until 1995 or 1996.

However, Mr. Boltho believes that the further integration of Europe, if achieved, will accelerate economic growth there-and, through rising prosperity, undermine protectionist tendencies. He noted that freight would be speeded up; even now, he said, a truck can sit for 80 minutes before getting across a border in Europe. He anticipates "huge possibilities for economies of scale" from the elimination of differing national regulations about such things as tractor windshields and tire sizes. European companies will become much more efficient — and much tougher competitors for the U.S.

Also undermining protectionism are the multinational companies, both operating on their own and through joint ventures. They are crossing borders, creating jobs and, Mr. Boltho said, torpedoing the whole "bloc logic."

In any event, the U.S. should resist any trend toward protectionist blocs. While acknowledging "the political pressure to do something" about America's trade problems, Mr. Behravesh wonders why the U.S. would want to hurt its own multinationals. Why shoot down Boeing? How could the U.S. benefit by narrowing its trade to the Americas in a world of blocs? "If the U.S. focuses on inter-American trade," Mr. Behravesh noted, "it would be at huge cost."

Source: *The Wall Street Journal*, October 21, 1991. Reprinted with permission of THE WALL STREET JOURNAL, 1991 Dow Jones & Company, Inc. All rights reserved worldwide.

CHAPTER 12
Trade and the Environment

Objectives of the Chapter

With increasing global integration in commodities flows and factor flows, we are also experiencing increasing integration insofar as one country's economic decisions can end up affecting the environment of other countries. Just as national borders cause complications in issues of trade and finance, national borders make addressing cross-border environmental problems difficult. Private activities that cause externalities are usually solved within a country by either tax/subsidy policies or by redefinition of property rights. Neither of these solutions is easy to apply when external effects drift from one country to another. In general, though, the fewer are the countries affected and/or the fewer are the goods involved, the easier it is to negotiate some international accord to correct environmental externalities.

After reading this chapter, you should understand

1. the reasons why solving environmental externalities is more difficult in the international sphere than within a single country
2. how and why traditional trade barriers rarely fit the specificity rule in correcting environmental problems
3. the factors that lead to success or failure of environmental protection measures
4. current debates on issues such as rain forest depletion, global warming, and extinction of animal life

Key Terms

CITES — the Convention on International Trade in Endangered Species of Wild Fauna and Flora, signed in 1973 by over 100 nations. Calls for strict regulation of trade in products related to species threatened with extinction.

GATT Article XX — lists general exceptions to its main free-trade rules, including allowing trade barriers that are necessary to protect human, animal, or plant life, and that relate to the conservation of exhaustible natural resources. GATT is wary of the use of Article XX by countries simply seeking protection for their import-competing industries.

Montreal Protocol a document signed in 1987 by over 50 nations; it was designed to ban trade in (and, later, production of) ozone-depleting chlorofluorocarbons.

Warm-up Questions

True or False? Explain.

1. T / F   The specificity rule rules out tariffs to correct pollution that is not caused by trade itself.

2. T / F   International treaties to protect endangered species were first introduced in the 1960s.

3. T / F   Arguments about environmental issues are strongest between countries of equal development levels.

4. T / F   Assigning property rights for air to victims will help resolve the problem of air pollution; assigning those property rights to the polluters will not.

5. T / F   If there were a single "world government," there would be less need to use trade policy to address environmental concerns.

Chapter 12: Trade and the Environment

Multiple Choice

1. As per capita income rises in a developing country, we can expect
   a. carbon dioxide emissions to go up
   b. poor sanitation to be reduced
   c. clean water to be more available
   d. concern for environmental issues to go up
   e. all of the above

2. If factories in Country A emit fumes into the air that eventually produce acid rain in Country B, a World Court could address the externality by
   a. taxing factories in Country A
   b. subsidizing research into emission controls in Country A
   c. giving Country B "ownership" of the air and the right to charge Country A for its cleanup
   d. none of the above (since there is no such World Court to enforce the measures, no matter how globally efficient they may be)

3. The trade ban on ivory has been successful in reducing the excessive slaughter of elephants because
   a. virtually all production and consumption involved international trade
   b. CITES provided for a multinational police force to stop poaching
   c. the specificity rule failed
   d. poachers were forced to watch the movie "Dumbo" eight times for every elephant they killed

4. If we want to reduce greenhouse-gas emissions, our best option would be to
   a. ban petroleum imports into the United States
   b. ban petroleum exports from Saudi Arabia
   c. ban the use of petroleum in all industrialized countries
   d. tax consumption of petroleum in OECD countries

5. Which of the following is *not* part of GATT's stance on trade?
   a. Any tax on imports must not exceed that on import-competing products.
   b. Freer import policy for the cleanest foreign country must be matched by freedom of imports for polluter countries.
   c. Any trade barrier which reduces greenhouse-gas emissions is permissible.
   d. Tariffs which are implemented to conserve natural resources must not be used merely to shut out foreign goods.

Problems

1. The citizens of Leinster are worried that the gas produced by the yeast used in the Saxon bakeries will cause a greenhouse effect. What policies would you prescribe to correct this international environmental externality?

2. It has recently been suggested that "it would be wrong for the World Bank or anybody else to insist upon rich-country standards of environmental protection in developing countries.... (T)he migration of... 'dirty' industries to the third world is desirable."

    a. What economic reasoning could make such a buildup of polluting industries in developing countries look like a net gain for the world?

    b. Is the North American Free Trade Agreement (NAFTA) likely to raise pollution in Mexico? in the United States?

3. Why did the Montreal Convention succeed in limiting global emissions of CFCs, whereas the world has been unable to limit the emissions of CO_2? What differences between the two cases explain the differences in outcomes?

4. Suppose that, in order to help fight global warming, North America (NA) and the European Union (EU) reach a pact to tax fossil-fuel consumption at $448 per ton of emitted carbon within their two areas. Describe the most likely effects of this decision on

   a. the welfare of NA and EU

   b. the welfare of the world as a whole

   c. international competition in manufactures

Discussion Topics

1. Is it "fair" for high per capita income countries, whose concern for the environment is a result of those high incomes, to expect developing countries to adopt the same environmental standards?

2. Do you foresee the development of a World Court that could enforce property rights between countries? What characteristics of that court would be necessary for it to be successful?

Final Thought

Private property began the instant somebody had a mind of his own.

—e.e. cummings, 1951

THE WALL STREET JOURNAL
August 30, 1994

GATT Is Threatened by the Squeamish...

By Julius L. Katz

It seems amazing, but the world's foremost free trading nation could end up destroying history's largest free trade agreement. The Uruguay Round of the General Agreement on Tariffs and Trade is facing uncertain ratification prospects in the U.S. Congress. Opposition has come not only from the traditional defenders of trade restrictions, but also from many who normally support free trade. They worry about the World Trade Organization, the body set up under GATT to adjudicate disputes and enforce the treaty. But these critics wildly exaggerate the threat the WTO poses to U.S. sovereignty, and they'd forsake a treaty that could be one of the great growth engines of coming years.

The principal criticism directed at the WTO is that, because of the one country-one vote procedure, the U.S. lacks veto power and can have decisions imposed on it by a majority of the WTO's 111 members. In fact, the WTO strengthens the voting system now employed by GATT and maintains a dominant role for the U.S. At the insistence of the U.S., the voting procedures were drawn to ensure against an abuse of power by the majority.

Most WTO decisions, as is the current practice, will be made by consensus, i.e., without objection. Indeed, on certain important matters — such as most-favored-nation obligations — consensus is required. Other matters, when there is no consensus, still require more than a simple majority — usually two-thirds or three-fourths of WTO member votes.

What is of key importance, however, is that no decision affecting the rights and obligations of the U.S. — such as an amendment of the GATT and related agreements — can be imposed without U.S. consent. Theoretically, U.S. resistance could lead to its expulsion, but this is not a serious practical possibility. A world trade organization without the world's leading trading power would not be much of an organization.

Opponents of the WTO — including Ralph Nader writing on this page Aug. 17 — suggest that the U.S. will frequently be the defendant in dispute-settlement cases, because we have higher labor and environmental standards than most of the rest of the world, and because the rules of the newest GATT round require "least-trade-restrictive" approaches to environmental regulation.

The facts are that the U.S. has been, and is likely to be, the plaintiff in many cases, as we seek to enforce GATT's rules. We have frequently been frustrated in our efforts to open markets by procedures that permitted the defendant party to block the decision of a dispute-settlement panel. For example, U.S. complaints against Europe, Japan and Korea over agricultural trade restrictions took years to resolve, and the European Community blocked the U.S. from bringing a complaint against subsidies for Airbus, the European consortium. This is why the U.S. fought for the more effective dispute-settlement mechanism that is now a part of the WTO.

Does this mean that if we lose a case, our laws could be rewritten in the WTO? Absolutely not. Nothing that the WTO does changes U.S. law; only Congress can change U.S. law. Failure to accept the ruling of a dispute panel could result in retaliation against U.S. exports, but this is no more than what we would insist on if our rights were violated. If we expect other countries to observe international trading rules, we must also be prepared to observe the rules we helped to write.

It is true that the Agreements on Sanitary and Photo-Sanitary Measures and on Technical Barriers to Trade require least-trade-restrictive approaches, because we wanted to ensure that health and safety measures and technical standards were not disguised barriers to trade. Clearly, we do not want such measures to be the "most trade restrictive." The agreements provide an appropriate balance. Nations may determine their own health, safety and other standards, with whatever risk tolerances they deem appropriate. Those standards must, however, be based on some scientific justification and be applied to domestic as well as imported goods.

There have been numerous cases where nations have wrongly restricted imports of U.S. agricultural products for alleged animal or plant diseases. Examples include citrus and apples to Japan, cherries to Korea and meat to Europe. The agreement will finally provide a means of challenging such unwarranted trade barriers, while letting nations take legitimate actions in support of public health and safety.

Some claim that WTO procedures will be somehow undemocratic because dispute-settlement panels will be closed to the public and the press, and neither transcripts of proceedings nor the legal arguments of the contending parties will be made public. But it is inaccurate to call the process "secret." It will be the practice of the U.S. Trade Representative to solicit the views of interested parties and to disclose fully the results of panel decisions, including the reasons for the decisions.

Finally, the argument has been

made that the WTO would disrupt U.S. federal-state relations, because state laws and regulations could be challenged in the WTO as being out of step with international trade rules. This is not a new problem or one that is peculiar to the WTO. In matters of trade, the federal government has a history of collaborating with the states; such cooperation continues. Most recently, the National Association of {State} Attorneys General concluded an agreement with the U.S. Trade Representative providing for specific rules in notification and participation by the states in international trade proceedings.

It would be wrong to let various misconceptions about the WTO get in the way of the swift ratification of the Uruguay Round Agreement, signed by more than 100 nations in April. The Uruguay Round will cut foreign tariffs on U.S. exports by 43%. It will eliminate tariffs for a broad range of our most competitive products — such as paper, construction equipment, steel and pharmaceuticals. New rules will protect patent and copyright holders, open markets for our service industries, end harmful subsidy wars, and provide a new mechanism to resolve disputes and ensure rights.

The WTO ensures that member countries agree to the obligations of all of the agreements, not just those they like. Thus, for the first time, developing countries, including the fastest-growing markets of the world, will undertake obligations to open their markets and to be bound by the rules of the multilateral trading system.

Mr. Katz is president of Hills & Co., which advises U.S. companies on their trade and investment interests abroad. He served as deputy U.S. trade representative, 1989-93, and was chief U.S. negotiator for the Nafta accord. (See related article: ". . . While Nafta Speeds Right Along" — WSJ August 30, 1994)

Source: *The Wall Street Journal*, August 30, 1994. Reprinted with permission of THE WALL STREET JOURNAL, 1994 Dow Jones & Company, Inc. All rights reserved worldwide.

CHAPTER 13
Trade Policies for Developing Countries

Objectives of the Chapter

Chapter 13 examines the interactions between developing countries and the world economy and the trade policies practiced or advocated by many developing nations. It begins by offering perspectives on the link between growth and foreign trade, on the changing pattern of comparative advantage in the Third World, and on the collective political voice gained by the developing countries after World War II. The New International Economic Order movement urged that incomes of developing countries be raised through cartels to restrict trade in primary products; schemes to stabilize primary-product prices; and preferential tariff reductions to foster developing-country exports of manufactures.

Several kinds of alternatives to free trade have been proposed specifically for developing countries. New industries can be nurtured by restricting imports of manufactured goods. Price-raising cartels can be used to increase the prices of primary product exports. Finally, there are attempts to increase exports of manufactured goods to industrialized countries.

After studying this chapter, you should know how to

1. contrast the growth rates for high-, middle-, and low-income countries
2. identify the forms taken by the increased political awareness and voice of developing countries in the international arena
3. explain how declining prices for primary products can work against developing countries
4. explain the concept of import substituting industrialization and how this strategy for development has been implemented, and evaluate its performance relative to a strategy of promoting exports of manufactured goods

Key Terms

Engel's law — the income-elasticity of demand for food is less than one. As per capita incomes rise in the long run, then, demand will shift away from food and the relative price of food will fall.

Import substituting industrialization (ISI) — a strategy for development that calls for the governments of developing countries to identify large domestic markets, as indicated by substantial imports over the years; to ensure that the technologies of production can be mastered by local manufacturers or supplied by foreign investors, or to use subsidies to make it profitable for potential investors or state enterprises to set up high-cost local production facilities.

New International Economic Order (NIEO) — refers to a new system of international economic relations, advocated by the Third World. It would include, but is not limited to, commodity price manipulating schemes and preferential tariff cuts favoring developing countries.

NICs (Newly industrializing countries) — commonly identified as South Korea, Taiwan, Hong Kong, and Singapore (these are also referred to as "the Four Tigers"). Their rates of growth over the period 1980–92 have been as high as 8.5 percent per year. Hong Kong, the richest of the group, had a higher 1992 GDP per capita than Britain.

OPEC (Organization of Petroleum Exporting Countries) — established in 1960, this cartel had a membership of thirteen producers by 1975. OPEC was successful in engineering enormous increases in the price of crude oil during 1973–74 and 1979–80. Because of supply conditions, it is unlikely that cartels in other primary products could achieve anything like OPEC's success

UNCTAD (The United Nations Conference on Trade and Development) — since 1964, a permanent forum for the discussion of developing countries' concerns about international trade and investments.

Warm-up Questions

True or False? Explain.

1. T / F   All OPEC countries are both wealthy and developed.

2. T / F   Developing countries all have the same problems and potentials.

3. T / F   Engel's Law means trouble for food producers in a prospering world.

4. T / F   A cartel which is optimal for its members is also optimal for the world.

5. T / F   At the current rate, per capita incomes in the developing countries should catch up to per capita incomes in the industrialized countries by the year 2000.

Multiple Choice

1. The optimal monopoly markup is
   a. higher with more elastic demand for cartel sales
   b. higher with less elastic demand for cartel sales
   c. lower with less elastic demand for cartel sales
   d. higher with more elastic supply schedules

2. An international cartel that maximizes its profits is optimal for
   a. the member countries and the world
   b. the member countries but not the world
   c. the consuming countries and the world
   d. no country at all

3. Which of the following is *not* a valid argument in favor of ISI?
   a. There can be large economic and social side benefits from industrialization.
   b. For a large country, replacing imports can bring better terms-of-trade effects.
   c. Replacing imports of manufactures is a way of using cheap and convenient market information.
   d. GDP per capita has grown faster in countries with ISI.

4. Arguments in favor of having developing countries focus on exporting manufactures include
   a. strong support in industrialized countries for free trade in manufactured goods
   b. very low tariffs on manufactured textiles, apparel, and footwear in industrialized countries
   c. political preference for VERs among importing countries
   d. a downward trend in the prices of primary products

5. Which of the following causes a downward trend in the relative prices of primary products?
   a. slow productivity growth in the primary sector
   b. development of synthetic substitutes for primary products
   c. the nonrenewable nature of many primary products
   d. a high income elasticity of demand for food

Problems

1. You have been appointed as an advisor to the Saxon government, which is considering implementing measures to increase Saxon production of electronic equipment.

   a. What are arguments in favor of promoting such industrialization? Are there any arguments against it?

   b. What methods would you suggest the Saxon government use to encourage such industrialization?

2. Suppose that several nations have formed a buying cartel, taxing imports of a product instead of taxing exports as OPEC does. For example, suppose that the EC, the United States, and Japan all agree to tax and restrict their coffee imports. What is the formula for their "optimal" import tariff (or markdown from domestic price)?

3. Assume that you are the head of a diamond cartel called De Booz. If the price elasticity of demand for exports of diamonds is –0.5; the diamond cartel's share of world sales is 50%; and the elasticity of competing supply is 1.0, what is the optimal cartel markup rate for De Booz?

4. Instead of focussing exclusively on the export of raw rubber, the country of Malaysia is becoming more involved in the production and export of rubber-based goods such as surgical gloves. Discuss motives for choosing this new strategy and policies for implementing this new strategy.

Discussion Topics

1. If all countries desire to become industrialized, will no country produce primary goods?

2. In a broader sense of the word, is "development" always the same as "industrialized"? as "wealthy"?

Final Thought

> God said, I am tired of kings,
> I suffer them no more;
> Up to my ear the morning brings
> The outrage of the poor.
>
> —Ralph Waldo Emerson, 1867

THE WALL STREET JOURNAL
June 30, 1995

Big Auto Plant Sparks A Debate in Portugal Over How to Develop —
Jobs, Training Are Welcome, But Critics Say Relying On One Project Is Risky — East Europe Becomes a Rival

By Audrey Choi and Carlta Vitzthum
Staff Reporters of The Wall Street Journal

PALMELA, Portugal — What's good for Ford Motor Co. and Volkswagen AG is good for Portugal.

Or so went the official message earlier this year when the two partners opened AutoEuropa, their new joint-venture factory here. Once up to speed, the companies pledged, this $2.8 billion minivan plant will account for more than 15% of Portugal's exports, 4% of gross domestic product and 4,500 jobs. Edward Hagenlocker, president of Ford's automotive operations, even promised that AutoEuropa will "enhance Portugal's place in the mainstream of world economic developments."

That's what the government wants.

The biggest foreign investment ever made in Portugal, AutoEuropa has sparked a lot of debate. Some economists and consultants question whether the country is pinning too much hope on one project and whether highly subsidized, high-tech plants run by foreigners are the best development strategy. Critics contend that Portugal ought to build on traditional strengths such as pulp and paper, textiles and tourism. In the past, they note, some big foreign investments, such as a Renault SA factory in Setubal, didn't pan out.

Foreign investment, particularly in the car industry, can help build up local suppliers and train workers, acknowledges Emmanuel Figueiredo, a Lisbon economist and co-author of a European Union report on foreign investment in Portugal. "But in the long run," he says, "these companies are extremely mobile, closing down and relocating when [the host] countries lose their competitive edge." And some people say Portugal already has.

When it entered the European Union in 1986, Portugal was one of Europe's hottest bets for expanding multinationals. It was still emerging from 48 years of dictatorship and offering low wages, long workweeks and deep harbors.

But the fall of the Berlin Wall in 1989 shifted Europe's attention to the East, where skilled-manufacturing wages were only half those in Portugal. Direct foreign investment here plunged to $1.03 billion in 1994 after peaking at $2.28 billion in 1991, according to the Bank of Portugal, while it more than doubled in Eastern and Central Europe to about $7 billion.

Southern Europe's concern was hardly allayed at the EU summit this week in Cannes, France. EU leaders agreed to spend 6.7 billion European currency units ($8.92 billion) over the next five years to help Eastern European countries and 4.7 ECUs on countries bordering the Mediterranean. The sums for Southern Europe, though substantial, fell short of the "parity" sought by Spain and Portugal.

Meanwhile, AutoEuropa has trimmed employment and production targets even before starting up. In fact, as many as seven foreign projects in Portugal, including five in the auto sector, have recently been scaled back. Mr. Figueiredo's EU report says the foreign companies may have inflated their initial targets to get bigger government subsidies.

Even in scaled-back form, AutoEuropa will receive more than $800 million in development funds from the EU and the Portuguese state, with each giving roughly half. From 1991 to 1994, by contrast, a total of about $400 million from EU and Portuguese coffers was divided among Portuguese companies in traditional sectors. Michael Porter, a Harvard University business professor, believes that Portugal should pursue niche markets through these basic industries. Asked by some Portuguese businessmen how the nation could best develop, Mr. Porter wrote a report advocating worker training and disparaging "outdated solutions . . . through macroeconomic policies, an increase in economies of scale or high technology."

But going back to basics presents a quandary. New competition from abroad, including Eastern Europe, Southeast Asia and Latin America, has already forced most of Portugal's traditional industries to restructure. Steel, textile and footwear producers are slashing costs, idling thousands of workers. Unemployment climbed to 7.4% in the first quarter from 4.2% at the end of 1992, and many economists expect it to top 8% by year end.

So, practically any foreign investor promising jobs is eagerly courted, and government officials tout AutoEuropa as the way forward. By joining existing parts and assembly plants of General Motors Corp., Renault, Ford and Toyota Motor Corp., AutoEuropa can jump-start Portugal's car industry, officials say.

"We consider AutoEuropa a structural investment because it will contribute to the strength of the auto cluster in Portugal," says Fernando Faria de Oliveira, minister for trade and tourism. "AutoEuropa totally changes the car industry here not only because of its size but because of its impact on the parts industry."

Karel Willaert, AutoEuropa's executive director, says that with investment "you don't get many big fish. If you get one, the whole region is going to develop because other industries will come." Already, 47 joint-venture suppliers have sprung up around AutoEuropa. Its workers have gone through 18 months of rigorous training; nearly a third were sent to Ford's premier factory in Hermosillo, Mexico. For now, the plant here will make a single model, to be sold as the Ford Galaxy and VW Sharan and expected to be on the market throughout Europe by late summer.

Portugal has already received huge inflows of foreign investment and assistance, and its per-capita income rose to 65% of the EU average last year from 51% in 1985. Aid from the EU has included $20 billion for roads and other infrastructure projects. Under the EU's latest five-year budget, Portugal is to receive almost $10 million a day until the year 2000.

But what Portugal needs most is jobs, says Rui Oliviera Costa, who heads the General Workers' Union. AutoEuropa "will be important in terms of macroeconomics," he adds, "but it won't be important in terms of people and jobs."

Instead of directly generating more than 4,500 jobs, as first projected, the factory now is expected to create about 3,000 directly, plus 1,500 at suppliers. The plant has a capacity of 180,000 minivans a year, but production this year is estimated at only 60,000. Last year, 160,000 minivans were sold in Europe.

If the project does go sour, it wouldn't be the first to do so in Portugal. Renault arrived in the late 1970s and was supposed to help build up a domestic car industry. Offered special benefits in Portugal's then closed market, it formed a 70-30 venture with the government that quickly dominated the market and was profitable. But EU membership ended Renault's special status, and the collapse of the Portuguese car market in recent years has pushed the operation deep into the red.

"Renault says our quality is among the best in the group, but they say it's cheaper to produce in Slovenia," a glum Manuel Vestias says. After more than a decade working at the Setubal plant, Mr. Vestias, a 35-year-old with few transferable skills, has scant other job prospects if it closes.

But Renault says it must consider its bottom line. It came to Portugal because it "thought Southern Europe had great strategic importance," explains Sergio Leitao Gomes, a spokesman for Renault Portuguesa. "Now, having consolidated a position in Europe, it is starting a new phase, looking at the world."

The Setubal factory is the smallest of five European plants that assemble the Renault Clio, and one of the larger plants could easily pick up the slack if Setubal closed. Local unions oppose a closure, and the Portuguese government is threatening to sue Renault.

Portugal is also crossing swords with Total SA over the French oil giant's commitment to buy into the Portuguese national oil company, Petrogal SA. After joining a consortium that bought an initial 25%, Total hasn't decided whether to exercise its option to raise its stake.

Other projects have done better. GM began a skeletal assembly operation in Azambuja in 1963; now, under GM's German unit, Adam Opel AG, the plant makes the Corsa Combo van and the S-van, both light commercial vehicles. Marc Verschueren, Opel Portugal's president, says it is a continuing battle to keep the plant competitive, given its remote location and small size, against larger, leaner facilities such as GM's new plant in eastern Germany or its operations in Poland.

Yet Mr. Verschueren cites lasting advantages in Portugal, such as good harbors; low corporate taxes; wages about a quarter those in Germany and half those in Britain and Spain; a ready supply of eager workers; and a 44-hour workweek, the longest in Western Europe.

"If you compare it with Germany, it's heaven on earth," he says.

AutoEuropa executives insist that they, too, intend to stay. Albert Caspers, president of Ford of Europe and the initial force behind AutoEuropa, says, "It is absolute nonsense to think we would go and invest $2.8 billion if we don't intend to have a lasting commitment there." Mr. Willaert of AutoEuropa notes that AutoEuropa is Europe's only minivan maker and that because of its modern equipment, it can be retooled quickly to make another model.

Meanwhile, Trade Minister Faria de Oliveira says Portugal is modernizing its whole economy and trying to help its homespun industries. "Many sectors are improving," he says. "Between 1986 and 1994, total exports of goods and services rose from $7.7 billion to $24 billion because our companies responded well to open markets." But one wary Portuguese economics professor warns against "putting all your eggs in one basket. Exports from just one factory will be equivalent to those of the whole textile industry."

Source: *The Wall Street Journal*, June 30, 1995. Reprinted with permission of THE WALL STREET JOURNAL, 1995 Dow Jones & Company, Inc. All rights reserved worldwide.

THE WALL STREET JOURNAL
October 13, 1995

U.S. May Be Losing Its Trade-Bully Status
WTO Levels the Playing Field For Settling Disputes

By Eduardo Lachica
Staff Reporter of The Wall Street Journal

GENEVA — The U.S. is no longer the intimidating trade bully it used to be, foreign trade diplomats contend.

For one thing, the U.S. lost the very first case that Hong Kong brought before a World Trade Organization body that polices the global textile trade. The Hong Kong delegation argued that the emergency import curbs the U.S. imposed on woolen shirts from the territory weren't justified. The threat of similar intervention also persuaded the U.S. to rescind import limits on luggage from the Philippines and synthetic yarn from Thailand.

"I've never seen the U.S. lift so many of its [temporary import limits] on textiles," chortles Timothy Tong, Hong Kong's deputy representative to the WTO. "It looks like the new rules are having a deterrent effect on abuses of the system."

To further improve their odds, many Asian countries are working hard to frustrate a U.S. bid for two of the seven seats on a WTO appellate body that may have the final say in some of the most contentious trade disputes. U.S. trade negotiators say they want two seats because the European Union is also demanding a pair.

That raises a good question: Are U.S. politician Pat Buchanan and other WTO-bashers right when they gripe about America's diminishing place in the "new world order"? Not quite, says Renato Ruggiero, the WTO director-general. What the trading world is seeing, he contends, is simply the implementation of new rules that can protect the "rights and obligations of all WTO members, not just those of the U.S. and the European Union."

Indeed, it's likely that the U.S., the most litigious of all WTO members, will continue to win its fair share of disputes. "There aren't many countries with the experience and resources to conduct a WTO case as well as the U.S.," says Christopher Parlin, a former U.S. trade official who argued many Geneva cases in previous U.S. administrations. Indeed, the U.S. quickly resolved one of its two complaints against South Korea this year by persuading Seoul to extend the allowable shelf life of imported meat products. The U.S. believes it also has a winnable case against the allegedly discriminatory taxes that Japan imposes on imported whiskey, cognac and other distilled spirits.

But legal experts don't expect the U.S. to repeat its stunning record of wresting favorable settlements in 47% of its complaints in the first four decades of the General Agreement on Tariffs and Trade, the WTO's predecessor. For one thing, the dispute-settlement process is no longer the exclusive playground of the so-called "quad" powers — the U.S., the EU, Canada and Japan. Many smaller countries such as Costa Rica, Nicaragua and Venezuela are getting in the act, too.

Nor can the U.S. block the adoption of unfavorable rulings with impunity as it has in the past. Robert Hudec, a University of Minnesota professor and a leading authority on WTO dispute-settlement procedures, sees "less

---

Disputes

Some cases involving the U.S. lodged with the World Trade Organization's dispute-settlement body this year

COMPLAINANT: Venezuela, Brazil
  ISSUE: U.S. standards for reformulated and conventional gasoline
  STATUS: Panel hearing complaint

COMPLAINANT: U.S.
  ISSUE: Korean measures on shelf-life of imported meat products
  STATUS: Settled

COMPLAINANT: U.S., Canada, EU
  ISSUE: Japanese taxes on imported distilled spirits
  STATUS: Panel requested

COMPLAINANT: U.S., Mexico, Guatemala, Honduras
  ISSUE: EU measures on bananas
  STATUS: Consultations

COMPLAINANT: Japan
  ISSUE: U.S. import duties on autos
  STATUS: Settled

COMPLAINANT: U.S., Canada
  ISSUE: EU duties on grain imports
  STATUS: Panel requested

Source: World Trade Organization

room for arm-twisting" by the big powers under the new rules and consequently a more-level playing field for smaller countries.

WTO officials say the 18 complaints brought to the WTO in the first nine months of this year represent a heavier caseload than anything they saw under the old GATT system. The U.S. is a complainant in six of the cases and a defendant in three. The European Union is appearing in only one case as a complainant but in seven as a defendant. Japan is a defendant in four cases.

The new dispute-settlement rules are a product of GATT's Uruguay Round agreements, which also transformed the old GATT secretariat into the WTO on Jan. 1. The rules provide for good-faith consultations to enable disputants to resolve their differences amicably. If consultations fail, the complainant can ask the WTO's dispute-settlement body, or DSB, to appoint a panel to hear the case. The DSB, a kind of committee of the whole in which all WTO members are represented, can then act on the panel's recommendations.

A losing country can seek a review by the appellate body — a major Uruguay Round innovation — that the WTO is expected to name later this month. The proceedings have to follow strict time guidelines.

While the appellate body's composition is still of concern to the U.S., it has no serious quarrel with the way the DSB has operated under its first chairman, Ambassador Don Kenyon of Australia. But the U.S. is still unhappy that WTO disputes are heard behind closed doors.

"We're still discussing with other members what documents can be publicly available and what can't," says Andrew Stoler, the deputy U.S. representative to the WTO. The U.S. is pressing for more transparency in the procedures.

The U.S. may learn soon enough how fairly the system works. In a few months a WTO panel is due to rule on a complaint that Venezuela and Brazil have brought against certain standards that the U.S. Environmental Protection Agency has adopted for reformulated and conventional gasoline. The Latin countries claim that the standards discriminate against imported gasoline. — Bhushan Bahree contributed to this article.

Source: *The Wall Street Journal*, October 13, 1995. Reprinted with permission of THE WALL STREET JOURNAL, 1995 Dow Jones & Company, Inc. All rights reserved worldwide.

THE WALL STREET JOURNAL
February 28, 1995

Now in First World, Asia's Tigers Act Like It
They Trade, Aid and Compete Like Other Developed Lands

By Dan Biers
Staff Reporter of The Wall Street Journal

HADONG, Vietnam — English-language teacher Haminah Osman uses all her wiles to coax simple sentences from her 12- and 13-year-old Vietnamese students, who sit bundled against the winter cold coming through the paneless classroom windows.

Miss Haminah, who at 33 has put her career as a television producer on hold to teach the language of the modern world to the youth of impoverished Vietnam, is a spiritual descendant of the altruistic youth who joined the U.S. Peace Corps in the 1960s. But she's not American, she comes from Singapore. The pint-size economic dynamo has just started sending volunteers abroad to help the less-privileged.

Miss Haminah's presence in Hadong, a Hanoi suburb, is one of the clearest signs that Singapore and the other fast-growing Asian "tigers" — Taiwan, South Korea and Hong Kong — are graduating from "newly industrializing countries," or NICs, as economists now call them, to full-fledged members of the First World.

"They're basically the new developed economies," says Kenneth S. Courtis, senior economist at Deutsche Bank Capital Markets (Asia) Ltd. in Tokyo.

The implications for the rest of the world, particularly Asia, are enormous. For the Third World, the tigers are a welcome new source of foreign assistance, albeit in modest amounts, that can reduce dependence on major aid-giving nations such as Japan and the U.S. For the First World, the tigers are becoming serious competitors in strategic industries from shipping to semiconductors. For the entire world, the tigers are widening the scope of their direct investment abroad to include more sophisticated industries, including automobiles and electronics.

Of course, much still separates the four tigers from the First World giants. A large portion of the tigers' industry relies on foreign capital and technology. Their schools don't rank with the top universities of the West, which have played a crucial role in developing technology and encouraging innovation. And some of their economies remain highly controlled by less-well-developed bureaucracies.

Yet by many standards, the tigers are now part of the developed world. Life expectancy at birth in Hong Kong is 80 years, several years longer than in the U.S. Singapore's infant-mortality rate per 1,000 live births is five, well below the U.S. level of nine.

A global competitiveness report last year placed Hong Kong and Singapore among the world's top four economies, along with Japan and the U.S. The survey applauded Singapore's organizational abilities, strong foreign trade and good infrastructure. Hong Kong, it said, benefited from "business-friendly monetary and fiscal policies." Taiwan was ranked 18th and South Korea 24th, ahead of Spain, Portugal and Italy.

Even in technological innovation the tigers are making a mark. In the year ended Sept. 30, 1993, the U.S. issued 1,453 patents to applicants from Taiwan, which has been luring trained native sons back from California's Silicon Valley. The Taiwan total is one more than the number of U.S. patents issued to Italy, which has nearly three times the population.

By one of the most widely used yardsticks to determine a country's development, gross national product per capita, three of the tigers are First World material. The World Bank considers countries to be "high income" if per-capita GNP tops $8,626 a year. Hong Kong, Singapore and Taiwan are well above that; they fare even better when their economies are measured in terms of the purchasing power of their national currencies. Under that system, Hong Kong's per-capita figure is about one-fifth greater than that of its colonial rulers, the British.

Earning Their Stripes
Based on 1993 data

COUNTRY	LIFE EXPECTANCY	GDP PER CAPITA	EXPORTS (billions)	IMPORTS (billions)	FOREIGN AID DISPERSED (millions)
Hong Kong	80.0	$22,900	$135.2	$138.7	N.A.
Singapore	75.8	18,800	74.0	85.2	$12.4*
South Korea	70.3	10,100	82.2	83.8	176.0
Taiwan	75.0	10,600	84.7	77.1	61.0
U.S.	75.8	24,700	464.8	603.4	9,011.0

*For year ended March 31, 1994
N.A.=Not available
Source: OECD, CIA Handbook of International Economic Statistics

South Korea's per-capita GNP in 1993 was $7,670, the lowest among the tigers but 23 times greater than in 1972, when it was still a largely agrarian state. "The economy 20 years ago wasn't far from where North Korea is now," marvels Gareth Evans, branch manager of Baring Securities Ltd. in Seoul.

If South Korea can maintain 8% economic growth for the next few years, it will soon pass the high-income mark. Already, Seoul is preparing to apply for entry to the Organization for Economic Cooperation and Development, or OECD, a group that coordinates economic policies among the world's 25 wealthiest nations.

With the impressive growth of the tigers have come new international responsibilities, such as providing aid, usually loans and technical assistance, and volunteers to help the world's poor.

Aid from Singapore, in the form of technical help in such areas as communications and urban development, amounted to $12.4 million in the year that ended last March 31; Singapore's Foreign Ministry expects the figure to grow 8% to 10% by the next fiscal year. Still, it's dwarfed by Japan's massive $11.26 billion in foreign aid in 1993, according to the OECD.

Seoul's official development assistance is growing, too. It reached $176.4 million in 1993, up a third from the previous year, the Korea International Cooperation Agency says. Taiwan's foreign-aid program, which the OECD says has nearly tripled since 1989, reached $61 million in 1993. The people of Hong Kong have made their mark through charity, with annual donations doubling to $152.7 million from 1989 to 1993, according to the Inland Revenue Department.

The tigers also help poorer countries develop through corporate joint ventures and other direct investments. One example is an ambitious attempt to build a new city center for Vietnam's crowded and creaky Ho Chi Minh City, formerly Saigon. The project is spearheaded by Central Trading & Development Group, a Taiwan concern.

Central Trading has already put up an export-processing zone in Ho Chi Minh City and is building an 11-mile road to connect it to National Highway 1, Vietnam's main transportation artery. Company officials envision the new thoroughfare flanked by a $242 million development called Saigon South that is to include universities, hotels, parks, sports facilities and commercial and residential zones.

That represents a sharp break from Taiwan's past foreign investment, which typically involved moving low-technology industries such as toy and shoe manufacturing offshore, particularly to China, to escape Taiwan's spiraling wages. Taiwan personal-computer maker Acer Inc. has more than a dozen assembly plants abroad, including two in the U.S. and several in Europe.

Microtek International Inc., a Taiwan manufacturer of color-image scanners and laser printers, employs about 120 people in Los Angeles and Portland, Ore., who perform advanced research and development and other services.

South Korea's conglomerates are also investing aggressively in the First World. Samsung Group, for example, announced in October that it would put $700 million into a huge complex in Britain to make everything from microwave ovens to semiconductors. Escalating wages in South Korea mean production costs may be cheaper in the developed West.

In 1993, South Korea led the world in shipbuilding, with 40% of the global market, says Mr. Evans, of Baring Securities. The country was the world's sixth-largest car producer that year with 2.1 million units, albeit mostly for the domestic market. In addition, he says, Samsung Electronics Co. recently became the world's leading maker of dynamic random access memory chips, which are used in personal computers. And Pohang Iron & Steel Co. has cracked the difficult Japanese market, selling steel to Mitsubishi Motors Corp. as the high yen erodes the competitiveness of Japanese steel suppliers.

Taiwan's Acer, meanwhile, has entered the ranks of the world's top 10 computer companies in terms of units shipped, a spokesman says.

"Like the Sonys that came out of nowhere in the '60s and the Hondas in the '70s, you are going to have high-tech companies coming out of these [tiger] economies that you have never heard of before," says Mr. Courtis of Deutsche Bank, citing Acer as one example.

Already, Mr. Courtis says, South Korea spends more on research and development as a proportion of GNP than do several Western nations; Seoul plans to boost such investment even more.

Source: *The Wall Street Journal*, February 28, 1995. Reprinted with permission of THE WALL STREET JOURNAL, 1995 Dow Jones & Company, Inc. All rights reserved worldwide.

CHAPTER 14
The Political Economy of Trade and Agriculture

Objectives of the Chapter

Previous chapters addressed the task of measuring and judging economic consequences of all trade policies. This chapter puts more emphasis on the economic consequences of trade policies toward agriculture and agricultural trade, and on the political and economic causes of all trade policies. Chapter 14 focuses on the political and institutional factors that influence the decision making of trade policy officials.

The special treatment given to agriculture by different countries defies the precepts of comparative advantage. In this regard, four issues are addressed: the different types of agricultural policies, the international patterns in agricultural policy, food security in the Third World, and trends in the welfare cost of agricultural policies.

After studying this chapter, you should be able to

1. explain why trade legislation is often biased in favor of producers' groups
2. describe the various factors which influence whether producers or consumers tend to win the battle over the tariff issue, including inefficiency of the tariff, group size, sympathy for the group, and representation in government
3. relate agricultural tariff policies to the developmental pattern and to the antitrade bias
4. correlate domestic policies on farm income support and agricultural trade policies

Key Terms

Antitrade pattern of agricultural policy
governments tend to tax exportable-good agriculture and to subsidize (protect) importable-good agriculture.

Developmental pattern of agricultural policy
as a nation becomes more developed, its policy switches from heavily taxing agriculture to heavily subsidizing it.

Free riders — people who think the common cause will stand or fall regardless of their contribution, and who therefore do not contribute in the hope of riding free if the cause succeeds.

Nominal protection coefficient — the ratio of the price received by domestic producers to the world price of the same product at the nation's border. If NPC > 1, producers of the good are protected by the government; if NPC < 1, producers of the good are effectively taxed.

Sudden-damage effect — refers to public sympathy for groups whose incomes fall due to import competition, either suddenly or during a general depression.

Switch-over goods — goods that countries convert from importables to exportables by offering generous subsidies to domestic producers.

Tariff escalation — refers to the tendency of tariffs and other import barriers to be higher on finished goods sold to consumers than on intermediate manufactured goods, sold to industry (inputs).

Trade concessions — in international trade negotiations it is customary to define cuts in one's own import barriers (thereby letting in more imports) as trade concessions, for which the liberalizing country ought to be compensated with reciprocal cuts abroad.

Warm-up Questions

True or False? Explain.

1. T / F   Most trade barriers protect a numerical majority of the population.

2. T / F   An NPC which is greater than one is indicative of government protection of consumer interests.

3. T / F The shrinkage of the agricultural sector increases its lobbying effectiveness.

4. T / F The free rider problem afflicts the small-group opposition more seriously than it afflicts the large-group opposition.

5. T / F Tariffs on consumer goods tend to be lower than tariffs on the inputs which are used to produce those goods.

Multiple Choice

1. The beneficiaries of U.S. support-price programs for wheat include
   a. Russia
   b. Canada
   c. wheat consumers in the United States
   d. European taxpayers

2. The nominal protection coefficient (NPC) is
   a. equal to the effective rate of protection
   b. equal to the nominal rate of protection
   c. the degree of protection experienced by the economy as a whole
   d. a measure of the protection of an industry by all trade barriers and all subsidies to import-competing domestic producers of the good

3. Which of the following statements is *wrong*?
   a. The drift from taxing agriculture in earlier stages of development to protecting it in more developed economies is easily explained by the prevalence of majority rule.
   b. Policy toward agricultural prices in the developed countries tends to be biased toward raising them, rather than keeping them as low as possible.
   c. By protecting the industrial sector, most countries implicitly tax exportable agricultural products.
   d. The pattern of protection of import-competing agriculture can be partially explained by the popular political goal of self-sufficiency in food.

4. Agricultural policies in developed countries tend to
   a. discourage trade and domestic production
   b. discourage trade but favor domestic production
   c. increase trade but discourage domestic production
   d. increase both trade and domestic production

5. The most likely explanation for the widespread use of trade barriers is
   a. domestic producers' ignorance
   b. domestic consumers' ignorance
   c. exporters' ignorance
   d. trade officials' use of a welfare measure other than the "one-dollar, one-vote" measure used in economic theory

Problems

1. Leinster is a democracy. Referring to the factors that influence who "wins" the tariff battle, speculate on the likelihood that bakers in Leinster will receive tariff protection.

2. Suppose that the Egyptian government is considering implementing some new strategies regarding trade in agricultural products:

   a. Egypt pays a fixed world price of 100 Egyptian pounds for each bushel of wheat the country imports. The government is considering two different policies, each of which would let Egyptian flour mills (on behalf of flour consumers) pay only 70 pounds per bushel. One policy is a subsidy of 30 pounds on each bushel of wheat consumed; the other is a subsidy of 30 pounds on each bushel they import. Which policy would inflict the greater net national loss on Egypt?

b. Egypt gets a fixed world price of 100 Egyptian pounds for each bale of cotton the country exports. The government is considering two different policies, each of which would give Egyptian cotton producers only 60 pounds for each bale they sell. One policy is a tax of 40 pounds on each bale of cotton they sell. The other is a tax of 40 pounds on each bale of cotton they export. Which policy would inflict a greater net national loss on Egypt?

3. Consider the following hypothetical data for a wheat-producing country:

   Domestic wheat price (P_{prod}) = $10 per bushel
   World wheat price (P_{world}) = $20 per bushel
   Input cost markup due to government policies = $2 per bushel
   Government subsidies = $1 per bushel
   Unit value added at free trade prices = $15 per bushel

   a. Calculate e.r.p., NPC, and PSE.

   b. Are producers subsidized or taxed in this case?

   c. What are the advantages of the e.r.p. over the NPC?

   d. Which of the three is the best measure of government impact on farm incomes?

   e. Is the pattern you observe here more typical of a high-income or a low-income country?

4. The United States and Thailand have a comparative advantage in rice production; Japan has a comparative disadvantage in rice production. In which of these countries do you think farmers get the greatest percentage of their net income protection from their government? In which do they get the least? Why?

Discussion Topics

1. Why do you think farmers receive greater protection in "developed" countries than in "developing" countries?

2. Try to think of ways of forcing government officials to employ the "one-dollar, one-vote" yardstick when they consider the implementation of new trade barriers.

Final Thought

> *A good farmer is nothing more nor less than a handyman with a sense of humor.*
>
> — E.B. White, 1944

CHAPTER 15
Payments among Nations

Objectives of the Chapter

This chapter looks at how international exchange of goods, services, and financial assets are recorded in official statistics. Two sets of statistics are presented: the balance of payments accounts and the international investment position accounts. The trade, current, capital, and official settlements accounts are specialized accounts within the balance of payments accounts, and are derived by grouping international transactions according to common characteristics.

After studying Chapter 15, you should know

1. what information the balance of payments accounts record
2. the distinction between debit and credit entries
3. the meaning and scope of various accounts' balances
4. why the current account balance equals the difference between national product and national expenditure
5. the concept of an overall balance of payments surplus or deficit
6. the meaning and usefulness of the balance on international investment
7. the historical status of the United States as net creditor or debtor with respect to the rest of the world

Key Terms

Balance of payments the systematic set of accounts that record all economic transactions between residents of that country and the rest of the world during a given period of time.

Capital account records the values of financial assets purchased and sold abroad by private residents (not monetary authorities) of the home country.

Capital inflow either an increase in foreign assets in the nation, such as when a foreigner purchases a U.S. stock; or a reduction in the nation's assets abroad, such as when an American sells a foreign stock.

Capital outflow — either an increase in the nation's assets abroad, such as when an American purchases a foreign asset; or a reduction in foreign assets in the nation, such as when a foreigner sells his American assets.

Current account — records the values of goods and services sold and purchased abroad, plus net interest and other factor payments and net unilateral transfers and gifts.

International investment position
measures a nation's stock of foreign assets and liabilities at a point in time.

Net foreign investment
the part of national saving invested abroad instead of being channeled into domestic capital formation ($S = I_d + I_f$). It is also the difference between purchase of financial assets (lending) abroad and asset sales to foreigners (borrowing), that is, a country's accumulation of net claims on other countries.

Official balance (official settlements balance)
equals the sum of the current account balance plus the private capital account balance. An imbalance in the official balance must be financed (or paid for) through official reserves transactions.

Official international reserves transactions
the changes in domestic official reserve assets and in domestic official liquid liabilities to foreign officials. It is derived by drawing the line through the balance of payments accounts so as to divide private transactions from official "accommodative" transactions.

Reserve assets — assets held by a nation's monetary authorities as a kind of "war chest" to enable them to intervene in the foreign exchange market if and when they decide to do so. Reserve assets include foreign key currencies, gold, official reserves at the IMF, and holdings of Special Drawing Rights (SDRs).

Trade account (or merchandise account)
records the value of goods sold and purchased abroad by residents of the home country. The value of goods exported (credits) minus the value of goods imported (debits) is the **merchandise trade balance**.

Warm-up Questions

True or False? Explain.

1. T / F   A negative net foreign investment on this year's balance of payments accounts means the country is a net debtor.

2. T / F   A nation running a current account surplus is accumulating foreign assets.

3. T / F   Because the balance of payments accounts must balance, sub-accounts like the capital account must balance too.

4. T / F   If GDP, consumption, and domestic investment are all constant, when government spending rises relative to taxes, the country will run a trade deficit.

5. T / F   The "statistical discrepancy" component of the balance of payments accounts is a refuge for scoundrels.

Multiple Choice

1. If a U.S. firm borrows one billion dollars in Mexican pesos from Citibank's Mexico branch and uses the money to build a factory in Mexico, the transaction will enter the U.S. balance of payments as
   a. a credit on short-term private capital inflow and a debit on direct investment payments
   b. a credit on long-term private capital inflow and a debit on long-term private capital outflow
   c. a credit on long-term private capital inflow and debit on direct investment
   d. a credit on short-term private capital inflow and debit on short-term private capital outflow

2. An economic transaction is recorded in the balance of payments as a credit if it leads to
   a. a payment to foreigners
   b. the receipt of a payment from foreigners
   c. a decrease in foreign exchange reserves
   d. neither an inflow nor an outflow of value

3. Which of the following is recorded as a debit item in the U.S. balance of payments accounts?
   a. An Italian firms pays $5 million in dividends to the holders of its stock in the United States.
   b. The French Club Med hires four American scuba diving instructors for its new resort on the Italian island of Sardinia.
   c. Toyota builds a factory in the United States to manufacture Celicas.
   d. Remittances from Cambodian immigrants in the United States flow to their relatives in Thailand's refugee centers.

4. Borrowing from abroad is
   a. a capital import and, therefore, a debit item
   b. a capital export and, therefore, a credit item
   c. a capital import and, therefore, a credit item
   d. a capital export and, therefore, a debit item

5. If a country's net foreign investment amounts to –$15 billion, this implies
   a. an equivalent current account deficit
   b. an equivalent current account surplus
   c. an equivalent trade balance surplus
   d. an equivalent overall balance deficit

Problems

1. Number-crunchers in Leinster have been working hard to come up with information about flows of funds between Leinster and Saxony. Suppose they have derived the following data for the current year in Leinster. (All numbers are in billions of the Leinster currency — the Leinster lira.)

National Product	100.0
Consumption	60.0
Government Purchases	15.0
Formation of Leinster Capital	15.0
Exports to Saxony	20.0

   a. What is the value of imported goods and services from Saxony?

   b. Is Leinster, on net, lending to Saxony or borrowing from Saxony?

2. Consider the following information:

   ■ Donald Trump buys a cottage in France for $1,008
   ■ American manufacturers export $998 in baseball bats
   ■ Profits from Costa Rican coffee plantations owned by residents of Seattle equal $1,002
   ■ Interest paid on a U.S. Treasury bond to a Japanese citizen is $1,004
   ■ An Irish worker in San Francisco sends $996 home to her mother in Dublin
   ■ A German tourist spends $1006 on a fling in Las Vegas
   ■ A Greek billionaire buys a hot dog stand in New York for $1,006
   ■ Bill Clinton imports $1,002 of wine from France
   ■ The Federal Reserve officially **buys/sells $X** in foreign exchange

   Assume that this is a complete list of international transactions for the United States this year. In addition, the numbers have been collected quite accurately, with the exception of the missing data on the Fed's transaction in foreign exchange. With this information,

a. place each of these transactions in their proper place in the balance of payments accounts,

b. find the trade deficit,

c. and find what the Fed's action was (did it buy or sell foreign exchange, and what was the amount).

d. Can you tell from the data whether there is a floating or a fixed exchange rate?

3. Which of the following transactions would contribute to a U.S. current account *surplus*?

   a. McDonald's makes a barter trade with Russia, providing hamburgers for the Kremlin in exchange for potatoes from Russian state farms.

   b. The United States borrows $100 million long term from Kuwait to buy $100 million of Kuwaiti oil this year.

   c. The United States sells Bosnians $100 million in automatic weapons, paid for with $100 million in bank deposits.

d. The U.S. government makes a gift of $100 million to the people of Rwanda to pay for emergency hospital care.

e. The U.S. government sells $100 million in long-term bonds to Japan, getting bank deposits in Japan and promising to repay the loan in five years.

f. American soccer fans buy 1998 World Cup tickets from a French scalper, paying with dollars (cash).

4. Given the following figures (in millions of dollars) from the U.S. balance of payments and international assets position in 1978, was U.S. domestic investment (real capital formation) above or below U.S. savings in 1978? By how much?

U.S. merchandise exports	141,884
U.S. merchandise imports	176,071
U.S. current account balance	−10,743
Decrease in U.S. official reserve assets	732
Increase in U.S. official holdings of foreign assets	31,001
U.S. assets abroad, end of 1978	450,050
U.S. liabilities abroad, end of 1978	373,345

5. Calculate the value of all foreign investments in the United States at the end of 1983 from the following data:

   U.S. investment abroad = $887.5 billion
   U.S. net creditor position = $106.0 billion
   U.S. official reserve assets = $33.7 billion

Discussion Topics

1. Is running a trade deficit always bad?

2. Should a country run an official balance surplus rather than an official balance deficit?

Final Thought

It has been said that figures rule the world; maybe. I am quite sure that it is figures which show us whether it is being ruled well or badly.

— Johann Wolfgang Goethe, 1830

THE WALL STREET JOURNAL
February 10, 1995

The Dollar Depreciation Mystery

By Charles Wolf Jr.

The Mexican peso's precipitous fall has gotten a lot of attention lately. But the dollar's own depreciation is, in many respects, even more puzzling. Last year, the dollar fell 11% relative to the Japanese yen, 9% relative to the German mark and 6% relative to the British pound. While the dollar depreciated, the U.S. economy's performance continued to be much stronger and more vigorous than that of the European and Japanese economies whose currencies appreciated.

In contrast with those economies, U.S. gross domestic product growth has been rapid, unemployment has decreased, productivity and corporate profits have risen, prices have been stable, and the dollar's relative purchasing power has increased. Under these circumstances, one might have expected the dollar's exchange value to rise, rather than fall. Indeed, George Soros reportedly lost about $1 billion betting that this would happen.

The explanation usually offered is the U.S. current account deficit: the excess of U.S. outlays for imports of goods and services over receipts from exports. While this is surely a part of the explanation, the larger part lies in the size and composition of U.S. capital exports. Indeed, the U.S. has been the world's largest capital exporter at the same time that it has been the world's largest capital importer.

Underlying the surge of U.S. investment abroad has been the proliferation and expansion of international and "emerging market" global equity funds. Mutual fund managers tend to be less concerned with exchange-rate risks than with other considerations: the outlook for aggregate and sectoral growth in specific foreign countries; the competitive strength of specific foreign firms; the domestic, regional, and global market shares that these firms can acquire; their dividend policies and management capabilities; and the increased interest of U.S. mutual fund shareholders in risk diversification through investment in markets outside the U.S.

These major movers of U.S. capital outflow have been sufficiently bullish about buying into foreign holdings to be willing to pay a higher dollar price for foreign exchange.

But a larger share of capital imports into the U.S. represents foreign bank loans to U.S. banks, rather than equity investments. (U.S. tax withholding on earnings from equity investments reduces the incentives of foreign investors and portfolio managers to buy U.S. equities.) These bank IOUs tend to be responsive to changes in interest rates, and are more passive with respect to changes in exchange rates. They tend, therefore, not to have a major effect on exchange rates.

Thus, the net impact on the dollar's exchange rate is greater per dollar of capital exports than per dollar of capital imports. Capital exports can have this dramatic effect because they are so huge. In 1993, U.S. capital exports were the largest of any country, rising to $148 billion, principally due to this surge of U.S. investments in foreign equities by mutual funds, pension funds, and individuals (totaling $120 billion), as well as U.S. direct investment in places like Mexico.

For the first half of 1994, the corresponding figures are $50 billion for total U.S. capital outflows, of which $37 billion represents increased holdings of foreign securities, and $33 billion is direct investment abroad. (Reductions by U.S. banks in their claims on foreign banks account for most of the difference between total outflows in the first half of 1994, $50 billion, and the sum of portfolio and direct investment, $70 billion.)

U.S. capital imports have also been the world's largest, necessarily exceeding the magnitude of our capital exports by an amount sufficient to provide financing for the current account deficit. In 1993, total capital inflows into the U.S. reached $231 billion. Of this amount, more than 40% represented increased holdings by foreign governments and individuals of U.S. government assets, with the remainder divided among foreign direct investment in the U.S., bank loans, and foreign investment in U.S. equities and bonds. For the first half of 1994 the corresponding figure for total capital inflows into the U.S. was $137 billion, of which about $20 billion consisted of increased foreign government holdings of U.S. assets, $60 billion represented loans to U.S. banks, and the remainder was divided among direct investment and increased holdings of U.S. securities.

On this reasoning, the dollar might continue to depreciate even if the U.S. current account deficit diminishes, because U.S. portfolio and direct investment abroad might continue to be large. However, to the extent that the most lucrative niches in foreign equity markets have already been, or soon will be, filled, and the next-best equities are less attractive, U.S. capital exports will recede and the dollar's value will appreciate. Also pointing in this direction is the plunge in the value of the Mexican peso. Mexico's setback may dim the luster of emerging markets, thereby reducing the flow of U.S. capital abroad.

To assess whether the dollar's foreign exchange value is more likely to rise or fall, look at the capital account, not just at the current account. The value of the dollar will depend on what happens to U.S. portfolio and direct investment abroad, rather than what happens to the current account deficit.

Mr. Wolf is dean of the RAND Graduate School of Policy Studies in Santa Monica, Calif.

Source: *The Wall Street Journal*, February 10, 1995. Reprinted with permission of THE WALL STREET JOURNAL, 1995 Dow Jones & Company, Inc. All rights reserved worldwide.

CHAPTER 16
The Foreign Exchange Market

Objectives of the Chapter

This chapter deals with the nature and organization of the foreign exchange market. At its most basic, the equilibrium exchange rate can be thought of as the price which equates the public's supply of and demand for a money. For example, the exchange rate on the French franc (expressed as American dollars per French franc) would be determined by the supply of francs arising from French purchases of American goods, services, and assets, and by the demand for French francs arising from American imports of French goods, services, and assets.

You might want to track a few of the major currencies and related commentaries in the daily listings in the financial press.

After studying Chapter 16, you should be able to identify

1. what an exchange rate is
2. what the reciprocal of the exchange rate means
3. the organization of the modern foreign exchange market
4. the distinction between spot and forward exchange rates
5. determinants of demand and supply for foreign exchange
6. how a system of flexible foreign exchange rates works
7. how a system of fixed foreign exchange rates works

Key Terms

Appreciation (depreciation)
    an increase (decrease) in the market price of a currency under a floating exchange rate system.

Clearing   permitting payments to be made between entities who want to hold or use different currencies.

Fixed exchange rate a rate whose officially declared value is maintained by central bank intervention. (Also referred to as a pegged exchange rate.)

Floating exchange rate
a rate whose value is determined purely by the market forces of supply and demand, with no direct intervention of the central bank. (Also referred to as a flexible exchange rate.)

Foreign exchange market
a computerized communications network embracing all the major financial centers in the globe, where sellers and buyers of any national money can quickly and efficiently carry out any desired currency exchange.

Foreign exchange market intervention
the act or policy of buying and selling foreign exchange on the part of the central bank in order to manipulate or peg the exchange rate.

(Foreign) exchange rate
the price of one country's currency expressed in terms of another country's currency. (Note: in this text, the exchange rate is expressed in terms of domestic currency units required to purchase one unit of a foreign currency.)

Forward exchange rate
the exchange rate applicable to foreign exchange transactions agreed upon today for later delivery (usually, in 30, 90, or 180 days).

Revaluation (devaluation)
an official increase (decrease) in the par value of a currency under a fixed exchange rate system.

Spot exchange rate the (past, current, or future) rate applicable to foreign exchange transactions requiring contemporaneous delivery.

Vehicle currency a currency used to accomplish an indirect trade between two other currencies. The American dollar is often used as a vehicle currency.

Chapter 16: The Foreign Exchange Market

Warm-up Questions

True or False? Explain.

1. T / F An increase in U.S. imports from France will give rise to a supply of francs in exchange for dollars.

2. T / F Central bank intervention is more prevalent under the floating exchange rate system than under a pegged exchange rate system.

3. T / F If Americans suddenly refuse to lend money to Mexico, we would expect the dollar to appreciate relative to the peso.

4. T / F Art appreciation courses have nothing to do with exchange rates.

5. T / F If a currency is undervalued in a fixed exchange rate system, officials from that country's central bank will have to sell their currency to keep it pegged.

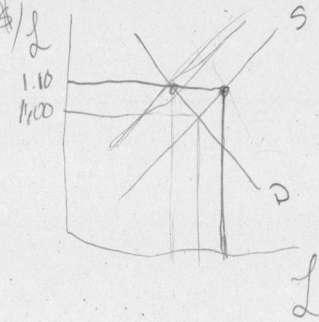

Multiple Choice

1. If the exchange rate between the Canadian dollar (C$) and the American dollar (US$) changes from C$1.340/ US$ to C$1.325/ US$ but the Canadian government wants to maintain a fixed exchange rate of C$ 1.340/ US$, what should the Bank of Canada do?
   a. Stop trading with the United States so that fewer U.S dollars will flow into Canada.
   b. Sell U.S. dollars (buy Canadian dollars).
   c. Sell Canadian dollars (buy U.S. dollars).
   d. Purchase British pounds and sell French francs.

2. If a dollar is valued at 400 Mexican pesos in the foreign exchange market, what is the value of one peso?
   a. $250
   b. $0.0025
   c. $0.04
   d. $1.25
   e. none of the above

3. Which of the following statements is *false*?
   a. British imports of Florida oranges will create a demand for U.S. dollars.
   b. If all Americans decide to buy German cars, the dollar will appreciate relative to the mark.
   c. The American dollar is often used as a vehicle currency.
   d. Australia, Canada, Hong Kong, New Zealand, and Taiwan all use currencies called "the dollar."

4. When American residents buy bonds from Her Majesty's Treasury in London, in the foreign exchange market it leads to
   a. a demand for American dollars
   b. a supply of British pounds
   c. a supply of American dollars
   d. another Boston Tea Party

5. The demand curve for foreign currency slopes downward because
   a. at lower exchange rates, foreign goods look cheaper to home country residents
   b. at higher exchange rates, the home currency can buy more foreign goods
   c. the quantity supplied of the foreign currency rises as the exchange rate falls
   d. marginal utility theory says that individuals substitute into any commodity whose price has fallen

Problems

1. The currency of Leinster is the Leinster lira (Ll); the currency of Saxony is the Saxon scudo (Ss). Consider the following diagram of the foreign exchange market in Saxony:

Figure 16.1

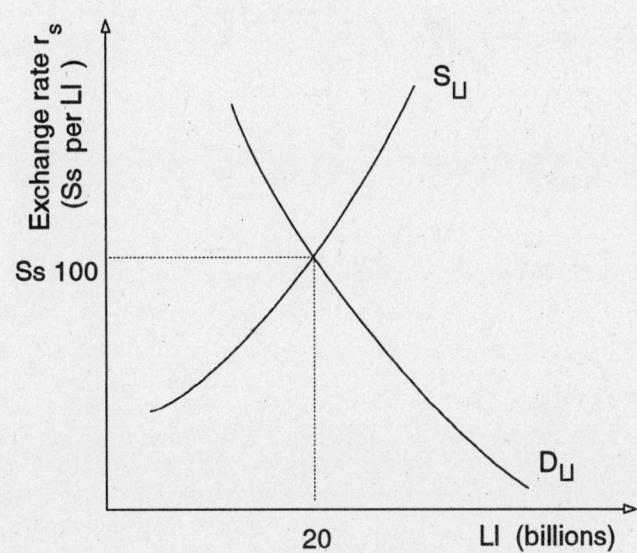

   a. What is the equilibrium price of one Leinster lira in Saxony?

   b. Can you also determine what the equilibrium price of the Saxon scudo is in Leinster?

   c. Suppose that a doctor in Leinster shows that eating Saxon bread can reduce the level of cholesterol in one's blood. What would you expect to happen to the exchange rate between lira and scudos in a floating exchange rate system?

   d. If the Saxon finance minister had wanted to peg the exchange rate at the value you determined in (a), what must she do to counteract the impact on the exchange rate of the event described in (c)?

2. Suppose that the Saxon scudo appreciates relative to the Leinster lira. Determine whether the economic agents listed below would see that appreciation as a good thing or a bad thing.

   a. someone who imports goods priced in scudos

   b. someone who exports goods priced in scudos

   c. someone who exports goods priced in lira

   d. someone who has a retirement account denominated in scudos

   e. someone who expected the lira to depreciate

3. For the most part, the exchange rate between U.S. dollars and the French franc is floating. What effect will each of the following events have on the $/F exchange rate?

   a. the French government bans the import of American movies

   b. Americans learn that drinking red wine from France will prevent heart disease

   c. an American mutual fund purchases stock in Renault

   d. Parisian terrorists buy chemicals from a company in New Jersey

   e. New York foreign exchange speculators believe the French franc is going to depreciate in the next few hours

4. Assume, instead, that government officials in the United States are trying to keep the exchange rate between the dollar and the French franc pegged. For each of the events described in Problem 3, what actions must these officials take to return the exchange rate to its previous level?

5. You have been given one million yen to play with. Use the following exchange rates to show how you can make a riskless profit in terms of yen.

>one German mark = 70 yen in Munich
>one yen = one American penny in Tokyo
>one American dollar = three German marks in New York

Discussion Topics

1. What do you see as the benefits and costs of each country having its own currency?

2. What problems would you foresee in a world where some countries have floating exchange rates while others try to keep their exchange rates fixed?

Final Thought

All things that are exchanged must be somehow compared. It is for this end that money has been introduced, and it becomes in a sense an intermediate; for it measures all things.

— Aristotle, 384–322 BC

CHAPTER 17
Forward Exchange

Objectives of the Chapter

This chapter extends the discussion of exchange rates begun in Chapter 16 by explicitly introducing the aspect of future exchange rate changes and the risk posed by rate fluctuations. Contracts to exchange currencies in the future, at a price determined in the present, are called forward contracts. These contracts can be used both by people wishing to avoid uncertainty and by people who are willing to take on risk by betting on the future movements of exchange rates.

After reading Chapter 17, you should be able to

1. differentiate between spot exchange rates and forward exchange rates
2. understand the use of forward rates to hedge and to speculate
3. explain the relationship between the forward exchange rate and the expected future spot rate
4. explain the relationship between the forward exchange rate, the spot rate, and international interest rates

Key Terms

Covered interest arbitrage
          buying a country's currency spot and selling it forward, while making a net profit off the combination of higher interest rates in that country and any forward premium on its currency.

Covered interest parity
          the condition where the forward rate on a currency exceeds the spot rate by the percentage that its interest rate is lower than the other country's interest rate.

Covered international investment
: when the exchange rate at which anticipated foreign investment returns will be redeemd is determined in the present through a forward contract. The agent is protected from exchange rate risk when "covered."

Exchange rate risk when the value of an economic agent's income, wealth, or net worth changes as exchange rates change unpredictably in the future.

Forward exchange contract
: an agreement to buy or sell a foreign currency for future delivery at a price set now (the "forward exchange rate").

Future spot rate the spot exchange rate that will end up prevailing at some date in the future.

Hedging the act of exactly matching assets and liabilities, such as foreign currencies, so as to avoid exchange rate risk.

International interest rate differential
: the difference between home and foreign interest rates.

Long position a net asset position (for example, owning a foreign currency).

Short position a net liability position (for example, owing a foreign currency).

Speculation deliberately assuming a net asset (long) position or a net liability (short) position in an asset, such as a foreign currency, in the hope of making a profit from price changes.

Uncovered interest parity
: when the expected rate of appreciation of a currency equals the percentage point amount by which its interest rate is lower than the other country's interest rate.

Uncovered international investment
: when the exchange rate at which anticipated foreign investment returns will be redeemed is not determined until the trade occurs at the future spot rate. The agent is exposed to exchange rate risk when "uncovered."

Warm-up Questions

True or False? Explain.

1. T / F The forward exchange rate is the same as the future spot rate.

2. T / F Speculating means taking only a short position, not a long position.

3. T / F If German interest rates are higher than American interest rates, we would expect the DM to be at a forward discount relative to the dollar.

4. T / F Hedgehogs are afraid of risk.

5. T / F If a speculator believes that the future spot rate on the British pound will be higher than the current forward rate, the speculator will buy the pound forward.

Multiple Choice

1. Suppose that an American speculator anticipates that the spot rate on the yen in 180 days will be higher than today's 180-day forward rate on the yen, which is $0.0072. Which of these investments is best if she is right?
   a. Sell one million yen today in the forward market for delivery in 180 days.
   b. Buy one million yen today in the forward market for delivery in 180 days.
   c. Buy dollars today in the spot market.
   d. Buy dollars today in the forward market for delivery in 180 days.

2. Covered interest parity is a condition where
   a. the forward value of a currency will tend to exceed its spot value by the same percentage as its interest rates are lower than foreign interest rates
   b. the spot value will tend to exceed its forward value by the same percentage as its interest rates are lower than foreign interest rates
   c. the domestic and foreign interest rates are equalized
   d. the spot and forward rates are equalized

3. Suppose you are an established speculator with an excellent reputation, but you do not have any liquid funds at the moment. You believe that the dollar is going to rise again. What would you do?
   a. Borrow dollars in the United States and sell the dollars in the spot exchange market.
   b. Buy foreign (nondollar) currencies forward.
   c. Sell foreign (nondollar) currencies forward.
   d. Borrow yen in Japan and sell them on the spot market.

4. If today's spot rate on the British pound is $2 and the one-month forward rate on the pound is $2.10 (ignoring any interest earnings or costs),
   a. a speculator who had purchased 100 British pounds forward today will make a profit of $10 one month from now
   b. a speculator who had purchased 100 British pounds spot today will make a profit of $10 one month from now
   c. a speculator who had sold 100 British pounds forward today will make a profit of 10 pounds one month from now
   d. a speculator who had sold 100 British pounds spot today will make a profit of 10 pounds one month from now
   e. none of the above

5. Assume that the interest rate in the United States exceeds Japan's interest rate by 4 percentage points (on an annual basis). If you were a speculator, you would take a long position in yen
   a. if the value of the yen is expected to increase by 2 percentage points on an annual basis
   b. if the value of the yen is expected to fall by 4 percentage points
   c. if the value of the yen is expected to fall by less than 4 percentage points
   d. if the value of the dollar is expected to fall by more than 4 percentage points

Problems

1. Imagine that you are a student, but you also work in your parents' bakery in Saxony. You have just shipped off a load of bread to Leinster and are supposed to be paid Ll 10,000 in 60 days. You observe that the forward rate on the Leinster lira is Ss 95/ Ll. You also guess that the spot rate may vary between Ss 85 / Ll and Ss 105/ Ll over the next 60 days.

   a. If you decide to lock in the exchange rate with a forward contract, how many Saxon scudos will you receive in 60 days?

   b. If, instead, you decide to wait to sell the Leinster lira at the spot rate which will prevail in 60 days, how much could you gain compared to the assured return in (a)?

   How much could you lose compared to the assured return in (a) ?

   c. What will determine which option you choose?

2. (Sometime later...) You have graduated to become a Saxon economist, and the finance minister of Saxony has asked you to consider the following information:

   ■ The annual interest rate on 180-day government bonds in Saxony is 8% ; the interest rate on similar bonds in Leinster is 6% .

   ■ In today's exchange markets, the spot rate is Ss 100 / Ll ; the 180-day forward rate is Ss 110 / Ll .

   a. Will funds be more likely to flow from Saxony to Leinster or vice versa?

b. What will be the impact of these funds flows on the spot and forward exchange rates?

c. Assuming rigidity in the forward rate and in interest rates, at what spot exchange rate will investors be indifferent regarding whether they put their funds in Leinster or in Saxony?

3. (Much later...) Despite the finance minister's protests, you decide to become a foreign exchange speculator in your spare time. You observe that the 180-day forward rate on the Leinster lira is Ss 100/ Ll. Based on all the information you have collected, you expect that, in 180 days, the lira will have appreciated to Ss 120/ Ll.

   a. Based on your expectations, how would you use the forward foreign exchange market to try to earn a profit in Saxon scudos?

   b. What will determine whether or not you actually make a profit?

   c. If there are many speculators in Leinster and Saxony, all acting on their expectations, what does this tell you about the relationship between the forward rate and the future spot rate?

4. (Finally...) You have retired from government service in Saxony and now spend your time thinking deep economic thoughts for your own amusement. You notice the following information in the newspaper:

- interest on one-year Saxon government bonds   = 8%
- interest on one-year Leinster government bonds   = 6%
- current spot rate on the Leinster lira   = Ss 100/ Ll

Furthermore, during your deep thinking you have formed the expectation that the spot rate on the Leinster lira is going to rise to 102 Ss/ Ll by the end of the year.

a. Does uncovered interest parity hold?

b. If not, at what current spot rate would the expected uncovered differential be zero?

c. How might the current spot rate be driven to this new level?

5. Consider the following information from today's edition of *The Greed Gazette*:

- U.K. interest rate = 7%
- U.S. interest rate = 4%
- spot exchange rate = $2 / £
- forward exchange rate = $1.95 / £

(You may assume that all data is of the same periodicity.)

a. If you have $100 to play with, explain how you can make the most money. In particular, should you invest in the U.S. or the U.K.?

b. At what forward rate would you earn zero profits, and so have no incentive to play this game?

Discussion Topics

1. "Speculator" is often used as a pejorative term. Why do you think that is? Can a speculator ever increase global welfare while he is earning profits?

2. Could the purchase of a foreign equity (stock) be motivated as much by expectations of exchange rate changes as by expectations of changes in the price of the equity?

3. If all economic agents became risk-lovers, would there still be a need for forward contracts in foreign exchange?

Final Thought

There are two times in a man's life when he should not speculate: when he can't afford it, and when he can.

— Mark Twain, 1894

THE WALL STREET JOURNAL
March 9, 1995

In Europe, Strengthening of Currencies Is Causing Headaches for Many Exporters

By Terence Roth
Staff Reporter of The Wall Street Journal

Life in Europe's "safe haven" economies can be pretty scary for exporters these days.

In the world-wide scramble to unload U.S. dollars, investors have been pouring money into islands of financial stability such as Germany and Switzerland. That's driving up the value of the German mark and Swiss franc, and raising concerns among exporters in those countries. Worried that their goods may become overpriced on the world market, some are considering moving more of their operations to cheaper locales.

Nicolas Hayek, chairman of Switzerland's largest watchmaker, is a good example. Last year, a sharp drop in the dollar caused SMH Swiss Corp. for Microelectronics & Watchmaking Industries Ltd., the parent company for Swatch watches, a currency loss of 140 million francs ($123 million at the current exchange rate). The dollar's latest plummet has caused the company to make plans to transfer part of its production from Switzerland to China, Thailand and France.

"I do this with great regret, but I have no choice," Mr. Hayek says.

At Deutsche Aerospace AG, the Daimler-Benz AG unit that is Europe's largest aerospace company, every decline in the dollar sends the finance department scrambling. Last year, the company thought it could safely base its planning on an exchange rate of 1.65 marks to the dollar. But the dollar has plunged below 1.39 marks from a level of 1.55 marks only a few weeks ago, and many currency analysts expect the dollar to continue falling toward 1.30 marks in the weeks ahead. Yesterday the dollar rebounded a bit, but it was viewed by many traders as a mere pause in the downward path.

"It hits us very hard," says a Daimler-Benz spokesman. "Our income is in dollars. Our expenses are in other currencies, especially marks."

Other major currencies, such as the French franc and the Dutch guilder, have also moved up against the dollar.

Central bankers like strong currencies because they make prices of foreign goods and commodities, particularly energy, cheaper. And that helps keep inflation at bay at home. But business and fiscal planners worry that the export surge that drove the recovery in major European economies last year could ebb if European products become too expensive abroad.

To be sure, currency-hedging instruments can help ease the sting of currency swings on corporate profits. And only about 15% of European exports go to the U.S. or countries in Latin America and Asia that use the dollar as the chief reference currency for trade.

German manufacturers say they will suffer only a little — if the mark's strength is short-lived. "For us, the currency crisis has no immediate effect," says Monika Steilen, a spokeswoman for Germany's Hugo Boss AG. "We have closed our orders up to next winter."

But trade analysts contend that few companies would be immune to a strengthening currency, especially at a time when important overseas markets such as the U.S. show signs of slowing.

Germany could see exports shrink by 0.8% for every pfennig that the mark rises against a basket of 18 currencies, including the dollar, according to Stephan Schneider, an economist in Frankfurt for S.G. Warburg & Co.

"If the dollar stays on this level, we might have to follow the trend of shifting more production capacity to foreign countries," says Horst Schmidt, who heads the order-financing department at engineering firm Schloemann-Siemag AG. He says more foreign clients now will want to negotiate contracts in dollars to unload the mark's burdensome strength onto the German supplier.

And price pressure is increasing even more. In current negotiations with a buyer from Southeast Asia, Mr. Schmidt says Schloemann-Siemag will have to lower its price to defend the deal against foreign competition.

Linotype-Hell AG, a maker of printing technology, has already reduced the range of parts it produces itself and boosted the amount it obtains internationally, because it can buy more as the mark strengthens. The group now meets less than 50% of its needs in-house.

In Switzerland, Pictet & Cie., a Geneva private banker, estimates that the Swiss franc's upward trend cost Swiss companies an average 6% to 7% in earnings last year on conversion. After the Swiss franc's recent rise, Pictet has now lowered its estimate for Swiss companies' 1995 average profit growth to a maximum 17% from 19%.

Bank Vontobel's chief analyst, Beat C. Philipp, says, "unless expectations of a rising franc are broken," its strength will make life extremely difficult for Switzerland's tourist industry and the wealth of small and medium-size manufacturers that have most of their production at home. Mr. Philipp adds, "In a worst-case scenario, we are in danger of having a country which has lost its industrial base and has a fully overvalued currency."

European companies also worry about losing market share in Europe and other regions to U.S. and dollar-based exporters that are reaping a huge competitive advantage as exchange rates swing in their favor.

Siemens AG's medical-technology division does one-third of its $5.4 billion annual business in the U.S., where the products it sells are 70% locally made. Even then, each one-pfennig rise in the mark against the dollar reduces the division's profit by three million to four million marks. "The lower dollar still hurts us somewhat, directly or indirectly," says Siemens chief economist Armin Sorg.

"You can only hedge so much, then you're left hanging," says Wilhelm Schmelzer, chairman of auto-parts maker Glyco-Metall-Werke & Co. in Wiesbaden. "It's becoming more difficult for German car makers to sell cars out there, and it could begin affecting suppliers like us."

Things are already serious for Barco NV, a Belgian maker of advanced graphics systems and other high-tech equipment. The company exports as much as 95% of its production, and a quarter of its sales, totaling about 10 billion Belgian francs ($351 million), is dollar-denominated.

Unfortunately, "we didn't hedge anything this time," says finance director Antoon Van Petegem. "We didn't expect the dollar to fall much below 31 Belgian francs." The Belgian franc has been trading at about 29 to the dollar.

"It's painful to see all our serious efforts to restrain wages and boost competitiveness wiped out by currency swings," says Mr. Van Petegem.

Source: *The Wall Street Journal*, March 9, 1995. Reprinted with permission of THE WALL STREET JOURNAL, 1995 Dow Jones & Company, Inc. All rights reserved worldwide.

CHAPTER 18
What Determines Exchange Rates in the Long Run?

Objectives of the Chapter

This chapter summarizes economists' theoretical and empirical findings about the determinants of the long run trends in exchange rates. One factor that appears to be important is the difference in rates of inflation between countries; this is explained in the purchasing power parity hypothesis. The monetary approach to exchange rates then explains inflation rates as functions of relative demands and supplies of domestic and foreign monies. Linking the two, we get a model which links exchange rates to "fundamentals" such as incomes and money supplies.

After studying Chapter 18, you should understand

1. the purchasing power parity hypothesis (PPP)
2. the quantity theory of money in a two-country world
3. the effect on the exchange rate of a change in real GDP
4. the effect on the exchange rate of a change in money supply

Key Terms

Law of one price   states that a single commodity will have the same price everywhere, once the prices are expressed in the same currency. This is another way of stating the hypothesis of PPP; it seems to be true chiefly for commodities that are standardized and that are heavily traded internationally.

Monetary approach to exchange rates
seeks to explain exchange rates by focusing on demands and supplies for national moneys.

Nominal bilateral exchange rates
the exchange rates we see quoted in the foreign exchange markets.

Nominal effective exchange rate
> the weighted-average exchange rate value of a country's currency, where the weights reflect the importance of other countries in the home country's total international trade.

Purchasing power parity (PPP) hypothesis
> states that the home and foreign prices of goods will be equalized, so that $P = r_s \times P_f$ overall, where r_s is the exchange rate, and P and P_f are the domestic and foreign price level, respectively.

Quantity theory of money
> theorizes that in any country the money supply is equated with the demand for money, which is directly proportional to the value of nominal gross domestic product (or $M = kPY$). Here, money serves mainly as a medium of exchange.

Real exchange rate (RER)
> the ratio of the foreign price level to the domestic price level, multiplied by the nominal exchange rate, or $(P_f/P)r_s$. If purchasing power parity holds, the real exchange rate equals 1.

Warm-up Questions

True or False? Explain.

1. T/F   The purchasing power parity hypothesis probably does not hold for goods that are not traded between countries.

2. T/F   All other things being equal, if the rate of money supply growth in France is higher than the rate of money supply growth in the United States, we could expect the dollar to appreciate relative to the French franc.

3. T/F   All other things being equal, if income levels in France increase more slowly than income levels in the United States, we could expect the dollar to appreciate relative to the French franc.

Chapter 18: What Determines Exchange Rates in the Long Run?

4. T/F The quantity theory of money stresses that moneys (whether domestic or foreign) are used only as a medium of exchange to purchase goods and services.

5. T/F If the inflation rate in the United States is lower than the inflation rate in France, the French franc will depreciate.

Multiple Choice

1. All other things being equal, which of the following would *not* cause the price of a foreign currency (r_s) to fall?
   a. A rise in the home country's expected inflation rate.
   b. A rise in the foreign country's expected inflation rate.
   c. A drop in the foreign country's real income.
   d. A rise in the foreign country's money supply.

2. All other things being equal, if the British government increases the money supply by 5 percent while the British economy is experiencing a 5 percent expansion in real GDP, the exchange rate on the pound will be
   a. unaffected
   b. higher
   c. lower
   d. a mystery

3. In the long run, countries with faster inflation have had
   a. appreciating currencies
   b. no change in the value of their currencies
   c. depreciating currencies
   d. sometimes appreciating, and sometimes depreciating currencies

4. All other things being equal, the price of a foreign currency (r_s) would be raised by
   a. a drop in the foreign country's money supply
   b. a drop in the foreign country's real GDP
   c. a rise in the foreign country's expected inflation rate
   d. a rise in the home country's real GDP

5. The purchasing power parity hypothesis (PPP) has greatest explanatory power
   a. in the short run
   b. in the long run
   c. for exchange rates in lower-income countries
   d. for goods like housing and services
   e. for salaries of international economics professors

Problems

1. The monetary authorities in Saxony are prone to flooding their country with new scudos, whereas the Leinster government authorities are loathe to increase the supply of lira. In light of this, what would you expect to be the long run trend in the exchange rate between the scudo and the lira?

2. Suppose that the U.S. price level in 1996 is at 120 (where 1990 = 100), and the price level in Italy is at 180 (where 1990 = 100). The exchange rate in 1990 was 1,500 Italian lira per $1. What would be the equilibrium exchange rate between the lira and the dollar in 1996 according to the purchasing power parity hypothesis?

3. Calculate the 1996 real exchange rate (U.S. dollars per British pounds) assuming the following hypothetical data:

$$r_s = \$2/£$$
$$P_{UK} = £150$$
$$P_{US} = \$200$$

4. What would happen to the exchange rate if foreign residents' demand for money suddenly rises by 20%?

5. The "Cambridge k" from the money demand formula $M^D = k \times P \times Y$ is thought to depend on behavioral variables that do not change much in the short run. Suppose that some sort of financial innovation in the United States causes the variable "k" to be smaller. (A good example might be the proliferation of credit cards.)

   a. What impact would this have on the demand for money?

   b. What impact would this have on the exchange rate between, say, dollars and pesos?

Discussion Topics

1. Discuss how a substantial movement away from free trade would nullify the purchasing power parity hypothesis.

2. If a country wants to peg its exchange rates, should it peg nominal exchange rates or real exchange rates?

3. What would you expect to happen to the value of the currency of a country engaged in a war (relative to the currency of a noncombatant country)? Relate your answer to the observation that few countries maintain fixed exchange rates during periods of war.

Final Thought

In the long run we are all dead.

— John Maynard Keynes, 1923

THE WALL STREET JOURNAL
March 13, 1995

Is the Big Mac a Mere Cheeseburger Or a Benchmark for Currencies?

By Jathon Sapsford
Staff Reporter of The Wall Street Journal

Those with an appetite for lofty economic debate might consider Japan, which is having a big yen attack. McDonalds Co. (Japan) Ltd., the Japanese arm of the fast-food giant, is planning to cut prices of key menu items this spring. The company says the move is partly the result of the strong yen, which has sharply reduced the cost of such imported ingredients as beef and potatoes.

Company officials say that they have yet to decide which fast-food items will be affected, but that a cheaper Big Mac is likely. That could cut the cost in Japan of the big double cheeseburger by as much as 100 yen — down from the current price of 380 yen, or $4.23.

For economists, the impending burger devaluation is food for thought. Many use the famous burger to make judgments about the theoretical values of currencies. Indeed, the price of the Big Mac, a favorite of fast-food junkies everywhere, has long been a centerpiece of a debate over what economists call Purchasing Power Parity.

Call it the benchmark burger. Supporters of the PPP theory say the average $1.80 price of a Big Mac in the U.S. — less than half the current cost in Japan — would suggest the yen is wildly overvalued compared with the dollar. After all, the ingredients for the burger are roughly the same whether it's made in Tokyo or Tulsa.

And with the dollar recently hitting a new low of 88.75 yen, many say it was only a matter of time before either the dollar rose or the Big Mac fell. "It makes sense," says Marshall Gittler, an analyst at Merrill Lynch Japan Ltd. "But please don't quote me on that because I'm a vegetarian."

The theory, however, has its detractors. "A lot of people like the Big Mac measure," says Dick Beason, economist at James Capel Pacific in Tokyo. "But to me, it really doesn't make any sense."

Mr. Beason says the PPP theory would only work in a perfect world where trade barriers were nonexistent, and such costs as labor and rents were the same for all of McDonald's 15,000 outlets worldwide. Still, Mr. Beason says he's happy about the news. "My boy is a big fan of the Big Mac," he says.

Indeed, with more than 500 million burgers sold in Japan last year — more than four burgers for every Japanese — customers don't appear to think McDonald's Biggu Macku is a raw deal.

Source: *The Wall Street Journal*, March 13, 1995. Reprinted with permission of THE WALL STREET JOURNAL, 1995 Dow Jones & Company, Inc. All rights reserved worldwide.

CHAPTER 19
What Determines Exchange Rates in the Short Run?

Objectives of the Chapter

The last chapter offered explanations for long-run trends in exchange rates in terms of national price levels and the relative demands and supplies of monies. Short-run fluctuations in exchange rates, however, can be related to demands and supplies of all assets denominated in different currencies—what we call the asset market approach to exchange rates. Here, we revisit the international financial investors and incorporate the impact of interest rate differentials and exchange rate expectations into the determination of the current spot exchange rate.

When you have completed your study of this chapter, you should be able to explain

1. the impact on the current exchange rate of interest rates
2. the impact on the current exchange rate of expectations about future spot rates
3. what exchange rate overshooting is, and why it can occur
4. how short-run exchange rate movements can diverge from what would be predicted by market fundamentals

Key Terms

Asset market approach to exchange rates
explains exchange rates in terms of demands and supplies of all assets denominated in different currencies. The monetary approach to exchange rates is a variant of this approach in which only demands and supplies of the money asset are considered.

Bandwagon
a situation in which investors expect the recent trend in exchange rates to be carried on into the future.

Exchange rate overshooting
when the exchange rate is driven past its ultimate equilibrium rate (usually thought to be the PPP level) and then back to that rate later during the adjustment of the macroeconomy to an exogenous shock.

News — unexpected information about economic performance or political situations that can cause sudden, sometimes large, changes in exchange rates.

Speculative bubble — a self-confirming upward or downward movement in a price (here, the exchange rate), that is out of line with the changes in the fundamental factors that determine that price.

Warm-up Questions

True or False? Explain.

1. T / F   An expectation that the yen will appreciate can cause the yen to appreciate.

2. T / F   An increase in the domestic interest rate will cause the home currency to depreciate.

3. T / F   Overshooting occurs because international investors do not accurately predict future exchange rates.

4. T / F   International interest rate differentials drive exchange rates in the short run; international price differentials drive exchange rates in the long run.

5. T / F   Tossing a coin to determine whether the exchange rate will rise or fall in the next year will give a prediction almost as accurate as one based on an economic model of exchange rates.

Multiple Choice

1. If there is a sudden 5 percent decrease in the domestic money supply, we could expect
   a. the domestic currency to appreciate by 5 percent in the long run
   b. the domestic currency to appreciate by 6 percent in the short run
   c. the foreign currency to depreciate as demand for foreign assets decreases
   d. all of the above

2. Under the asset market approach, if both U.S. and British interest rates rise by three percentage points, we could expect
   a. the dollar to appreciate
   b. the dollar to depreciate
   c. the exchange rate on the pound to remain unchanged
   d. investors to move their funds to a third country

3. A bandwagon is
   a. the expectation that the recent trend of the exchange rate will continue into the future
   b. a coordinated attack on a currency by foreign exchange speculators
   c. the formation of a common-currency area
   d. how drummers and bass players get from one concert to another

4. If a country's nominal interest rate increases by the same percentage that the inflation rate has increased
   a. international investors will withdraw their funds from the country
   b. international investors will pour more funds into the country
   c. international investors will demand an increase in the real interest rate they are paid
   d. none of the above

5. Short-run prediction of exchange rates is difficult because
   a. unpredictable news affects exchange rates in the short run
   b. people don't understand the fundamentals that determine exchange rates
   c. speculative bubbles dominate exchange rate changes
   d. economic agents intentionally destabilize exchange rates

Problems

1. What impact will each of the following events have on the current spot exchange rate between the Saxon scudo (Ss) and the Leinster lira (Ll)? (You should assume that each event was not predicted in advance.)

   a. Leinster residents expect the scudo to appreciate.

   b. The new government of Saxony was voted in on a "Whip Inflation Now" (WIN) platform.

   c. A change in saving behavior causes the real interest rate in Leinster to increase.

   d. The minister of trade announces that Saxony has incurred a much larger trade deficit than had been predicted.

   e. An earthquake flattens the major telephone factory in Leinster.

   f. The minister of finance in Leinster is charged with embezzling one billion lira from the Treasury.

2. The current spot rate is 100 yen per dollar. Suppose that after a 20 percent increase in the money supply in the United States the domestic interest rate drops from 12 percent to 8 percent, while the Japanese interest rate remains at 12 percent.

   a. What is the new long-run equilibrium value of the exchange rate?

b. Calculate the overshooting necessary in the spot rate of the yen for interest parity to hold.

3. Consider the following information:

   ■ Today's spot exchange rate between the scudo and the lira is Ss 100/Ll.
   ■ People believe that in the next 90 days, the lira is going to appreciate to Ss 101/ Ll.
   ■ The 90-day interest rate in Saxony is 2%; the 90-day interest rate in Leinster is 1.5%.

   a. Does uncovered interest parity hold?

   b. If it does not hold, at what current spot rate would it hold?

4. When the United States was running large federal budget deficits in the mid-1980s, the dollar rose to very high levels, particularly against the yen. Using the asset market approach to exchange rates, explain this phenomenon. How does this analysis help to explain the correlation between budget deficits and trade deficits in the 1980s?

Discussion Topics

1. If the prices of goods and services are flexible even in the short run, will exchange rate overshooting occur?

2. Try to match recent changes in the exchange rate of some currency to political events in that country, such as elections or new criminal investigations; also compare changes in the exchange rate to economic "news" about the country's budget or trade balance.

Final Thought

The value of the pound is what the market says it is.

— Milton Friedman, 1976

THE WALL STREET JOURNAL
June 30, 1994

As Clinton Spends, the Dollar Weakens

By Allan H. Meltzer

The dollar has been falling and interest rates at home and abroad have been rising. The recent fall, about 6%, is not large by past standards. Since 1971, the dollar has lost 60% to 70% of its value against the Japanese yen and the German mark.

Standard economic and political fundamentals say the dollar should be strong, not weak. The U.S. economy has been expanding faster than its rivals, and we have raised interest rates while others have cut. Japan is unable to form a stable government. Germany's reunification has been slow, divisive and costly.

President Clinton was right to point to these fundamentals. What he failed to mention was his spending policies and the effect of these policies on the current and prospective supply of dollar securities that the market must absorb. His policies increase the supply of dollar securities — U.S. debt — just when the market wants less.

To reduce the supply of dollar securities, the U.S. has to borrow less, save more, increase the growth of exports, reduce the growth of consumption and imports. A serious government would work to reduce subsidies, cut entitlements and encourage investment, not consumption.

The Clinton administration is not serious. Instead of cutting subsidies and entitlement programs, the administration and its congressional leadership blocks the A to Z proposal that would reduce government spending. Proposed new entitlement programs for health and welfare may be phased in slowly, but $50 billion to $75 billion increases in annual spending would begin in a few years. And these estimates probably understate future increases in consumption spending and in the supply of dollar securities that world markets will be asked to absorb.

Inflationists in Congress, led by Sens. Paul Sarbanes (D., Md.) and Jim Sasser (D., Tenn.), oppose the modest and belated effort by the Federal Reserve to sustain growth and head off some of the increased inflation that seems likely by the end of the year. The Treasury and U.S. Trade Representative Mickey Kantor are fixated by the irrelevant bilateral trade balance with Japan. A falling dollar encourages the Germans and Japanese to buy dollars and inflate a bit. This gives a short-lived stimulus to U.S. exports but does nothing about America's long-term problem — rising entitlement spending.

The change is dramatic. From 1981 through 1990, the U.S. purchased abroad about $90 billion a year more than it sold. To finance this (current account) deficit, the U.S. sold assets to foreigners or borrowed. On average in these years, foreign central banks and governments provided about 15% of the total financing. Private purchasers willingly bought the rest. In 1992 and 1993, public and private shares reversed. The current account deficit remained near $90 billion, but central banks and governments financed 65%. For the year ended this April, Japan added $27 billion to its reserves and Germany $11 billion. Continued purchases at this rate will increase inflation in Europe and Japan.

The recent fall in the dollar suggests that many foreign central banks are unwilling to continue accumulating dollar securities at the 1992-93 rate. Since the amount the U.S. wishes to borrow will increase this year, the dollar must fall until private market participants want to voluntarily accumulate dollar assets that are offered for sale. A fall in the dollar means that U.S. land, buildings, corporations and capital can be bought on better terms. As the dollar falls, foreigners willingly invest more here. At the same time, with a lower dollar, the U.S. exports more and imports less, thereby reducing the amount it has to borrow.

Dollar weakness will not be solved by dramatic efforts at coordinated central bank intervention. Intervention is the monetary equivalent of King Canute holding back the tide. It may succeed in punishing the currency speculators, but if the fundamentals are with them — as they appear to be — the speculators will be back.

Some, remembering the Carter administration, call for a dramatic move by the Federal Reserve to raise interest rates by a point or more. This would make the dollar attractive, but the attraction would be short-lived. The dollar's current weakness is not primarily monetary. America's current and prospective inflation rates, though higher than in Japan, are not much different from Germany's and are below the rates in several European countries. If the rise in interest rates produces a sharp reduction in money growth, the economy would slow after a few months, reducing the return to capital and investment as well as foreign demand for dollar securities.

The Federal Reserve's best course is to bring the economy's growth rate to its long-term path with stable prices. Like the administration, the Fed claims the long-term growth rate is 2 1/2%. This assumes, somewhat optimistically, that productivity will grow about 1 1/2% a year over the long-term, despite the administration's policy of taxing savings and increasing consumption entitlements.

The dollar problem belongs to Congress and the administration. They can hope that foreign central banks will buy up the dollar securities and inflate. They can reduce current and prospective consumption spending to increase saving and investment. Or, they can let the dollar fall. The last choice seems most likely. The decline is unlikely to be a collapse or a one-way street. There will be short-term ups and downs. But if Congress agrees to the Clinton administration's spending policies, the dollar will continue to fall.

Mr. Meltzer, a professor of political economy at Carnegie Mellon University, is a visiting scholar at the American Enterprise Institute.

Source: *The Wall Street Journal*, June 30, 1994. Reprinted with permission of THE WALL STREET JOURNAL, 1994 Dow Jones & Company, Inc. All rights reserved worldwide.

C H A P T E R

20 Government Policies toward the Foreign Exchange Market

Objectives of the Chapter

This chapter lays out the foreign exchange options available to a country and explores some lessons of history about each of those options. Particular attention is paid to the decisions faced by a country that is trying to defend a fixed exchange rate. These range from whether to intervene in the foreign exchange market to the possibility of imposing exchange controls.

After studying Chapter 20, you should know

1. the variety of exchange rate policies countries have used
2. how a country can respond to pressure on the value of its currency
3. the implications of temporary vs. permanent imbalances in exchange rates
4. the benefits and costs of foreign exchange controls
5. how fixed rates have performed in the past
6. how flexible rates have performed in the past

Key Terms

Adjustable peg a system in which a country tries to keep its exchange rate fixed for long periods of time and only changes the pegged rate when there is a substantial disequilibrium at that rate.

Beggar-thy-neighbor policies
 policies (such as devaluations or tariffs) intended to benefit one country's economy at the expense of another. Such policies were widespread during the depression of the 1930s.

Bretton Woods system
 under this post-World War II agreement, countries were allowed devaluations and revaluations of an adjustable peg exchange rate when faced with fundamental disequilibria that would otherwise require drastic domestic adjustment to keep the exchange rate fixed.

Capital controls government limits placed on the use of the foreign exchange market to make payments related to international financial activity (as opposed to payments for goods and services).

Clean float exchange rates determined by a freely functioning foreign exchange market.

Crawling peg an exchange rate system in which the pegged rate is changed frequently according to a set of indicators or in response to monetary authority direction.

Deficits without tears
a situation in which a country's currency is considered an international reserve so that the country can finance its official settlements deficit by issuing its own currency. The United States had extraordinary leeway to finance its payments deficits by issuing dollars in the 1950s and 1960s.

Dirty float a synonym for managed float.

Dollar crisis denotes the situation prevailing toward the end of the Bretton Woods era, with the excessive build-up of dollar reserves in the hands of foreign central banks due to the large and persistent U.S. payments deficit. The gold backing of the dollar was questioned and, ultimately, the dollar was allowed to float freely in 1973.

Domestic adjustment
refers to the necessary changes in the level of a country's aggregate demand to ensure that supply and demand for foreign exchange are back to equality and to avoid any further pressure on the exchange rate.

European Currency Unit (ECU)
a basket currency composed of the currencies of the countries that are members of the European Union.

Exchange rate mechanism (ERM) of the European Monetary System (EMS)
maintains pegged exchange rates among ERM members' currencies with the currencies floating as a bloc against outside currencies such as the U.S. dollar.

Foreign exchange controls
restrictions on the ability of individuals to freely dispose of foreign exchange earned abroad and to acquire foreign exchange for spending abroad. For example, the excess demand for an officially undervalued foreign currency is dealt with by rationing the scarce supply available.

Chapter 20: Government Policies toward the Foreign Exchange Market **169**

Fundamental disequilibrium
a balance of payments surplus or deficit too great and/or too enduring to be financed. It is easy to detect with hindsight, but difficult to detect at the outset.

"Gnomes of Zurich" epithet coined by Britain's chancellor of the Exchequer for the speculators he thought were abandoning the British pound and making it increasingly difficult to defend a pegged exchange rate in the mid-1960s.

Gold Standard era from about 1870 to World War I, most nations tied their currency values to gold and allowed unrestricted import and export of gold. Officials were expected to adjust the whole economy to defend the exchange rate.

Leaning against the wind
occurs when a government intervenes in the foreign exchange market to moderate current movements in floating exchange rates.

Managed float an exchange rate which is generally floating but with government willingness to intervene to attempt to influence the equilibrium value of the rate.

Official intervention government attempts to influence the market exchange rate by buying or selling foreign currency in exchange for the domestic currency.

One-way speculative gamble
a bet which entails minimal or zero risk of loss for the gambler. A persistent payments imbalance under the Bretton Woods system, for example, clearly signaled the likelihood of a devaluation in the case of a deficit or a revaluation in the case of a surplus. There was, therefore, little risk of losing money by moving funds away from the currency to be devalued and toward the one to be revalued. At worst, speculators had to shoulder the transaction costs.

Par value the value of the exchange rate that government officials try to target. Often the government will allow some flexibility of the actual exchange rate in "a band" around this par value.

Pegged exchange rate
term used in place of "fixed exchange rate" because, in practice, no exchange rate stays fixed forever, but can be changed by government action.

"The snake in the tunnel"
a scheme set up by members of the EEC in 1971 whereby each currency would float inside a specified band against every other member currency (the snake), and a maximum limit was set on the difference between the most appreciating and most depreciating currencies (the tunnel). This was the predecessor to the EMS.

Special drawing rights (SDRs)
fiduciary reserve assets created by the IMF, beginning in 1970, as a supplement to existing reserve assets. The value of one SDR is determined by the weighted average of a basket of the currencies of the five countries with the largest share of world exports of goods and services — the U.S. dollar, the German mark, the Japanese yen, the French franc, and the British pound.

Sterilization
using monetary policy to offset the impact of official intervention on the domestic money supply.

Warm-up Questions

True or False? Explain.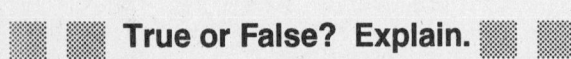

1. T / F   In its most strict form, an exchange control would require you to turn over all your foreign currencies to your government.

2. T / F   If a country fixes its currency to a basket of other currencies, it will experience more severe swings in the value of its currency than if it were fixed to a single other currency.

3. T / F   A clean float and a permanently fixed exchange rate are the polar cases of possible exchange rate systems.

4. T / F   Maintaining par may be pretty good for monetary authorities, but it is pretty bad for golf authorities.

Chapter 20: Government Policies toward the Foreign Exchange Market

5. T / F The stability of the gold standard era proves that pegging currencies to gold ensures international economic tranquility.

Multiple Choice

1. A government might want to keep the value of its currency high if it
   a. is nuts
   b. wants to help exporters
   c. wants to punish buyers of imports
   d. cares about national pride and honor

2. A government might want to devalue its currency if
   a. exporters have a strong lobbying arm
   b. import buyers have a strong lobbying arm
   c. policymakers worry about high domestic inflation rates
   d. foreign governments tell it not to

3. If monetary authorities in the United States want to "lean against the wind," they should
   a. sell the dollar when it is depreciating relative to the yen
   b. sell the dollar when it is appreciating relative to the yen
   c. buy the yen when it is appreciating relative to the dollar
   d. buy the dollar when it is appreciating relative to the yen
   e. work in Chicago instead of Washington, D.C.

4. Indicators that a government could use to "crawl" the pegged value of its currency include
   a. domestic holdings of the international reserve currency
   b. changes in the country's own money supply
   c. the difference between the domestic inflation rate and the inflation rate of the currency it pegs itself to
   d. all of the above
   e. none of the above

5. Which of the following is *not* used as a government strategy to defend a fixed exchange rate?
   a. imposing exchange controls
   b. buying and selling foreign currencies
   c. changing the demand for or supply of its currency by altering domestic interest rates
   d. swords and crossbows

Problems

1. Because Leinster produces its phones in a solar-powered factory, exports to Saxony fall off in winter and hit a peak in the summer. Consequently, Saxon demand for foreign exchange is relatively low in January but quite high in July. This is illustrated below.

Figure 20.1

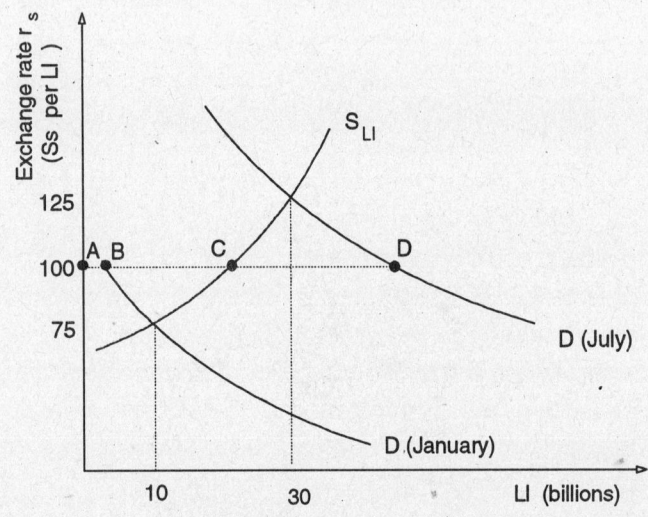

a. If Saxony and Leinster are on a clean float, how will this seasonality affect the exchange rate between the scudo and the lira?

b. Could Saxony defend a fixed exchange rate of Ss 100/ Ll under these circumstances? How? Why might the country want to defend a fixed rate?

Chapter 20: Government Policies toward the Foreign Exchange Market

2. As a matter of pride, government officials in Saxony decide to fix the value of the scudo at Ss 100/ Ll. However, the popularity of telephone communication (kids in Saxony have become hooked on "chat lines") has caused a sudden increase in the need for lira to import telephones. If the exchange rate were still determined in a clean float, this would force the scudo down to Ss 150/Ll. What options could government officials use to defend the scudo at Ss 100 / Ll?

3. Consider the following hypothetical data from a gold standard system:

    - value of the British pound, in gold = 1/7 ounce
    - value of the American dollar, in gold = 1/28 ounce

    a. What is the fixed exchange rate between the British pound and the American dollar?

    b. If the United States government is committed to maintaining the convertibility of the dollar, what is the maximum supply of dollars that can safely be printed if Fort Knox holds ten billion ounces of gold bullion?

4. How does a change in the price level eliminate payments imbalances under the gold standard?

Discussion Topics

1. Why would a country allow the use of foreign exchange for transactions in goods and services, but not for transactions in assets and financial instruments?

2. How would you tell the difference between a heavily managed float and a crawling peg?

3. Discuss why some former French colonies (particularly in Africa) peg their currencies to the French franc.

4. If the United States were to return to a pegged exchange rate, what other currency would you suggest we peg the dollar to, and why?

Final Thought

To attempt to increase the wealth of any country by introducing or by detaining in it an unnecessary quantity of gold and silver, is as absurd as it would be to attempt to increase the good cheer of private families by obliging them to keep an unnecessary number of kitchen utensils.

— Adam Smith, 1776

THE WALL STREET JOURNAL

March 20, 1995

What If the Dollar Doesn't Stay on Top?

By David Wessel

WASHINGTON — The incredible shrinking value of the dollar raises a frightening prospect: That the greenback is losing its status as the world's premier currency and is headed for the near-irrelevancy of the British pound.

So what?

Well, the U.S. would suffer — and not just in lost prestige — if the German mark replaced the dollar as the world's reserve currency. But the economic implications, though measured in tens of billions of dollars a year, may not be as profound as emotions about this possibility suggest.

As previous U.S. Treasury secretaries have done in dollar crises past, Robert Rubin declares unequivocally that the U.S. must and will maintain the dollar as the world's main reserve currency.

But if it can't? "A cool, dispassionate analysis would suggest that it doesn't make any consequential difference," says Richard Cooper, a Harvard University international economist and former U.S. official.

For all its recent weakness, the dollar won't be replaced soon as the world's reserve currency, the one that foreign governments trust so much that they hold their extra money in it. The dollar remains the global currency of choice, maintaining the role it assumed with the decline of the British pound after World War I. Unless unexpected inflation undermines its worth, the dollar's reign seems secure for now.

No other nation as yet has the economic size or financial markets to unseat the dollar. When Pennzoil Co. collected $3 billion from Texaco Inc. back in 1988, it knew without a doubt that it could instantly sink the proceeds in U.S. Treasury bills. No one can have that same confidence about doing huge transactions in German or Japanese markets; they are too small. As a result, the U.S. has the world's biggest financial-services industry. And the lack of progress toward a single European currency defers the day when Europe can truly be a rival.

But the dollar has been losing market share to the mark and yen as those economies have matured and

Losing Market Share
U.S. dollar as a percentage of government currency reserves
Source: International Monetary Fund

the Cold War threats have diminished. Twenty years ago, about 80% of foreign-currency reserves around the world were held in dollars, the International Monetary Fund says. Today, it is down to 60%, a measure that reflects both diversification into other currencies and the dollar's falling value.

Because the dollar is still dominant, the U.S. enjoys lower interest rates than it otherwise would — and that may be the most significant benefit. Foreign businesses, investors and governments with cash to spare prefer dollar-denominated securities; the more demand for those securities, the less the U.S. has to pay to borrow.

If the mark supplanted the dollar, the U.S. could still borrow in dollars — just as Germany borrows in marks today — but it would pay more. With nearly $5 trillion in U.S. government debt outstanding, paying just one-hundredth of a percentage point more interest would add $500 million to the annual interest tab.

The U.S. also benefits handsomely from the growing willingness of Russians, Mexicans and others to hold greenbacks — the paper money — because they don't trust their own currencies. The Federal Reserve estimates that roughly two-thirds of the $360 billion in U.S. currency is held overseas. To get these dollars, these foreigners have traded something of value — marks, gold, oil, fur hats, tequila. In return, the U.S. has given them a piece of paper. This swap amounts to an interest-free loan to the U.S. government. It saves the U.S. roughly $15 billion a year in interest; that is more than twice Microsoft Corp.'s annual sales.

That's about it. Everything else is more a matter of convenience than economic significance, the equivalent of having English spoken widely.

Take oil prices, now quoted in dollars. Some OPEC members, unhappy about selling their oil in ever-less-valuable dollars, are talking about pricing it in a basket of currencies; they have talked of this before and never gone very far. At first blush, the U.S. seems to benefit from the fact that oil is priced in dollars. The dollar is weak; U.S. consumers pay more for German chocolate but don't pay more for oil. Ah, the advantage of being the reserve currency.

But the Japanese and the Germans, by paying in cheaper dollars, are enjoying lower oil prices now. No wonder they decline the honor of serving as the world's main reserve currency.

Overall, the U.S. clearly benefits economically because the dollar is the world's principal reserve currency. But that status itself is less valuable than the global confidence it implies. If Germany and Japan gain market share against the dollar because they prosper and cultivate open financial markets, that isn't worrisome. If, however, the dollar loses ground to the mark and yen because of doubts that the U.S. will preserve the dollar's value by properly managing its economy, then alarm bells will sound.

Source: *The Wall Street Journal*, March 20, 1995. Reprinted with permission of THE WALL STREET JOURNAL, 1995 Dow Jones & Company, Inc. All rights reserved worldwide.

THE WALL STREET JOURNAL

April 19, 1995

IMF Chief Slams Fed for Ignoring Dollar

Camdessus Calls for Increase In U.S. Interest Rates; Economic Threat Cited

By David Wessel
Staff Reporter of The Wall Street Journal

WASHINGTON — The head of the International Monetary Fund said the U.S. Federal Reserve is shirking its responsibility as protector of the world's prime currency by failing to raise interest rates to boost the dollar.

"A country which is responsible for the key currency of the world has the responsibility of maintaining reasonable stability of it," IMF Managing Director Michel Camdessus told reporters at a briefing here yesterday, echoing complaints from Japanese and German officials.

Mr. Camdessus said the Fed, both for domestic and international reasons, should have raised short-term interest rates when the Germans and Japanese cut them recently. "The U.S. economy — as well as the world economy — is certainly threatened by a too-low dollar," he said. Mr. Camdessus also faulted "the culture of the fund" for not doing more to avert Mexico's financial crisis. "We are possibly at times — not always but at times — a little bit too much on the soft side" in conversations with member countries, he said. But he also renewed his call for a substantial increase in IMF resources so it can respond to future crises. He even offered to sell some of the IMF's $40 billion of gold to subsidize loans to poorer countries.

The IMF chief's unusually sharp criticism of the U.S. may have been intended as a reply to criticism by Europeans for responding too generously to U.S. pleas for aid to Mexico. But it will do nothing to smooth the already tense relationship between Mr. Camdessus and Treasury Secretary Robert Rubin.

The Fed's spokesman, Joseph R. Coyne, wouldn't respond to Mr. Camdessus's blunt remarks on the dollar, which elaborate on a written statement he issued last Friday. But Fed officials have made clear that the domestic economy is their chief concern and that they see plenty of evidence the Fed's interest-rate increases have produced the desired slowing of the U.S. economy without a significant acceleration of inflation.

"We have a primary responsibility for maintaining the purchasing power of the dollar, which is largely a matter of controlling inflation," Fed governor Lawrence Lindsey said yesterday, predicting that the inflation rate will peak at about 3.5% this year but go no higher. "There are already signs that the economy is slowing to a sustainable pace. There is reason to believe that slowing is likely to continue...."

The dollar continued its fall against the Japanese yen, trading at 80.63 yen late yesterday, down from 82.06 the day before. In early Tokyo trading Wednesday, the dollar touched a new low of 79.85 yen. Yesterday, the dollar declined to 1.3530 German marks from 1.3685.

Mr. Camdessus said he personally favors an attempt by the U.S., Japan and Germany to recreate the high-profile public cooperation on the dollar that marked the Plaza and Louvre accords of the 1980s. But he allowed that he is in "a possibly distinguished minority."

In the absence of such a campaign, he said, the industrialized countries should address the underlying economic causes of the weak dollar — namely further deregulation of the Japanese economy and opening of its market for foreigners, and further reduction of government budget deficits in the U.S. and Europe.

The U.S. favors the first. But Clinton-administration officials observe that, financial market commentary to the contrary, textbook economics suggests that reducing the U.S. budget deficit would further weaken the dollar. The huge budget deficits of the Reagan years, for instance, were accompanied by a surging dollar.

Mr. Camdessus's comments on U.S. economic policy, unwelcome in Washington, illustrate one of his defenses to criticism that the IMF wasn't public enough in its assessment of Mexico's economic policies last year. Countries are ambivalent about the IMF surveillance, he said. "They love surveillance on others. They hate it when it is on them."

In previewing proposals he will make to the IMF's policy committee, which meets here next week, Mr. Camdessus made a strong pitch for more resources for the IMF. But there aren't any signs that the major industrialized countries that control the IMF are inclined to give the agency the money — and certainly not as long as the often-controversial Mr. Camdessus is in charge.

Among other things, he called for a doubling of member countries' investments in the IMF, known as quotas, and for expanding the group of 11 countries that have agreed to lend money to the IMF in emergencies. The U.S. and other industrialized countries are opposed to the first, which would require congressional approval, but willing to consider the second.

Source: *The Wall Street Journal*, April 19, 1995. Reprinted with permission of THE WALL STREET JOURNAL, 1995 Dow Jones & Company, Inc. All rights reserved worldwide.

CHAPTER 21
How Does the Open Macroeconomy Work?

Objectives of the Chapter

This chapter sets up a model which allows us to relate two important goals of macroeconomic performance: internal balance (achieving full employment and price stability in the economy) and external balance (achieving balance in the country's overall balance of payments). Using the IS-LM-FE framework, we can see that an economy will not necessarily achieve both balances at the same time. In fact, an event that might move an economy toward full employment could worsen its trade balance, and vice versa.

Before tackling this chapter, you might want to review the concept and determination of the equilibrium national income and the spending multiplier in a closed economy (take a look at your dusty old macroeconomics textbook).

After studying Chapter 21, you should understand

1. the dependence of imports on the level of national income
2. the concept (and determination) of equilibrium national income in an open economy
3. the spending multiplier for a closed economy versus an open economy
4. the impact of various economic changes on national product and on the balance of trade
5. the two goals of internal balance and external balance
6. price movements in the macroeconomy in the short run and in the long run, and the relationship of price competitiveness to international trade

Key Terms

External balance performance goal in which the country's economy has an overall balance of payments that is sustainable over time.

FE curve this curve shows all combinations of interest rate and national income which result in a zero balance in the country's overall international payments position (its official settlements balance is zero). The FE curve usually slopes upward because as national income rises the demand for imports rises; interest rates must rise to attract capital so that the current account deficit is offset by a capital account surplus. The FE curve is horizontal if there is **perfect capital mobility**.

Foreign-income repercussions

these refer to the feedback effect on the national economy of a domestic income-induced change in imports that affects foreign income and thus the country's exports. These repercussions increase the size of the simple spending multiplier.

Internal balance a performance goal in which the country's economy is producing at the full employment income level with price stability.

IS curve this curve shows all combinations of interest rate and national income which equilibrate the market for goods and services. The IS curve slopes downward because as interest rates fall, the demand for goods and services rises; product must rise to re-equilibrate the market for goods and services.

LM curve this curve shows all combinations of interest rate and national income which equilibrate money demand and money supply. The LM curve slopes upward because as national income rises, so does money demand; with a fixed money supply, interest rates must rise to re-equilibrate the money market.

Locomotive theory this says that growth in the largest countries may be sufficient to raise world growth overall. This theory comes from the observation that growth in the United States, Europe, and Japan tends to result in growth of other countries because these large countries import more when their incomes rise.

Marginal propensity to import

the ratio of a change in import volumes to the change in real national income causing the import change. Graphically, it is represented by the slope of the import function.

Open economy spending multiplier

this takes into account the leakage from the spending stream caused by the marginal propensity to import. For a small economy, the open economy multiplier is smaller than the closed economy multiplier. For a large country, however, the open economy multiplier may be augmented by foreign-income repercussions.

Spending multiplier the ratio of a change in national income to the change in autonomous spending that caused the income change. It is greater than one because an initial increase in autonomous spending (independent of income) generates many successive changes in induced spending (dependent on income).

Warm-up Questions

True or False? Explain.

1. T / F If a country's residents don't save and don't import, the spending multiplier will be infinite.

2. T / F When government spending rises, the trade balance tends to worsen.

3. T / F If U.S. interest rates rise, capital will flow into the U.S. in both the short run and the long run.

4. T / F If both domestic money demand and international capital flows are very sensitive to interest rates, both the LM curve and the FE curve will be flat.

5. T / F An increase in the foreign price of goods worsens a country's trade balance.

Multiple Choice

1. If there is an unintended reduction in inventories then
   a. aggregate demand (expenditure) exceeds national product
   b. aggregate demand is less than national product
   c. aggregate demand is equal to national product
   d. aggregate demand is zero

2. Foreign income repercussions
   a. increase the impact of extra domestic spending on both national income and the trade balance
   b. dampen the impact of extra domestic spending on national income but increase the impact of extra domestic spending on the trade balance
   c. increase the impact of extra domestic spending on national income but dampen the impact of extra domestic spending on the trade balance
   d. dampen the impact of extra domestic spending on both national income and the trade balance

3. Which of the following will *not* shift the IS curve outward?
   a. an increase in domestic investment spending
   b. an increase in interest rates
   c. an increase in government spending
   d. a decrease in saving

4. Which of the following will *not* shift the LM curve inward?
   a. a decrease in the domestic money supply
   b. an increase in the demand for money
   c. a decrease in interest rates
   d. a decrease in saving
   e. c and d

5. Which of the following will *not* shift the FE curve outward?
   a. An increase in the level of national income.
   b. A decrease in imports.
   c. An increase in the level of foreign income.
   d. An increase in exports.
   e. A decrease in foreign interest rates.

Problems

1. An accountant in Leinster has found the following information:

    National income = Ll 100.0 billion
    Consumption = Ll 60.0 billion
    Domestic investment = Ll 15.0 billion
    Government spending = Ll 15.0 billion
    Exports to Saxony = Ll 20.0 billion
    Imports from Saxony = Ll 10.0 billion

    a. Does Leinster have a trade surplus or a trade deficit with Saxony?

    b. What is the level of total saving in Leinster?

    c. On net, is Leinster investing in Saxony, or is Saxony investing in Leinster?

2. Determine what impact each of the following events is likely to have on the level of national income and the trade balance of Leinster in the short run:

    a. Saxon teenagers discover the joys of the "chat line" and demand that their parents buy them telephones for their bedrooms.

b. The marginal propensity to import rises in Leinster.

c. A sudden research breakthrough allows Leinster to produce all electronic devices (including telephones) at a lower cost than ever before.

d. An import-competing telephone manufacturing plant opens in Saxony.

3. An economist (the cousin of the accountant in problem 1) has figured out the following data on the Saxon economy:

> Marginal propensity to save = 0.05
> Marginal propensity to import = 0.15
> Exports to Leinster = 1.0 trillion scudos
> Imports from Leinster = 2.0 trillion scudos

a. Does Saxony have a trade surplus or a trade deficit with Leinster? How big is it?

b. What is the open economy multiplier in Saxony?

c. Suppose Saxon bakers decide to buy new ovens worth Ss 500 billion. What will happen to the level of income in Saxony?

d. Keeping in mind that Saxony is a small country, what is its trade balance with Leinster now?

4. Suppose that in Japan, the marginal propensity to save suddenly falls from 0.2 to 0.1 at the urging of the U.S. trade representative. How would the United States benefit from this? (Hint: What will be the impact of this reduction in Japanese marginal propensity to save on (a) the equilibrium level of national income in Japan and (b) Japan's trade balance with the United States?)

5. Consider the graph below:

Figure 21.5

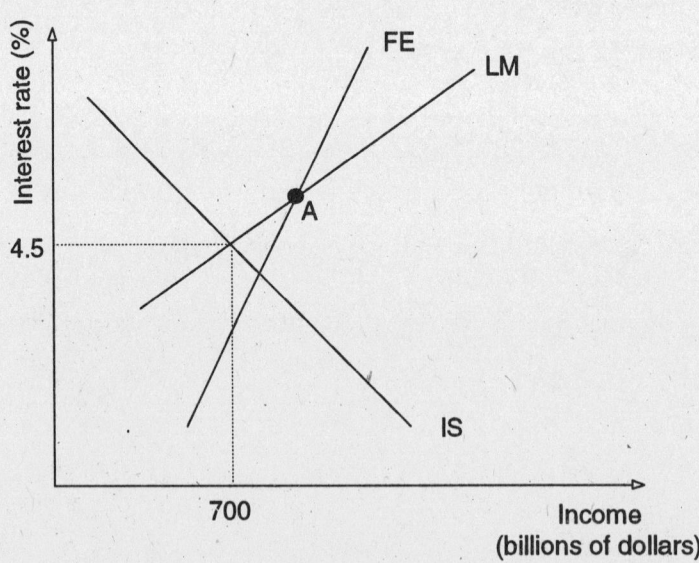

a. What is equilibrium GDP in this country?

b. What is the interest rate in this country?

c. Does this country have an overall balance in its balance of payments?

d. If consumption spending should rise in this country, what will happen to the levels of income, interest rates, and the international payments balance?

e. If, instead, exports from this country rose, what would happen to these three macroeconomic indicators?

6. Explain the meaning of an FE curve that is

   a. vertical

   b. horizontal

   c. upward sloping

Discussion Topics

1. Americans have been criticized for having very low saving rates. If we suddenly increased our marginal propensity to save, what would be the impact on GDP and our current account balance? Would you say this is an improvement?

2. Foreign income repercussions tie one country's GDP changes to another country's GDP changes. Is this interdependence good or bad? Why?

Final Thought

Macro-economics: a laudable attempt to explain how large parts (or the whole) of an economy work, without pretending to know how the component parts work.

— Ralph Harris, 1964

CHAPTER 22
Internal and External Balance with Fixed Exchange Rates

Objectives of the Chapter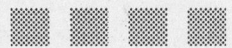

Reconciling the policy goals of full employment, price stability, and overall payments balance is a difficult undertaking for a government determined to keep the exchange rate fixed. Starting from some disequilibrium states, the choice of fiscal and monetary policies that would move the economy toward both internal and external equilibrium (or balance) might be quite easy. Starting from some other disequilibrium states, the choice is less obvious.

Chapter 22 analyzes the effects of fiscal and monetary policies on the product market, the money market, and the foreign exchange market. A set of recommendations for the proper policy mix is then derived for the case of imperfect capital mobility. Finally, the analysis of the feedback from the balance of payments to the money supply and the case of perfect capital mobility highlights the limitations of discretionary monetary policy under fixed exchange rates.

After studying the chapter, you should know

1. the connection between official intervention in the foreign exchange market and the domestic money supply
2. how official intervention affects a country's balance of payments and macroeconomic performance goals
3. the reasons for, and methods of, sterilized intervention by monetary authorities
4. how monetary and fiscal policies affect internal and external balance under fixed exchange rates
5. the ineffectiveness of monetary policy (and the effectiveness of fiscal policy) with perfect capital mobility
6. when aggregate demand policies can achieve both internal and external balance, and when they cannot
7. how, under imperfect capital mobility, an appropriate mix of monetary and fiscal policies can achieve internal and external balance in the short run
8. when a country might want to abandon its defense of a fixed exchange rate
9. how much the trade balance will respond to a change in the exchange rate

Key Terms

Aggregate demand policy dilemma
refers to the difficulty of improving the levels of both national income and the balance of payments by manipulating only the level of aggregate demand.

Assignment rule a guideline for assigning goals to fiscal and monetary policies. In particular, fiscal policy should aim at achieving internal balance, while monetary policy should aim at achieving external balance.

Capital flight when investors flee a country (and take their capital with them) because of doubts about government policies.

Central bank the official monetary authority that controls monetary policy and also (usually) undertakes the official intervention in the foreign exchange market.

Endogenous shocks shocks determined by factors within the model or system.

Exogenous shocks shocks determined by factors outside a model which are independent of other factors in the model or system.

External shocks sudden changes in international capital flows or in international trade.

Internal shocks sudden changes in domestic spending or in the financial sector (money demand or supply).

J curve when the price effect of a currency devaluation occurs more rapidly than the volume effect, the initial impact of a devaluation is to worsen the current account. After a period of months, the volume of imports falls and the volume of exports rises, causing the current account to improve. A trace of this time pattern in the current account results in the "J" shape.

Monetary-fiscal policy mix
a short run solution to the aggregate demand policy dilemma; it exploits the opposite impacts of fiscal and monetary policies on the interest rate and, in consequence, on the balance of payments. Under fixed exchange rates and with imperfect capital mobility the policy mix suggested by the assignment rule will allow a country to achieve both internal and external balance in the short run.

Perfect capital mobility
under this situation, a practically unlimited amount of lending shifts between countries in response to the slightest change in one country's interest rate.

Rules of the game ("classical medicine")

under fixed exchange rates or under the gold standard, the "rules of the game" require that the monetary authorities refrain from sterilizing payments imbalances. Instead, they should actively make their domestic lending change in the same direction as the payments imbalance, so as to speed up the elimination of payments imbalances, even at the short run cost of sacrificing the goal of internal balance.

Unsterilized intervention

under a fixed (or managed) exchange rate regime, the monetary authorities have to intervene in the foreign exchange market to satisfy any private excess demand for or supply of foreign exchange. If the monetary authorities allow such operations to affect the money supply, it is called unsterilized intervention. If, instead, they undertake offsetting purchases or sales of government bonds in the open market, so as to prevent a balance of payments surplus or deficit from having any net effect on the money supply, it is called **sterilized intervention**.

Warm-up Questions

True or False? Explain.

1. T / F   Easier monetary policy worsens the balance of payments in the short run.

2. T / F   Contractionary monetary policy can correct a situation where a country has rapid inflation and a payments deficit.

3. T / F   Money is easy; economics is hard.

4. T / F   Sterilized intervention (sterilization) is impossible under perfect capital mobility.

5. T / F   If both import and export demand are perfectly inelastic, a country's trade deficit could be reduced by revaluing its currency.

Multiple Choice

1. Expanding aggregate demand can achieve internal and external balance only if the economy is experiencing
   a. a payments surplus and unemployment
   b. a payments surplus and inflation
   c. a payments deficit and inflation
   d. a payments deficit and unemployment

2. A payments deficit can be completely sterilized if monetary authorities
   a. sell government bonds in the open market
   b. purchase government bonds in the open market
   c. decrease their lending to commercial banks
   d. sell foreign exchange to match the private excess demand for foreign exchange

3. The appropriate monetary-fiscal mix in the case of payments deficit and unemployment is
   a. easier fiscal policy and easier monetary policy
   b. easier fiscal policy and tighter monetary policy
   c. tighter fiscal policy and easier monetary policy
   d. tighter fiscal policy and tighter monetary policy

4. Under fixed exchange rates, if capital is perfectly mobile,
   a. both monetary and fiscal policy are powerful
   b. neither monetary nor fiscal policy is powerful
   c. fiscal policy is powerful but monetary policy is not
   d. monetary policy is powerful but fiscal policy is not

5. A devaluation will improve the trade balance if
   a. the country is small
   b. demand for both imports and exports is perfectly elastic
   c. we look at the trade balance a number of months after the devaluation
   d. all of the above

Problems

1. The Prime Minister of Saxony has a problem: he is up for re-election. The electorate is angry about the high inflation rate and about Saxony's payments deficit with Leinster.

   a. If the Prime Minister has promised to defend the fixed exchange rate of Ss 100 / Ll, can he use domestic monetary and fiscal tools to achieve both internal and external balance?

   b. Suppose the Prime Minister decides to abandon the fixed exchange rate and allow the scudo to devalue to Ss 150 / Ll. Can he count on a devaluation to reduce the Saxon trade deficit? (Remember, Saxony is a small country.)

2. If the development of new telecommunication technology were to make capital perfectly mobile between Saxony and Leinster, what will this do to

   a. the ability of Saxony's fiscal authorities to increase the level of national income?

   b. the ability of Saxony's monetary authorities to increase the level of national income?

3. Consider a country that currently has full employment, a balanced current account, limited capital mobility, and a fixed exchange rate. Which of the following disturbances can be remedied with standard aggregate demand tools, and which might require surrendering the country's fixed exchange rate?

   a. a loss of export markets

b. a reduction in savings and a corresponding increase in home demand for domestic goods

c. an increase in government spending

d. a shift in residents' spending from imports to domestic goods

e. a reduction in imports with an equal increase in savings

f. an increase in residents' demand for the domestic currency

4. The demand for petroleum and petroleum fuels is relatively inelastic. In light of this, would you counsel an OPEC leader to further improve his country's trade balance by devaluing its currency?

Discussion Topics

1. Since monetary policy and fiscal policy are not officially coordinated in the United States, would the assignment rule be applicable?

2. Could a country change the level of capital mobility between it and other countries? How? Why might it want to change the level?

3. The OPEC shocks in the 1970s resulted in high unemployment, rapid inflation, and payments deficits for many countries. What sorts of policy dilemmas did this combination of problems cause?

Final Thought

The budget should be balanced, the Treasury should be refilled, public debt should be reduced, the arrogance of officialdom should be tempered and controlled, and the assistance to foreign lands should be curtailed lest Rome become bankrupt.

— Cicero, c. 63 B.C.

THE WALL STREET JOURNAL
March 24, 1995

Why Isn't Weak Dollar Narrowing U.S. Trade Deficit?

Effect Will Come Over Long Term, Not Immediately, Economists Say

By Amanda Bennett
Staff Reporter of The Wall Street Journal

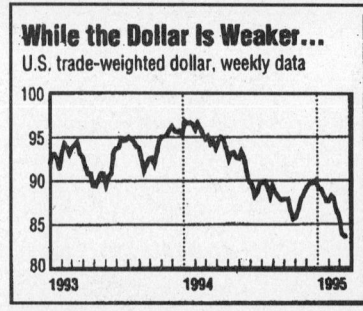
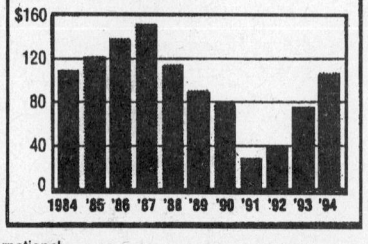

Sources: St. Louis Federal Reserve. Datastream International.

It's an economic axiom: A lower dollar should mean more American exports, and fewer imports.

As lower-cost U.S. goods become more appealing abroad and more-expensive imports are shunned at home, that should lead to a narrower trade deficit. But even as the dollar has been plunging to postwar lows against the mark and the yen, the U.S. trade deficit continues to soar. On Wednesday, the Commerce Department reported that the trade gap ballooned to a record $12.2 billion in January as merchandise exports declined and merchandise imports grew.

So why isn't the currency free-fall working its magic on the trade deficit? The answer, say economists, is time. For all the turmoil in the currency markets, the dollar's weakness is relatively recent. If it persists, they say, the trade deficit will shrink. "These things work very slowly," says Robert Lawrence, professor of international trade and investment at Harvard's John F. Kennedy School of Government. "You see very little effects in the short period," he says.

Still, Prof. Lawrence and others say the exchange rate is only a mechanism mediating myriad complex economic relationships among nations. In the end, they say, the trade gap — now in its 14th year — won't go away until the budget deficit does, or at least until the U.S. domestic savings rate or level of taxation rises enough so that Washington can fund that deficit domestically instead of borrowing abroad as it does now.

That's because of another economic axiom: The more money we borrow abroad, the more foreign goods we will ultimately buy, and the bigger the trade deficit. "We are a low savings country," says James Tobin, at Yale, a Nobel laureate in economics. "We import capital to finance part of our investment. The counterpart of that is a trade deficit."

While the U.S. dollar has been weak against the yen and the mark for quite some time, it has been strong against other world currencies, especially the Mexican peso and the Canadian dollar.

However, William R. Cline, a senior fellow at the Institute for International Economics in Washington, says that the trade-weighted real exchange rate, a widely used index of the dollar's value against all world currencies, shows that the U.S. currency's value has been overall fairly stable for the past five years.

By that index, it is only in the past several months that the dollar's overall value has begun to decline. It takes about two years for changes in U.S. exchange rates to affect trade balances, Mr. Cline says. Thus, even if the dollar's current weakness persists, he wouldn't expect to see the U.S. overall trade balance to be affected before late 1996 or 1997.

The effects of exchange rates aren't absolute, either. Mr. Cline says he would have expected to see some impact by now on U.S.-Japanese trade from the dollar's weakening against the yen. The slower Japanese economy and the growing U.S. economy blunted that impact, though, by damping overall Japanese demand for goods and services, and increasing demand from the U.S.

Although the U.S. trade deficit reached a record monthly high in January, many economists say the gap itself doesn't overly concern them.

"I don't consider it a big problem," says Richard Cooper, a professor of economics at Harvard University. He says that in real terms, the U.S. current account deficit — which includes not only trade in goods and services, but also investment income and government grants — peaked in 1986 and has been declining since then.

"Our current account deficit is around 2% of gross domestic product. This is undesirable, but it is not in any sense a catastrophe. It doesn't spell doom in any respect."

What does trouble Prof. Cooper and others is what that trade deficit represents. "My problem with the trade deficit is that it is a consequence of the unwillingness of the current generation of taxpayers to pay fully for what they are consuming. They don't want to pay fully for government. They don't want to pay for the goods and services they want. If they won't do it, we turn to foreigners to do it."

Part of the problem, though, is that increasing taxes or reducing the budget gap to reduce the trade deficit probably wouldn't be altogether pleasant. "Suppose that — miracle of miracles — we cut government spending and reduce the deficit," asks Peter Kenen, a professor of economics at Princeton. "The government would spend less, and employ fewer people. There would therefore be less available money to buy foreign goods." Domestic purchases would fall too, he says, freeing up more domestic production for export. The trade gap would narrow, but only at the cost of a slower domestic economy.

Not everyone agrees that the trade-off would be worth it.

"The economy is doing very well" even with a large trade deficit, says Prof. Tobin at Yale. "We don't have to have a trade surplus in order to be prosperous."

Source: *The Wall Street Journal*, March 24, 1995. Reprinted with permission of THE WALL STREET JOURNAL, 1995 Dow Jones & Company, Inc. All rights reserved worldwide.

CHAPTER 23
Floating Exchange Rates and Internal Balance

Objectives of the Chapter

From the discussion of stabilization policy under fixed exchange rates, it appears that when the economy finds itself in one of the two cases of aggregate demand-policy dilemma explored in Chapter 22, letting the exchange rate float freely (rather than attempting to juggle monetary and fiscal policies) would solve all our troubles. Since external balance would automatically be assured, we would just have to worry about tuning monetary policy (and fiscal policy, if feasible) for internal balance. However, the exchange rate movements that achieve external balance will have a feedback effect on our domestic economy and internal balance.

This chapter compares the effectiveness of monetary and fiscal policies under different exchange rate regimes and the relative ease of stabilizing national income in a country beset by various domestic and foreign shocks.

After studying Chapter 23, you should know

1. the effectiveness of monetary policy under flexible rates
2. the effectiveness of fiscal policy under flexible rates
3. which exchange rate regime performs better in the face of internal shocks
4. which exchange rate regime performs better in the face of external shocks

Key Terms

G-7 countries Canada, France, Germany, Great Britain, Italy, Japan and the United States.

International macroeconomic policy coordination
the joint determination of several countries' macroeconomic policies to improve joint performance. An example is the 1985 Plaza Agreement among the G-7 countries.

Warm-up Questions

True or False? Explain.

1. T / F The impact of fiscal policy under floating exchange rates depends on the degree of international capital mobility.

2. T / F Erratic monetary policy will cause more disruptions under a flexible exchange rate regime than under a fixed exchange rate regime.

3. T / F When exchange rates float, foreign trade shocks are more disruptive to the domestic economy.

4. T / F International macroeconomic policy coordination is a frequently (and successfully) used tool among western countries.

5. T / F Under floating exchange rates, an increase in the foreign interest rate can cause our exports to rise because it causes our currency to depreciate.

Chapter 23: Floating Exchange Rates and Internal Balance

Multiple Choice

1. In the short run under floating exchange rates, expansionary fiscal policy
   a. causes a depreciation of the home currency
   b. causes an appreciation of the home currency
   c. may cause a depreciation or an appreciation of the home currency
   d. has no effect on the value of the home currency

2. In general, the success of the exchange rate regime a country adopts to stabilize its economy depends on
   a. the volume of trade
   b. the success of sterilization policies
   c. the type of shocks to which the economy is more vulnerable
   d. the economic power of the country

3. A fixed exchange rate regime with no sterilization offers the most protection against
   a. export demand shocks
   b. domestic monetary shocks
   c. import supply shocks
   d. international capital flow shocks

4. If the people who run the monetary policy of a country are inept and erratic, a good way to protect the domestic economy would be to
   a. have a big jail to put the monetary authorities in
   b. have a fixed exchange rate regime
   c. have a flexible exchange rate regime
   d. have a barter economy

5. International macroeconomic policy coordination has been infrequent because
   a. people speak different languages, making meetings very difficult
   b. countries do not always agree on goals that are mutually consistent
   c. the gains to coordination may be small
   d. all of the above (even "a" !)

Problems

1. Recall that Saxony was suffering from a trade deficit and an income level that put inflationary pressure on the economy. Suppose the Saxon prime minister decides to surrender fixed exchange rates and let the scudo float instead.

   a. What will happen to the exchange rate in order to achieve external balance?

   b. How will that exchange rate movement affect internal balance in Saxony?

   If the prime minster wants to reduce the level of income in Saxony using aggregate demand policy,

   c. what will be the impact on internal balance of a contractionary monetary policy?

   d. what will be the impact on internal balance of a contractionary fiscal policy?

2. Government officials like the prime minister tend to put the Saxon economy through frequent political business cycles. If you are interested in protecting the level of income in Saxony from such election-year gyrations, would you suggest that Saxony choose a fixed exchange rate regime or a floating regime?

3. Suppose the residents of Leinster believe that the Saxon government is about to fall (perhaps due to Saxon citizens' dissatisfaction over inept policy). As a result, they pull all of their funds out of Saxony. What would be the impact of this on Saxon economy if

   a. Saxony has a floating exchange rate?

   b. Saxony has a fixed exchange rate instead?

4. Consider a country which is currently at its desired level of income. Determine whether the following events will be least disruptive (cause the smallest fluctuation in domestic income away from the desired level) under a *fixed* exchange rate or under a *floating* exchange rate:

   a. an increase in the country's exports

   b. an increase in the country's domestic money supply

   c. a increase in the flow of capital out of the country

d. an increase in tax rates

e. an increase in the country's imports

f. an increase in the country's saving rate

5. Below are drawn the IS-LM-FE curves for Leinster.

Figure 23.5

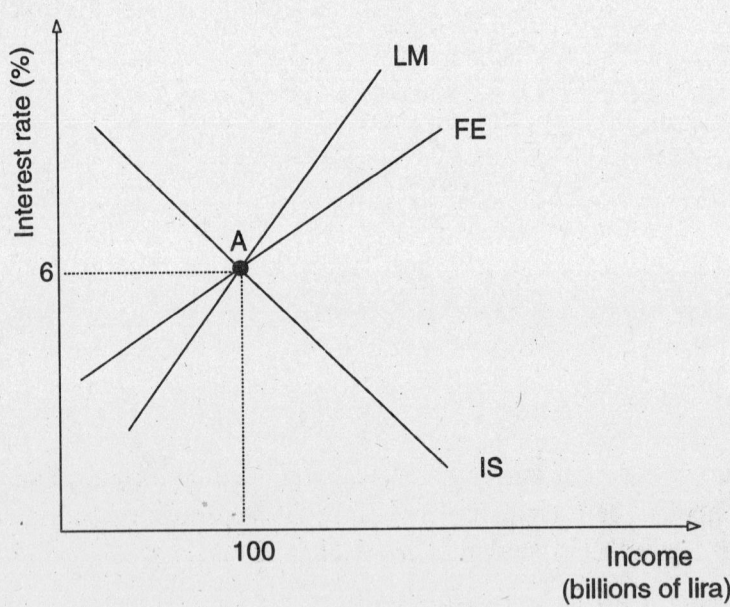

During a month-long celebration (when citizens honor their patron saint Padraic) domestic spending rises dramatically. What would be the impact of this on the economy of Leinster if

a. the exchange rate on the lira is fixed with unsterilized intervention

b. the exchange rate on the lira is fixed with sterilized intervention

c. the exchange rate on the lira floats

6. Assuming that exchange rates are floating, complete the following table:

Event	Direction of U.S. interest rates	Impact on U.S. GDP	Impact on value of the $
a. The Fed cuts U.S. money supply.	up	down	up (appreciate)
b. The Bundesbank cuts the German money supply.			
c. U.S. government spending increases.			
d. German government spending increases.			
e. Tax rates rise in the U.S.			
f. Tax rates rise in Germany.			
g. Exports of goods from the U.S. increase.			

Discussion Topics

1. It is clear that domestic economic conditions are dependent upon the exchange rate and the exchange rate regime. Who should decide which exchange rate regime a country chooses? The fiscal authority? The monetary authority? The residents?

2. Thinking back a number of chapters, consider the implications of a floating exchange rate regime for risk-averse people who must deal with foreign currencies in their business or leisure activities.

Final Thought

> ***Ms. Prism:*** *Cecily, you will read your Political Economy in my absence. The chapter on the Fall of the Rupee you may omit. It is somewhat too sensational. Even these metallic problems have their melodramatic side.*
>
> — Oscar Wilde, 1895

CHAPTER 24
National and Global Choices

Objectives of the Chapter

One of the key decisions that each country has to make is what exchange rate policy it should use. Although there is a clear trend toward floating exchange rates today, some countries still adhere to fixed exchange rates. Others choose a regime between the two extremes of a pure float and a permanently fixed rate. As you have seen in the previous two chapters, whatever exchange rate system a country chooses, it will have implications for domestic stability and domestic policymaking.

After studying Chapter 24, you should be able to discuss the advantages and disadvantages of fixed and floating exchange rates relative to various policy issues such as

1. the impact of domestic shocks on income levels
2. the power of government policies to affect income
3. the ability to conduct macro policy independent of other countries
4. the ease with which a country can trade in goods and services and in financial assets

Key Terms

European Central Bank
upon formal commencement of the European Monetary Union, this institution will formulate the common monetary policy for union members. A key goal is to achieve price stability in the union.

European Monetary Union
set up by the Maastricht Treaty. To join this union, a country has to meet five requirements regarding its inflation rate, exchange rate, interest rate, government budget deficit, and total government debt. If a majority of EU countries meet these criteria by the end of 1996, they could officially form the EMU in 1997.

Maastricht Treaty
an agreement signed in 1991 in which the European Union (EU) countries set in motion a process to create a monetary union and a common currency.

Monetary union a collection of nations in which exchange rates are permanently fixed and a single monetary authority conducts a common monetary policy for the countries of the union.

Price discipline argument
the suggestion that a fixed exchange rate system will result in reduced rates of inflation around the globe.

Warm-up Questions

True or False? Explain.

1. T / F If demand for a country's exports is highly variable, that country will be more stable under a fixed exchange rate than a floating one.

2. T / F Proponents of flexible exchange rates believe that a fixed-rate system generates widespread price distortions and gives misleading signals.

3. T / F An important argument for a flexible exchange rate regime is that, in such a system, business cycles are not easily transmitted from one country to other.

4. T / F Countries that belong to the European Exchange Rate Mechanism (ERM) have found it difficult to pursue independent monetary policy.

5. T / F Island nations always choose a floating exchange rate while continental nations choose a fixed exchange rate.

Multiple Choice

1. Inflation was relatively lower under
   a. the adjustable-peg system
   b. the floating exchange rate system
   c. the gold standard system
   d. the managed float system

2. One advantage of a fixed exchange rate system is that
   a. the economy is likely to be more stable
   b. the value of the foreign reserves of the country will not change much since the exchange rate is fixed
   c. destabilizing speculation is unlikely if officials are committed to keeping exchange rates fixed
   d. prices are kept fixed under a fixed exchange rate

3. Which of the following statements is most correct?
   a. The more stable national macroeconomic policy is, the better fixed rates are.
   b. The more flexible domestic prices and wages are, the better floating rates are.
   c. The more we insist on independent national policies, the more we prefer floating rates.
   d. The more we insist on output stability, the more we prefer fixed exchange rates.

4. If a country moves from a fixed exchange rate to a floating exchange rate system
   a. internal shocks will be more disruptive than before
   b. external shocks will be more disruptive than before
   c. both internal shocks and external shocks will be more disruptive than before
   d. both internal shocks and external shocks will be less disruptive than before

5. When Argentina pegged its peso to the U.S. dollar
   a. it reduced people's expectation of further inflation in the country
   b. it lost independent control over its money supply
   c. it reduced inflation from an annual rate of 3000% in 1989 to 4% (the same rate as in the United States) in 1994
   d. all of the above

Problems

1. You are an impartial economist who has noticed that Leinster is much more internally stable than Saxony.

   a. If you are hired by the government of Leinster to suggest the exchange rate regime that will keep income in the country constant, would you suggest a fixed rate or a floating rate?

   b. If, on the other hand, your services are bought by the government of Saxony, what exchange rate regime would you recommend to try to reduce the impact on income of instability in their own country?

2. Suppose that our imports were completely unaffected by our level of national income (i.e. our marginal propensity to import were zero), and suppose that our income also has no effect on our exports. Under these assumptions, compare the effects of expansionary fiscal policy under the following exchange rate regimes:

   a. fixed rates with sterilization
   b. fixed rates without sterilization
   c. floating rates

3. Try to make a case that Leinster and Saxony should form a monetary union and ultimately replace their separate currencies with a new common currency called the scalira.

4. If a country prefers to use monetary policy rather than fiscal policy to achieve its economic goals, would a fixed rate system or a flexible rate system provide the best environment for policymakers?

Discussion Topics

1. Consider the costs and benefits of having a fixed exchange rate among the U.S. dollar, the Canadian dollar, and the Mexican peso. Do you foresee a common currency for NAFTA along the lines of the "euro" proposed for ther EU?

2. Choose any country that interests you and try to determine to which, if any, currency it should peg its own currency.

Final Thought

> ...the Central Bank is the conductor of the orchestra and sets the tempo.
>
> — John Maynard Keynes, 1925

THE WALL STREET JOURNAL

July 28, 1995

Monetary Chaos Precedes Europe's Single Market

Consumers and Businesses Take Advantage of Cross-Border Anomalies

By Thomas Kamm
Staff Reporter of The Wall Street Journal

IRUN, Spain — The Repsol gas station is in Spain. The prices are indicated in pesetas. The attendant is Spanish. So how come most of the customers are French people, who conduct business in French and settle transactions in French francs?

Simple: the price. Since 1992, with Spain's first of four devaluations of the peseta, it has been much cheaper to buy gas in Spain than in France. Filling up a 50-liter tank costs the equivalent of $63 in Hendaye, on the French side of the border. But here in Irun, just 200 yards across the border in Spain, it costs $46.50.

And so every day, scores of people like Rita Sorondo cross the border — nothing more than an unmanned post since the European Union dismantled internal borders in 1992 — to fill up in Spain. "You have to be crazy to buy gas in France if you live near the border," says Mrs. Sorondo. "And I don't just buy gas here. A pack of Gauloises cigarettes costs 13.80 francs in France. Here it costs the equivalent of 8 francs. So now, I go from France to Spain to buy French cigarettes. It's illogical, but that's the way it is."

And that's why, even as the EU nears its 1999 deadline for establishing a common currency, monetary turmoil is rife among the 15 member states. The trade distortions threaten not only the EU's plans for monetary union, but its greatest creation to date: a common market where goods and people circulate as freely as between two U.S. states.

"We can't durably have a situation in which trade is as free as in the U.S., but where the Texas dollar suddenly devalues massively against the New York dollar," says George Jolles, president of France's Union of Textile Industries. "That's approximately what we have in Europe today."

Indeed, the scene at the Franco-Spanish border is a microcosm of the growing split within the EU between strong-currency and weak-currency countries that's prompting pressure for protectionism. The devaluing countries retort that they are simply making up for the years in which their currencies were overvalued and aren't deliberately distorting trade.

To many, 1992 is the year in which Europe became a single market. But that same year, another powerful — and conflicting — force was unleashed: the European Monetary System began to unravel. Currency speculation drove Britain and Italy out of the common exchange-rate mechanism, and only a significant widening of the authorized fluctuation margin in 1993 kept Spain and Portugal in.

The result is that some EU countries enjoy the benefits of free trade without suffering the constraints of defending monetary stability. And many businesses in countries like France and Germany feel the 25%-plus depreciation of the Italian lira and peseta over the past three years, and the lesser slide of the British pound and Portuguese escudo, has given these countries a huge and unfair trade advantage. "We feel that currencies have been transformed into commercial weapons," says Olivier Bouissou, head of a French trade group of shoe manufacturers.

As long as the impact was limited to a few gas stations, liquor stores or tobacco shops in border areas, these currency distortions were largely ignored. But today, people aren't just crossing borders to fill up their tanks; they're crossing them to buy the car whose tank they fill. Huge companies, even entire industries, are being hit by intra-European currency disarray. So, while some are already worrying about what to name Europe's future common currency, many business people are saying: Let's make sure free trade is still possible.

"Whether you're for the single currency or not, something has to be done in the period leading up to it or the system is going to implode," says Jacques Calvet, chairman of French auto maker PSA Peugeot Citroen SA.

In a parting shot before stepping down as chairman of Germany's Daimler-Benz AG, Edzard Reuter said a persistently strong German mark would leave much of German industry with no choice but to move production abroad. The German airline Lufthansa AG says foreign-exchange fluctuations will cost it 200 million marks ($145 million) this year.

Danone SA, the French food group, says currency movements cost it 1.63 billion francs ($340 million) of sales in the first half, and auto-parts group Valeo SA says first-half sales would have risen 16%, not 11%, without currency fluctuations. Conversely, Italian auto maker Fiat SpA concedes that without the lira's depreciation, it would never have recovered in one year from its 1993 record loss of 1.8 trillion lire ($1.12 billion).

"If this situation lasts much longer, whole parts of Northern Europe's industry will crumble in favor of Southern Europe," says Gerard

A Scorecard for European Union

The Maastricht Treaty stipulates that EU nations joining the planned monetary union must meet five economic criteria. They are:

■ **ANNUAL INFLATION** mustn't exceed that of the three best-performing nations by more than 1.5 percentage points.

■ **PUBLIC-SECTOR BUDGET DEFICIT** mustn't exceed 3% of gross domestic product.

■ **PUBLIC SECTOR DEBT** mustn't exceed 60% of GDP.

■ **LONG-TERM INTEREST RATES** mustn't exceed those of the three nations with the best inflation performance by more than two percentage points.

■ **THE EXCHANGE RATE** has to be kept within normal bands of Europe's Exchange Rate Mechanism for the previous two years.

This is how each of the 15 EU nations shapes up for monetary union in 1999. Those that don't make it first time around can join later. Table shows which of the criteria each country has met, based on estimates for 1996.

Country	Inflation	Budget Deficit	Debt	Interest Rates	Exchange Rate	Outlook
Austria	●			●	●	Deficit is problem, but surmountable
Belgium	●			●	●	Debt at over 130% of GDP is chronic
Denmark	●	●		●	●	Debt and political will are obstacles
Finland	●	●		●		Should make it
France	●		●	●	●	Must cut budget deficit
Germany	●	●	●	●	●	Should sail in, barring public backlash
Greece						No chance of making it
Ireland	●	●		●		On course to make it
Italy						No hope, unless rules are bent
Luxembourg	●	●	●	●	●	Top of the class
Netherlands	●	●		●	●	Government debt at 80% is too high
Portugal					●	Virtually no hope
Spain					●	Almost no chance
Sweden	●					Major debt and deficit troubles
U.K.	●	●	●	●		Could make it – if it wants to

Source: Deutsche Bank Research

Ruckebush, chief financial officer of Stephane Kelian SA, the French shoe manufacturer.

In 1993, Mr. Kelian, then chairman of the company that bears his name, transferred back to France the production of its cheaper shoes, which had been subcontracted to Spain and Portugal — just as the cycle of Southern European devaluations began, making it 30% to 40% cheaper to produce in those countries than in France. Publicly traded Kelian lost 3.85 billion francs in 1994, Mr. Kelian lost his job and the new chairman, Bernard Besson, has decided to transfer the production of midprice shoes back to Spain and Italy, possibly cutting 171 jobs.

Other companies, while avoiding mass layoffs, have had to scramble. Valeo, for instance, says the percentage of its sales outside France has risen to 61% from 50% in 1992. "We try whenever possible to produce in countries with weakened currencies and attractive labor costs, and sell in countries with strong currencies," says Chairman Noel Goutard. "We moved some of our machinery to our Spanish plant from our French plant. We transferred certain orders for plastic components from Germany to Italy. Now, we're moving them back to France because we've found a more competitive manufacturer."

With production facilities throughout Europe, Mr. Goutard says Valeo has been able to absorb most of the devaluations' effects. But it's been costly to France in terms of jobs, and it makes managing a company very difficult. "These fluctuations from one country to another are extremely disruptive," he says. "We go through incredible gymnastics, we have to arbitrate constantly, and that has a financial cost."

But devaluation has also meant opportunity for some. Car prices have long differed from one European country to another for similar cars, partly because of differing taxes, and partly because French and German car makers sometimes sell at smaller margins in other markets to compete with local car makers. But the Italian and Spanish devaluations, coming just as barriers to intra-European trade were lifted, have disrupted the market.

At a Peugeot dealer in the French town of Urugne, near the Spanish border, a midrange Peugeot 306 sells for 99,800 francs ($20,700). But nine miles away in Oyarzun, Spain, the same car sells for 79,000 francs ($16,400). So the Centrauto dealership there has two employees dealing full-time with French customers. "About half the cars we sell every month are for French people," says salesman Javier Eskudero.

French car makers are cracking down. Renault SA is rationing sales to dealers in Spain and Italy whose orders seem out of step with domestic demand. But the threat doesn't only come from people crossing the border. In Saint-Cyr-l'Ecole, in the western suburbs of Paris, Alain Fournier has started up a company called European Cars, where the most popular cars can be bought for an average of 20% less than at authorized dealers. The trick? Mr. Fournier buys the cars in Spain, Italy or Portugal and sells them in France.

"My whole business is based on currency and price disorder," says Mr. Fournier, who expects to sell 3,500 cars this year. All told, middlemen like him are believed to have captured between 5% and 7% of the French market.

Such a business can only thrive as long as there is currency disarray in Europe. But people like Mr. Fournier think they have a good future. Indeed, while some view the current disorder as a powerful argument for a common currency, skeptics say it also highlights how hard it will be to achieve monetary union.

The EU has delayed the deadline for the common currency to 1999 from 1997, but only half of its member states at most will meet the criteria. Many fear that leaving some countries outside of the monetary union could mean that currency and trade turmoil will continue beyond that deadline. "The consequences of a single currency between five, six or seven countries for the economic stability of the whole of the European Union . . . have not been sufficiently studied," French President Jacques Chirac has warned.

Some say that the prospect of being relegated to a secondary status within the EU is a powerful incentive to countries not in the core group of monetary union to get their houses in order so they can join. Already, inflation and higher raw-material prices are eating into the devaluations' positive effects in Italy and Spain. But try telling that to people on the French side of the Franco-Spanish border. Jean-Pierre Hiribarren, who runs a small carpentry shop in Hendaye that has been losing order after order to competitors in Spain, has few illusions. "By the time they're in, we will have had plenty of time to go bust," he says.

Source: *The Wall Street Journal*, July 28, 1995. Reprinted with permission of THE WALL STREET JOURNAL, 1995 Dow Jones & Company, Inc. All rights reserved worldwide.

THE WALL STREET JOURNAL
July 28, 1995

Now the Hard Part: Imposing a Common Currency

By Peter Gumbel
Staff Reporter of The Wall Street Journal

BRUSSELS — Forging a single currency is back at the top of Europe's political agenda, partly as a result of recent huge currency fluctuations. And this time, monetary union is being debated with a new realism.

No longer does the debate focus, as in the late 1980s and early 1990s, on the abstract issue of whether to abandon the German mark, the French franc and the other moneys for a yet-to-be-named Eurocurrency. Today's discussion concentrates on the big questions of how to make the plans work.

Dozens of practical problems connected with a new European currency are being puzzled over, away from the political glare, in government departments, banks, industry associations and elsewhere. They range from the technical, such as how retailers should display two sets of prices, to the practical, such as dealing with a shortage of software programmers.

Few are ready to bet that a single currency will actually come about in 1999 as planned, and many economists and politicians, notably in Britain, believe it never will. But business doesn't want to be left out if and when it does arrive. And as an army of business executives and technocrats try to figure out how to ease the problems, they lend a new credibility to the beleaguered project.

Drop in at Kredietbank NV's new headquarters in Brussels. The Belgian bank has looked at every aspect of a switchover, hoping to gain an edge over rivals. It is already a major player in securities denominated in European currency units, or ECUs, the artificial currency that a real Eurocurrency would replace. Maurits Verherstraeten, the bank's head of securities trading, says that if Europe doesn't forge a monetary union within five years, "it won't be possible for two decades." He adds: "We believe it has to happen — and we'll be ready for it."

Two hundred miles away in Paris, Jean-Marie Avadian, a managing director for payment systems at the French bank Societe Generale, worries that the huge investments and time spent on ensuring a smooth transition could leave it and other European banks at a competitive disadvantage to their U.S. and Japanese rivals. And the technical challenge of converting the bank's operations from francs into a Eurocurrency, he says, "is more complex than putting a man on the moon."

There are many other problems, including those same currency speculators who battered at Europe's semi-fixed exchange rates in 1992 and 1993. They will have a new chance to meddle during the period between the decision to go for monetary union and the day exchange-rate parities are irrevocably fixed. "There is no certitude about how the [currency] markets will react," says Pierre Simon of France's Cie. Financiere de Paribas.

The business community hopes that many uncertainties will be removed this year, when Europe's politicians are expected to pick a precise scenario for changing over to the new currency. Most agree that to prepare the public, the currency should be introduced in stages, with some financial operations transacted from the start, and the rest — including introduction of notes and coins — three years later.

But questions on the pace have sparked an intriguing tussle between France and Germany, the twin motors of European integration. Under Yves-Thibault de Silguy, a French technocrat who is the EU's commissioner for monetary affairs, the commission on May 31 published a scenario that largely reflects the views of France's political and banking establishment. It calls for a "critical mass" of transactions, including treasury-bill trading by banks and issues of government debt, to be conducted in the new currency from the start to lend credibility.

Until recently the Bundesbank, Germany's central bank, had advocated a far more cautious scenario that would limit the new currency initially to financial transactions between central banks. But under pressure from leading German banks, including Deutsche Bank AG, which backs the French approach, the Bundesbank did an about-turn last week, saying it now sees merit in the "critical mass" approach.

Even so, the Germans remain adamant that not every EU nation can join this new club. The Bundesbank is demanding strict adherence to economic criteria laid down in the EU's 1992 Maastricht treaty, including tough limits on debt and budget deficits that most EU nations don't yet meet. Bundesbank President Hans Tietmeyer and other officials repeatedly have raised objections they want resolved before the countdown begins.

The Bundesbank's caution reflects the German public's reluctance to give up the mark, a currency that Juergen Stark, a top government official, says "forms a large part of the Germans' self-image." The task of forging a compromise has been handed to the European Monetary Institute in Frankfurt, the precursor of a European central bank.

Under any scenario, the single currency will impose significant short-term costs on business, especially banks. The European Banking Federation estimates the minimum cost to the banks will be $10 billion to $13 billion, or 2% of annual operating costs over a three-to-four-year changeover period; software alterations could account for half of the cost.

Everyone is scrambling to devise ways to limit the technical problems and costs of operating two overlapping systems at the same time, one in national currency and the other in Eurocurrency. Smaller German banks are already fretting about this "double-currency chaos."

The new Eurocurrency also will require a massive campaign to win over a still skeptical European public. The best indication of the public's lack of readiness is contained in a recent opinion poll conducted by the Ipsos agency for France's Leclerc retailing group. Of the respondents, 79% said they know nothing, or very little, about the single-currency plans, and 59% feared it would disrupt their lives.

But the European Commission and other proponents of a single currency say it is worth the effort. Removing foreign-exchange costs within the EU alone could boost annual growth as much as 0.4%, the commission estimates, as well as make life easier for travelers. And the single-currency goal provides a powerful economic rationale for free-spending nations such as Spain and Italy to get their finances in order.

A single currency, its proponents hope, also would amount to a quantum leap for the cause of political and economic integration in Europe. Failure, on the other hand, would be devastating. Ulrich Cartellieri, a board member of Deutsche Bank, worries that it even could give rise to dangerous protectionism. For European economic policy, he says, failure would mean "a fatal loss of credibility."

Source: *The Wall Street Journal*, July 28, 1995. Reprinted with permission of THE WALL STREET JOURNAL, 1995 Dow Jones & Company, Inc. All rights reserved worldwide.

CHAPTER 25
The International Movement of Labor

Objectives of the Chapter

A necessary condition for world GDP to be maximized is that people work where their productivity, and presumably their salaries, are highest. Recognizing this, governments often encourage internal migration, as in the movement of people from the Rust Belt to the Sun Belt of the United States. A move from south to north across the U.S.-Mexico border is regarded as a different matter altogether.

Chapter 25 explores the welfare implications of the flow of humans and identifies the stakes of different groups within the sending and the receiving regions. It is important to remember, however, that economic analysis must be supplemented by sociological and political considerations in order to understand the different treatment of internal versus international migration.

After studying Chapter 25, you should be able to

1. describe the patterns of migration into North America and into the EU
2. illustrate and explain the welfare effects of migration in the labor markets of both the sending country and the receiving country
3. discuss the impact of migration on taxes paid and public goods and services received by the migrants themselves, and on revenue and spending totals for the sending and the receiving countries
4. point to both positive and negative externalities generated by international migration
5. evaluate the gradualism and selectivity of immigration policies

Key Terms

Average-income paradoxes
    the counterintuitive results that the receiving country can gain from immigration, even if its per capita income falls after the arrival of the new immigrants; and the sending country can lose, even if its per capita income rises after the departure of the new emigrants.

Brain drain
    the emigration mainly from developing countries of highly skilled and educated people toward better paying countries (usually industrial economies, but recently some OPEC nations as well).

Part V: Factor Movements

Gradualism in immigration policy
deliberate restrictions on net inflow of immigrants (assuring that it doesn't exceed a certain share of the population) in order to allow a peaceful transition into the economy.

Guestworker
a term used to indicate a temporary foreign worker, who does not intend to (or is discouraged from) permanently integrating in the host country society. In German, the term is *Gastarbeiter*.

Immigration Reform and Control Act (ICRA)
passed by Congress in 1986, this legislation was designed to reduce illegal immigration and give permanent residence to families of people who had illegally immigrated in earlier years.

Selectivity in immigration policy
deliberate twisting of regulations to encourage the inflow of highly skilled and educated workers and to discourage the inflow of unskilled and poorly educated ones.

Warm-up Questions

True or False? Explain.

1. T / F   There is a gain to workers who stay at home while others immigrate.

2. T / F   On average, immigrants tend to pay more in taxes than they receive in benefits from their consumption of public goods and services.

3. T / F   The country sending immigrants has a net gain from positive labor market effects and public finance effects.

4. T / F   The average per capita income of workers in a receiving country rises.

5. T / F   "Brain drain" is what you experience after taking a midterm exam.

Multiple Choice

1. In the absence of externalities, the countries sending large numbers of workers abroad
   a. lose only if their emigrants' gains are excluded from the net welfare calculations
   b. lose, with or without consideration of the emigrants' stake
   c. lose because per capita income falls
   d. gain, even when their emigrants' gains are excluded from the net welfare calculation

2. Ignoring externalities, the countries receiving immigrants
   a. gain only if their immigrants' gains are included in the net welfare calculation
   b. gain, with or without consideration of the immigrants' stake
   c. lose, because per capita income falls
   d. lose, because wage rates are kept lower than they would be otherwise

3. Which group definitely loses from international migration?
   a. the migrants
   b. the migrants' new employers in the receiving country
   c. the migrants' old employers in the sending country
   d. the migrants' fellow workers who did not emigrate

4. From a public finance point of view, the benefits of receiving immigrants, so far, exceeded the costs because
   a. they bring in skilled labor
   b. they raise total income
   c. they pay more in taxes than is spent on them in public goods and services
   d. they introduce new technology into the economy

5. The welfare (supply and demand) analysis of immigration
   a. assumes that factor price equalization is not achieved through trade alone
   b. implicitly assumes that factor prices will eventually be equalized through trade alone
   c. considers the factor price equalization theorem to be totally irrelevant
   d. acknowledges that commodity price equalization will not be achieved through immigration alone

Problems

1. Recall that Saxony is a relatively labor-scarce country while Leinster is relatively land-scarce. For years, some people have emigrated from Leinster in search of higher wages in Saxony. Without immigration, the labor markets in the two countries look like the graphs below. (To make comparison easier, wages in both countries are expressed in terms of the scudo.)

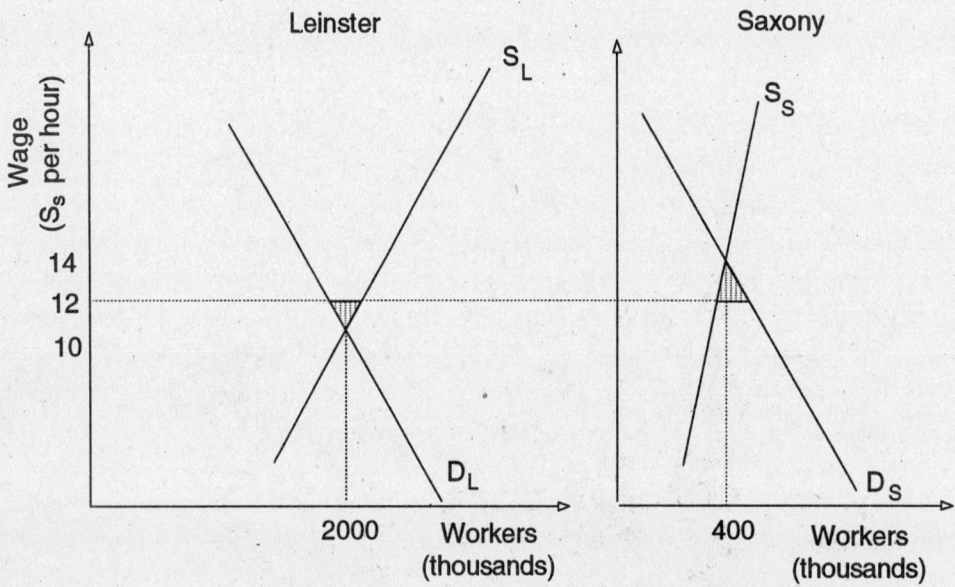

Figure 25.1

Suppose that pressure from some Saxons has caused the government to pass legislation that closes the border to any immigration from Leinster, reducing the inflow of workers to zero (and perhaps causing some immigrants to exit).

a. What will be the effect of this on wages in Leinster? in Saxony?

b. What will be the effect of this on the welfare of workers in Leinster? in Saxony?

c. What will be the effect of this on the welfare of employers in Leinster? in Saxony?

d. What will be the net effect on "world" welfare?

In light of your answers, which Saxons are likely to be part of that anti-immigration pressure group?

2. The purpose of the Immigration Reform and Control Act of 1986 was to restrict the entry of undocumented immigrants into the United States, while granting amnesty to some undocumented immigrants who were already here. In the model used in the text, suppose that the United States *restricts* the entry of all immigrants from Mexico.

   a. Illustrate the effect on U.S. firms, workers, and national welfare.

   b. Illustrate the effect on Mexican firms, workers, and national welfare.

c. Using (a) and (b), what is the effect on undocumented immigrants granted amnesty in the United States and on those who cannot enter? As a result, is the incentive for illegal entry into the United States decreased or increased?

3. Discuss how the movement of labor from Leinster to Saxony could be a substitute for the movement of goods between the two countries.

4. Explain whether you agree or disagree with the following statement:

> A country doesn't need to worry about labor emigration. When some workers emigrate, the marginal product and wages of the remaining workers actually goes up, making the home country better off.

Discussion Topics

1. Would you expect to see labor migration increase as barriers to the movement of goods between countries proliferate?

2. In 1994, voters in California passed Proposition 187 which was intended to stop the flow of undocumented immigrants, especially from Mexico. What groups would have voted for this legislation? Who would have voted against it?

Final Thought

We denounce the importation of contract labor, whether from Europe or Asia, as an offense against the spirit of American institutions.

— Republican National Platform, 1884

THE WALL STREET JOURNAL

November 2, 1995

Hot Thai Export to U.S.: 'Slave' Workers

Washington Calls for Crackdown But Isn't Optimistic

By Paul M. Sherer
Staff Reporter of The Wall Street Journal

BANGKOK, Thailand — Long notorious as a source of illegal drugs bound for the U.S., Thailand is emerging as a major hub for another type of clandestine merchandise: illicit cheap labor.

U.S. officials in Bangkok estimate that 2,000 people a month — Thais, Chinese, Indians, Pakistanis, Bangladeshis, Sri Lankans and even Nigerians — use Bangkok as a gateway to sneak into North America illegally. Prodded by the U.S. Embassy here, Thai authorities recently began cracking down. But U.S. officials aren't optimistic the flow can be stanched soon.

Well-organized Thai criminal syndicates smuggle the workers to the sweatshops and brothels of New York and California. The networks include procurers in poor Thai villages, travel agents, document forgers, corrupt immigration officials and airline employees, couriers who accompany the immigrants and U.S. factory and brothel operators who pay as much as $35,000 for each worker. Each worker must repay that amount through years of labor or, in the case of prostitution, sex with hundreds of men.

The trade in illegal workers was splashed across U.S. front pages three months ago after authorities raided a textile sweatshop in El Monte, Calif., where more than 60 Thais had been toiling 17 hours a day sewing brand-name U.S. clothing for less than $1 an hour. U.S. officials in Bangkok say the El Monte case represents a tiny proportion of the flow from Thailand to the U.S.

These officials think about 20 Thai travel agencies regularly supply travelers with false documents for visa applications. Two of Thailand's largest travel agencies, Roong Sarp Travel Service Co. and Takerng Tour Co., brought many of the women in the El Monte sweatshop to the U.S. on group tours, the workers say.

"We see people every day coming [with falsified documents]," says Timothy Scherer, consul of the U.S. Embassy in Bangkok. "We're convinced those documents are prepared for them by tour agencies who specialize" in travelers with improper documents. Takerng Tour and Roong Sarp Travel Service deny any involvement in alien smuggling.

Separately, Thai Airways International Ltd. is investigating employees believed to have smuggled hundreds of Thais into the U.S. at $1,600 a head. And since August, 11 Thai immigration and police officers have been accused of working with smugglers to pass people through Bangkok's international airport for $400 each.

The U.S. only recently began shifting resources to stop illegal immigrants at the source rather than after they have sneaked into the U.S. And Thai immigration police, while cooperating with the U.S., have their hands full trying to stem the tide of illegal immigrants into Thailand.

Thailand has long been an exporter of unskilled labor to Asia and the Middle East. As many as 200,000 Thais work, often legally, in such places as Taiwan, Japan and Saudi Arabia in construction, as maids and in the sex trade. Thai workers can earn $600 a month on a Taipei construction site or well over $2,000 a month in a brothel in Brunei. The $200-a-month jobs they leave behind are in turn often filled by illegals from Burma or China.

Thais continue to entrust themselves to smuggling gangs despite the pathetic tales told by workers who return from an overseas "hell factory," as the Thai media has dubbed the El Monte sweatshop.

Among those returnees is Kanang Isara, a 36-year-old seamstress who grew up on a rice farm in northern Thailand. When Miss Kanang flew to California four years ago, she had been promised work in a clothing factory at 10 times her Bangkok wages. Instead, Miss Kanang found herself working in slave-like conditions at the El Monte sweatshop.

"I was kept like in prison and treated like an animal," Miss Kanang says. She remembers what she was told in the factory by one of the Thai bosses: "If you run away, your house will be burned. Even if it takes 10 years, I won't forget."

Early last year, Miss Kanang left the sweatshop and returned to Bangkok. But she has been on edge since her phone rang a few weeks ago. On the line was her former boss from the sweatshop. "We will meet again," he told her.

"I'm afraid," she says softly.

Source: *The Wall Street Journal*, November 2, 1995. Reprinted with permission of THE WALL STREET JOURNAL, 1995 Dow Jones & Company, Inc. All rights reserved worldwide.

CHAPTER 26
International Lending and the World Debt Crisis

Objectives of the Chapter

International capital flows are sometimes courted, sometimes denigrated, and sometimes troublesome for the governments of the countries involved. Chapter 26 focuses on portfolio lending, which is the transfer of financial assets (rather than the movement of physical capital) between countries. After a welfare analysis of well-behaved international lending, an overview is offered of the post-World War II patterns of capital flows. At the end, the basic problem of the incentive to default on sovereign debt is investigated.

By the time you finish studying Chapter 26, you should be able to

1. classify the various types of international capital flows
2. illustrate and explain the welfare effect of allowing free international lending and borrowing
3. evaluate the case for taxing international capital flows
4. chronicle the rise and fall in private international lending since the first oil shock
5. evaluate the role of defective property rights in the recurrent sovereign debt crisis

Key Terms

Collateral — the value of the borrowers' assets that a lender can seize if the borrower falls behind on loan payments. It is easier to seize these assets if they are located within the legal jurisdiction of the lender's home country.

Debt service — repayments of principal and interest. The debt service ratio is a measure of a country's debt burden and it expresses debt service as a percentage of total export revenues or GDP.

Foreign investment — lending to, or purchasing ownership shares in, a foreign enterprise largely owned and controlled by the investor (direct investment) or in a foreign enterprise not owned or controlled by the investor (portfolio investment).

International capital flows
financial flows of credit and ownership claims between countries. Flows of physical capital goods are typically treated as ordinary trade flows, not capital flows, in the balance of payments accounts.

Petrodollars
the funds accumulated by Middle Eastern oil-producing countries in the wake of the OPEC price increases. These funds were often deposited in U.S. banks.

Sovereign
someone or something that has legal independence. This usually refers to national governments because (as in the case of debts they owe) they cannot be forced to repay, be sued, or have their domestic assets seized.

Transfer pricing
the price that is set on a transaction (for instance, the sale of a good or the making of a loan) between two related entities (for instance, two national units of a multinational firm). Transfer prices are sometimes used to shift capital or profits across borders, in order to avoid (or evade) being subject to taxation by a country.

World debt crisis
refers to the inability (or unwillingness) since 1982 of many developing countries to service their international obligations, and the large exposure of major Western banks to shaky foreign loans.

Warm-up Questions

True or False? Explain.

1. T / F Well-behaved international capital flows yield welfare results similar to those of international trade.

2. T / F Under sovereign debt arrangements, the interest rate is often higher to compensate for the likelihood of default.

3. T / F If new loans (which are intended to postpone default) equal only the repayments of interest and principal they were meant to induce, there is a high probability of ultimate default.

4. T / F Throughout the 1990s, the United States has lent more internationally than it has borrowed.

5. T / F Taxes and prohibitions on international lending are usually easy to enforce.

Multiple Choice

1. When a Japanese company buys a U.S. communications satellite, this flow is typically treated as
   a. a capital flow
   b. a trade flow
   c. a direct investment
   d. a portfolio investment

2. The property-rights problem of sovereign debt can be solved by
   a. making sure that sovereign debtors borrow only up to their collateral
   b. hoping that debtors will repay to protect their creditworthiness
   c. military threats
   d. helping debtor countries enhance their economic growth through fresh loans

3. Suppose that all barriers to international lending were stripped away. Who would gain and who would lose?
   a. Wealthy countries' lenders would gain; poor countries' borrowers would lose.
   b. Wealthy countries' lenders and poor countries' borrowers would gain.
   c. Wealthy countries' lenders would lose; poor countries' borrowers would gain.
   d. Wealthy countries' lenders and poor countries' borrowers would lose.

4. Which of the following factors *least* explains the world debt crisis of the early 1980s?
   a. the resistance to direct investment in the 1970s
   b. the world recession of 1982
   c. the second OPEC oil shock in 1979
   d. mistaken overlending by banks

5. The dominant international borrower in the past decade has been
   a. the developing countries
   b. the European Community
   c. the former Soviet Union
   d. the United States

Problems

1. The marginal productivity of capital (MPK) schedules for Saxony and Leinster are drawn below. (To make them easier to compare, MPK in both countries is expressed in terms of lira.)

Figure 26.1

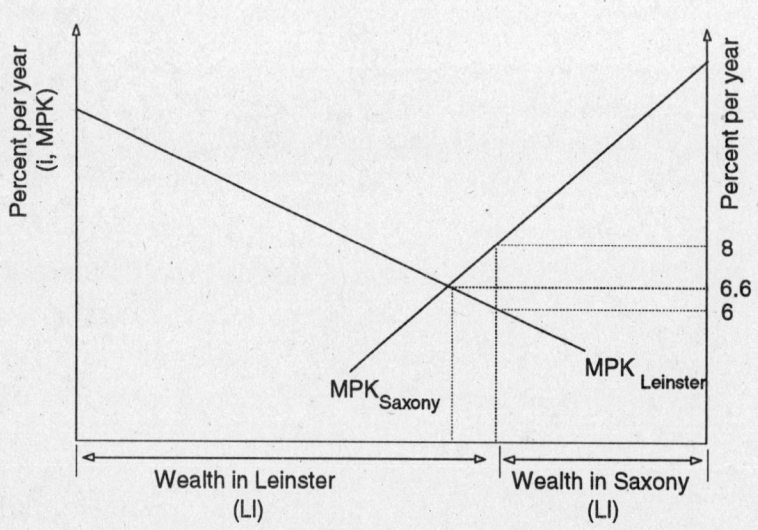

a. If the initial interest rate in Saxony is 8 % and the initial interest rate in Leinster is 6 %, is there an incentive for lending between the countries? In which direction will funds flow?

b. Given these curves, what will be the equilibrium rate at which funds will flow between the countries?

c. What is the impact of these funds flows on Saxon borrowers? Saxon lenders? Saxony as a whole?

d. What is the impact of these funds flows on Leinster borrowers? Leinster lenders? Leinster as a whole?

e. Does international lending between the two countries raise or lower "world" welfare?

2. Suppose that both Saxony and Leinster are thinking about levying a tax on funds borrowed or lent internationally.

   a. Why would Saxony want to levy such a tax?

   b. Why would Leinster want to levy such a tax?

   c. If both countries place a tax on international funds flows, what is likely to be the result?

3. The graph below depicts the costs and benefits of a Saxon government default on funds it has borrowed from Leinster (expressed in lira).

Figure 26.3

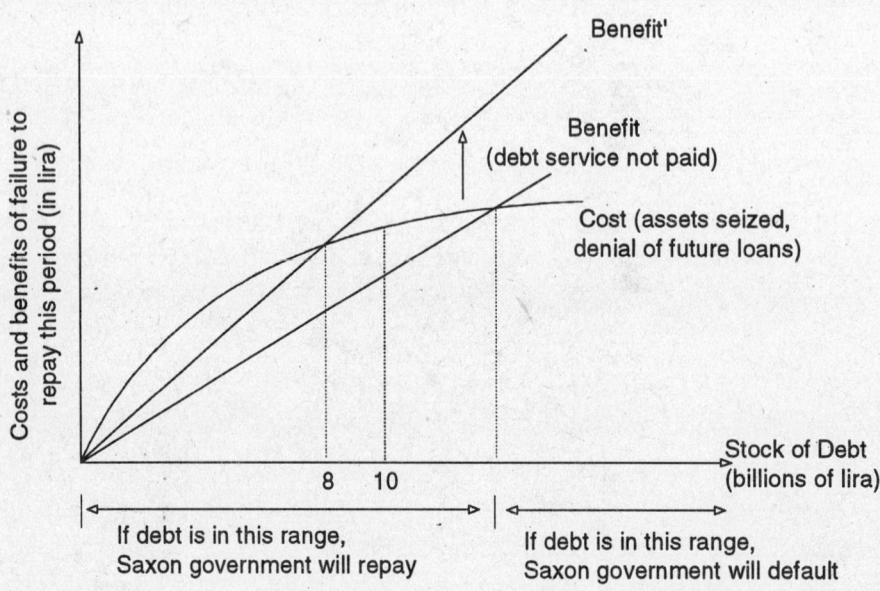

a. If Saxony currently owes Ll 10 billion, does it have an incentive to default?

b. Suppose that reduced saving rates in Leinster raise the real interest rate that Saxony must pay, rotating the debt service curve to the line labelled Benefit'. If Saxony's debt is still Ll 10 billion, does it have an incentive to repay now?

4. An American investment banker in Tokyo wrote:

> What flows in can flow out. As long as the United States takes more and more money from abroad, it is mortgaging its domestic economic decisions to foreign investors whose behavior could be fickle and irrational.

Do you agree or disagree with this statement?

Discussion Topics

1. The United States is currently the largest debtor nation in the world. How did we get there from our position as a creditor nation for most of the twentieth century?

2. Is it bad to be a debtor nation? Is it good to be a creditor nation?

Final Thought

> *Polonius:* Neither a borrower, nor a lender be:
> For loan oft loses both itself and friend;
> And borrowing dulls the edge of husbandry.
>
> — William Shakespeare, 1601

THE WALL STREET JOURNAL
May 17, 1995

The Challenge of Capital Flows

By Robert L. Bartley

BEIJING — As China enters the world economy, we should stop to ask about the features of the economy it's entering. The international economy, we should understand, is increasingly dominated by huge capital movements.

Every day billions of dollars move up and down satellite links at the speed of light, with enormous effects on national economies around the world. Saying this is by now almost a cliche, but at the same time it is poorly incorporated into our understandings and discussion. Instead, our discussion of the international economy is dominated by the issue of trade. We often fail to keep in mind that trade movements and capital movements are complementary, that for every buyer there has to be a seller, that surpluses and deficits in the trade accounts can only exist if they're financed in the capital accounts.

By definition, every nation's international accounts must balance. A trade surplus normally means capital exports, while trade deficits imply capital imports. The unexamined wisdom is that trade flows cause capital flows. Yet while capital moves at the speed of light, trade splashes along in ships.

Enormous swings in capital flows, and gyrations in exchange rates that often result, create enormous problems for even the most highly developed economies. Thus the remarkably high yen raises the question of whether Japan can sustain an economic recovery. And the correspondingly low dollar raises the issue of whether the U.S. will achieve a "soft landing" or slip into a mild version of stagflation, the combination of recession and inflation it experienced in the 1970s. In Europe, Jacques Chirac, newly elected as president of France, finds himself facing a dilemma between a mandate to cut high unemployment and the dictates of the traditional link between the franc and German mark.

In developing countries, which need foreign capital for rapid development, the impact of the flows is even greater. Developing nations of course have less margin for error. And as they become increasingly integrated into the world capital markets, they will face increasingly difficult demands and increasingly stringent judgments.

We have just had a dramatic example in the case of Mexico. Only a year ago, Mexico was considered the very model of a developing country. It had opened its trade with the North American Free Trade Agreement. It had conducted vast privatizations, with its premier companies being offered as American depository receipts on the New York Stock Exchange. It had instituted fiscal prudence, with an internal deficit not more than 1% of gross domestic product.

While it did experience a current account deficit, this seemed the normal counterpart of vast capital inflows into an exceedingly promising market. During 1993, indeed, the current account deficit did not prevent Mexico from maintaining its exchange rate while accumulating foreign exchange reserves, which reached $25 billion around the turn of the year. While some economists contended its currency was "overvalued," exports surged.

In retrospect, 1994 was a year of misfortunes and mistakes. Politically, Mexico experienced shocks: two apparently political assassinations, an armed uprising, albeit in retrospect a minor one, and political scandals suggesting corruption and drug money. Economically, its mistakes turned on increasing reliance on short-term debt and a failure to react to losses of foreign reserves by contracting monetary policy. Still, in November, with a new administration due at the end of the month, its foreign exchange reserves still exceeded its monetary base.

Between another political scandal and a new willingness to consider devaluation intended to bolster "competitiveness," a run on the peso quickly developed. Three weeks into its tenure, the new administration signaled a willingness to devalue. When this reached the market, Mexico lost $5 billion in foreign exchange reserves in a few hours. Counting the issue of dollar-linked obligations, its reserves were exhausted in a day's trading. With capital exiting at the speed of light, Mexico went overnight from a model of a successful developing nation to a model of a failed developing nation.

In the size of capital inflows in the last few years, Mexico stood second only to China. Now, I do not believe China will become another Mexico anytime soon. It is indeed likely to experience political shocks. A new leadership impends, and already there is concern with scandal and corruption, and stories of suicides. The incorporation of Hong Kong in 1997 will either be a highly positive signal to the capital markets, or if it goes badly, a highly negative one. But investment in China is primarily direct investment, while in the case of Mexico it was 80% portfolio investment, where flows may not merely stop but reverse. Though in Mexico it took only a year to develop a reliance on short-term capital, there is no sign of that in China and indeed no obvious mechanism for it to develop. That is to say, China is much less vulnerable than Mexico because it is much less integrated into the world economy.

Even so, the Chinese economy is already being buffeted by the impact of capital flows on its money, the renminbi. It is currently struggling with a new outbreak of inflation, which ironically is in part caused by strong investment inflows. Investment dollars are flowing into China at a pace exceeding imports, and Chinese monetary authorities are accumulating foreign reserves. But as they buy up the excess dollars, they are naturally issuing yuan, creating a rapid pace of credit expansion that shows up as inflation.

In developed economies, the purchase of dollars would be "sterilized" by the offsetting sale of government bonds in open market operations. But China does not yet have a commercial banking system or a functioning government bond market, let alone open market operations. The People's Bank of China can try to sterilize through more primitive mechanisms, but in the end has limited options in containing inflation.

China has recently started to let the yuan appreciate in foreign exchange markets, which would slow investment inflows. Since the People's Bank only needs to issue yuan for excess dollars, China could increase imports, ideally by allowing more foreign purchases by the private sector. The best solution is to restrict credit creation in subventions to state-owned enterprises, which had created rapid credit expansion even before the advent of the excess dollar problem. The worst solution is to continue credit creation and try to contain inflation through price controls, backing away from market-oriented reforms. The very worst solution, for which ample precedent exists, is to concentrate the price controls on food, subsidizing urban consumers at the expense of China's true producers in the rural sector.

Happily, China's government is aware of the problems caused by capital flows, and is developing institutions to manage them. The People's Bank law of last year set a path of evolution toward a modern central bank. The commercial banking law passed this month was the next logical step toward a monetary regime including a national bond market and open market operations.

We have to wish China all success in developing these institutions, since its smooth development would contribute to a successful world economy. And with the shocks of leadership changes, political development and Hong Kong lying ahead, we have to wish China's leaders all success in using these institutions to manage capital flows successfully. Perhaps they will succeed even better than our leaders in the highly developed economies.

Mr. Bartley is editor of The Wall Street Journal. *This is based on his remarks to the Beijing conference, "China and its Neighbors: Economic Relations in a Region of Economic Growth," organized by the Asia Society and Dow Jones & Co.*

Source: *The Wall Street Journal*, May 17, 1995. Reprinted with permission of THE WALL STREET JOURNAL, 1995 Dow Jones & Company, Inc. All rights reserved worldwide.

THE WALL STREET JOURNAL
January 30, 1995

Private-Capital Flows Can Hurt Poor Nations

By Tim Carrington

WASHINGTON — Hot money is the double-edged sword of economic development.

For five years, international investment managers ventured beyond established industrial economies in search of higher returns, transforming many of the world's poorer states, Cinderella-like, from bedraggled less-developed countries into sizzling emerging markets. But for the past five weeks, with Mexico in crisis, those managers have been taking their money home.

The dizzying reversal leaves the Cinderellas badly shaken and raises new questions about whether unfettered private-capital flows really facilitate long-term economic development. Testifying in Congress last week, Federal Reserve Chairman Alan Greenspan conceded that while global flows have underwritten economic gains around the world, "they also have some potential negative consequences." Similarly, Ernest Stern, managing director of the World Bank — soon to leave for a job at J.P. Morgan & Co. — sees a "downside" to the rush of private money, adding, "the outflows can be very disruptive." At the minimum, countries are seeking ways to avoid the trauma afflicting Mexico.

What's emerging is an amended view of global finance that may change the way that Brazil and others approach reform. Before Mexico's meltdown, and the world-wide plunge in emerging markets, the World Bank and International Monetary Fund held that private capital reinforced economic development. Investment managers, it was said, rewarded reform-minded privatizers and punished laggards who clung to statist policies and bureaucratic controls.

In fact, it's not so simple. Investment money speeds in and out of developing countries for reasons not always related to their policies. Jorge Mariscal, manager of Latin American equity research for Goldman, Sachs & Co., studied volatility in Mexico's financial markets in 1994 and found that 80% of the turbulence wasn't caused by economic or political events inside the country but by "a retrenchment in liquidity that was taking place around the world." Often, a rise of interest rates in New York sparked a sell-off in Mexico City. The December devaluation and ensuing crisis proved contagious, with investors dumping securities not just in Mexico but in markets as distant as Poland and Morocco for no other reason than that they, too, were called emerging markets. Today's hot money, according to Robert Hormats, vice chairman of Goldman Sachs International, is "less informed and more nervous" than the last decade's bank loans to developing countries. So, it whips in and out at the first sign of trouble-with no prospect of negotiation or rescheduling obligations. Moreover, reforms — even bold ones — take time. After eight years of change, Mexico's transition still had enough holes in it to give fretful investors reason to flee. In addition, the flows, and their ability to disrupt, far outstrip the capacity of the institutions established to guard stability. "The IMF was created with capital and instruments that weren't designed for the current world," says Ricardo Hausmann, chief economist at the Inter-American Development Bank. Hence, the only real safety net for Mexico's high-wire act is the one that the U.S. Treasury hopes to put up. Stanley Fischer, the IMF's first deputy managing director, recently raised the prospect that the world "needs some international facility available that's much larger than what we've got." He notes that if Mexico's crisis were to occur in nearly any other country, the U.S. wouldn't step in.

Meanwhile, developing nations have ways to make themselves less vulnerable to sudden shifts of hot money:

— Establish credible restraints on capital flows, such as reserve requirements for short-term investments. Portfolio flows face various restraints in Chile, and the country doesn't "seem to have suffered for it," says Lawrence Brainard, head of global-markets research at Chase Manhattan Bank. But he warns that countries shouldn't slide back into broader capital controls, which have a sorry history.

— Keep current accounts — trade in goods and services, plus certain financial transfers-in line. Economists put too much emphasis on Mexico's federal budget, which was in balance, and not enough on its current account, which had spiraled into a $28 billion deficit. The current account could be financed only by foreign capital, which obviously can be fickle.

— Build domestic savings. Like the U.S., most Latin American countries have relatively meager domestic savings, a shortfall that leaves them more dependent on foreign capital. The high-growth economies of East Asia were built mostly on high rates of domestic savings.

— When using foreign money, encourage long-term commitments, such as foreign direct investment in productive facilities. Overall, as one economist puts it, a country's foreign capital should be a blend of hot and cool, averaging out as lukewarm.

Source: *The Wall Street Journal*, January 30, 1995. Reprinted with permission of THE WALL STREET JOURNAL, 1995 Dow Jones & Company, Inc. All rights reserved worldwide.

CHAPTER 27
Direct Foreign Investment and the Multinationals

Objectives of the Chapter

Unlike portfolio investment, direct foreign investment (DFI) involves ownership and control. Firms undertake DFI for a number of reasons: locating a plant in a growing market; securing access to raw materials and minerals; avoiding trade barriers; seeking low wage labor; or pre-empting another foreign investor. DFI comes in a package that may or may not include equity finance, but usually does include management expertise, modern technologies, and technical skills in production and in marketing. Since this package is controlled by a multinational firm headquartered in the source country, it raises the host country's fears of interference by, and dependence upon, foreign economic powers.

While DFI was eclipsed by the portfolio lending which led to the world debt crisis, it is on the rise today. The United States has always shown a preference for DFI; in the 1980s Japan and the European countries have expanded their direct investments too. While North America and Europe are the major host regions for DFI, lending to Third World countries is on the rise as economic policies in those countries are reformed.

After studying Chapter 27, you should be able to

1. distinguish between direct foreign investment and portfolio investment
2. describe the historical and geographical patterns of DFI
3. explain the "Hymer view," the "appropriability theory," and the "tax evasion theory" of DFI
4. analyze the welfare effects of DFI in both the source and the host countries, and show how the measurement of welfare depends on the political status of the multinational investors
5. list the arguments for taxing or for subsidizing DFI based on considerations of market power, externalities, and politics

Key Terms

Appropriability theory
this explains DFI as a way for a firm to appropriate the potential gains from its firm-specific advantages; the firm seeks to earn returns from some key productive inputs.

Direct foreign investment (DFI)
any flow of lending to, or purchase of ownership in, a foreign enterprise that is largely owned (at least 10 percent ownership, according to U.S. balance of payments accountants) by residents of the investing country. Direct investment implies full or partial control of the enterprise and, usually, physical presence by foreign firms or individuals in the host country.

Firm-specific advantages
managerial, technical, and marketing skills and patents that accrue to a particular firm and help it overcome the inherent native advantage of local rival firms.

Foreign defensive investment
setting up enterprises abroad, that are less profitable than the home country's production facilities, with the stated purpose of shutting out competition from other countries.

Hymer view
the thesis that DFI is a way for an oligopolist to stifle competition and protect its market power. The Hymer view assumes imperfect competition in product markets.

Multinational firm
a firm that owns and controls enterprises in more than one country. The parent company is based in the home-country source for the DFI and has one or more foreign branches or subsidiaries. (These firms are also referred to as multinational corporations [MNCs] and multinational enterprises [MNEs].)

Worldwide unitary taxation
mandates that a multinational firm pay profits taxes to a state or country based on the average share of its world property, payroll, and sales in the state or country. The application of such a principle preempts transfer pricing and allows countries to collect what they consider to be their fair share of a multinational's profits.

Warm-up Questions

True or False? Explain.

1. T/F As of 1992, the United States was the biggest source country for direct foreign investment, and the majority of American DFI was in Europe.

2. T/F Hymer's view explains the potential political threat of multinational firms to a host-country government.

3. T/F The appropriability theory is not an appropriate explanation of DFI if the firm does not have any firm-specific advantages.

4. T/F Even though DFI raises some political concerns for host countries, these countries may still be better off subsidizing DFI rather than taxing it.

5. T/F Direct foreign investment is essentially a flow of financial capital.

Multiple Choice

1. A five percent ownership participation by General Motors in an Irish software developer is considered
   a. direct foreign investment
   b. portfolio investment
   c. official aid
   d. short-term lending

2. Apple Computer's direct investment in computer assembly plants in Singapore is
   a. mainly motivated by the desire to evade U.S. corporate taxes
   b. an example of defensive investment
   c. explained by Hymer's model of imperfect competition
   d. explained by the appropriability theory

3. When DFI brings positive technological externalities with it, a case can made for
   a. the source country subsidizing outward-bound DFI
   b. both the source country and the host country taxing DFI
   c. both the source country and the host country subsidizing DFI
   d. the host country subsidizing inward-bound DFI

4. Firms who engage in DFI are mostly from industries characterized by
   a. perfect competition
   b. imperfect competition
   c. pure monopoly
   d. cartels

5. In order to evade a higher tax burden, a multinational may engage in transfer pricing, in which the subsidiary in the high-tax country will
   a. be overcharged when buying from a less-taxed foreign branch
   b. be overpaid when selling to a less-taxed branch
   c. be charged above-market rates on loans it makes to the less-taxed branch
   d. borrow from the less-taxed branch at below-market interest rates

Problems

1. Some telephone executives in Leinster want to set up a telephone manufacturing concern in Saxony.

    a. Why might they prefer to do this rather than just exporting telephones to Saxony?

    b. What factors would be important in deciding whether they undertake portfolio investment in a Saxon firm, or direct foreign investment to set up their own plant in Saxony?

    c. What arguments could the Leinster government use to either encourage or discourage a flow of DFI out of Leinster?

    d. What arguments could the Saxon government use to either encourage or discourage a flow of DFI into Saxony?

2. To attract direct foreign investment some developing countries have offered to exempt the income of new enterprises from corporate taxes for three to six years — a technique referred to as a "tax holiday." Other common incentives include granting monopoly rights or setting up barriers to competing foreign products. How effective do you think these measures are?

3. Early in this book it was suggested that trade between countries is a substitute for factors' mobility between countries. How do the past three chapters on international factor mobility confirm or contradict that hypothesis?

4. In the 1980s the United States attracted more direct foreign investment than any other country. Why?

Discussion Topics

1. Why does most direct foreign investment go from one industrialized country into another industrialized country?

2. Could DFI be thought of as an inflow of both capital *and* skilled labor?

Final Thought

Capital as such is not evil; it is its wrong use that is evil.

— Mohandas Gandhi, 1937

THE WALL STREET JOURNAL
January 23, 1995

Foreign Capital Holds Key in Southeast Asia

By Marcus W. Brauchli

SINGAPORE — Is it possible to have too much money?

For Southeast Asia's economic dynamos, the answer could be yes — if it is foreign capital. Like high-octane fuel, heavy international investment in factories, stocks and bonds has been revving the economies of Malaysia, Thailand and Indonesia perilously close to overheating.

Even the region's First World bastion, Singapore, is uneasy: Hefty capital inflows are putting intense upward pressure on its currency. Finance Minister Richard Hu was almost relieved this month when investors, spooked by Mexico's financial crisis, started selling the Singapore dollar. "We'd like to see it soften a bit," he says.

That smaller capital inflows could be a tonic for Southeast Asia suggests how alluring the region has become for foreign investors. With Hong Kong reverting to China in two years, Singapore and its bustling Southeast Asian neighbors have emerged as a distinct, fast-growing marketplace for multinationals. International Business Machines this year will open a $100 million disk-drive factory in Singapore. General Motors has put at least that much into plants in Thailand and Indonesia.

With a population of 190 million, Indonesia is the region's biggest and favorite destination for foreign capital. Approved foreign investment last year totaled $24 billion — triple the level of a year earlier. That growth far outpaced the country's economic expansion of about 6.8%. The numbers may be even bigger this year; Exxon just agreed to develop a natural-gas field that could entail $35 billion in investment.

Such huge sums bloat Southeast Asia's economies. In Malaysia, the money supply is swelling a quarter faster than the economy, whose growth last year topped 8% for the

Hot Markets
Growth and inflation in selected Southeast Asian countries

Country	'94 GDP Growth	Latest CPI
Indonesia	6.8%	9.0%
Malaysia	8.5	3.8
Singapore	10.0	3.7
Thailand	8.1	5.0

Source: Smith New Court Securities, Ltd. estimates

seventh straight year. The huge cash overhang, says David W. Carbon, an economist at J.P. Morgan, could unleash a growth-eroding bout of inflation.

Foreign investment also spurs inflation by generating such a plethora of jobs that wages start to climb. In booming Thailand, where unemployment is negligible, workers generally spend their rising earnings, spurring price increases. Though the economy grew at about 8.1% last year — up only slightly from 7.8% in 1993 — inflation rose by some two-thirds to about a 5% pace.

What worries Singapore Finance Minister Hu is that a bulge of money and inflation may create a bubble. At the high end of Singapore's property market, some prices have doubled or more in a year. He believes that asset inflation such as the property and stock booms that collapsed in Tokyo and Hong Kong in the past five years is "really something to worry about."

But despite the risk of overheating, nobody wants to turn away foreign capital — or see it scared off by an event like the Mexico currency crisis. Without those funds, Southeast Asia might not enjoy a sustained economic boom.

In a recent issue of Foreign Affairs, Stanford economist Paul Krugman says the "miracle" of Asia's rapid economic growth was attained through increased mobilization of resources — chiefly capital and labor — not through gains in productivity. By contrast, the U.S. and other developed economies derive much of their growth from greater productivity each year. Because Southeast Asia has marshaled most of its capital and labor already, Prof. Krugman writes, it may have trouble keeping up its high growth rates.

Not necessarily, rejoins Lee Tsao Yuan, a deputy director of Singapore's Institute of Policy Studies, who a decade ago pioneered the trail Prof. Krugman is following. By drawing in foreign capital, she says, Singapore and other Southeast Asian countries can continue to flourish even as they train workers and bolster their productivity.

"Southeast Asia's success . . . is really a reflection that openness to international trade and investment are policies that work," she says. Since the mid-1980s, she says, Singapore's economy is producing more with less. "While I agree one cannot grow at 11% or 12% forever, the growth experience of Asia . . . has shown that maybe a country can grow faster than what has been the historical experience of Western countries."

Moreover, by raising productivity, countries can attract more foreign capital which itself adds to growth. "As long as you keep a surplus in your capital account, [achieving] growth is not a terrible problem," notes

Friedrich Wu, an economist at Singapore's DBS Bank. Finance Minister Hu says foreign capital has kept Singapore's economy expanding at a 10%-plus rate for two years, almost double what he reckons would be possible without the foreign lift.

In the end, economists say, the real question Southeast Asian leaders may have to ask isn't is it possible to have too much money, but can they wean their countries from the easy — but potentially volatile — growth it brings?

Source: *The Wall Street Journal*, January 23, 1995. Reprinted with permission of THE WALL STREET JOURNAL, 1995 Dow Jones & Company, Inc. All rights reserved worldwide.

ANSWERS

Solutions to Warm-up Questions and Odd-Numbered Problems

Chapter 2

True/False
1. False
2. True
3. False: the producers of the domestic import-competing good see lower prices for their goods.
4. True
5. True: but both are rare, at times!

Multiple Choice
1. a
2. a
3. c
4. a
5. c

Problems

1. a. The equilibrium price of bread in Leinster is 0.6 telephones per loaf; in Saxony the price is 0.2 telephones per loaf.

   b. Yes. Since the Saxon bread price is less than the price of bread in Leinster, there will be an incentive for Leinster bread consumers to buy Saxon bread; Saxon bread producers have an incentive to sell in Leinster where the price is higher.

   c.

   Figure 2.1c

   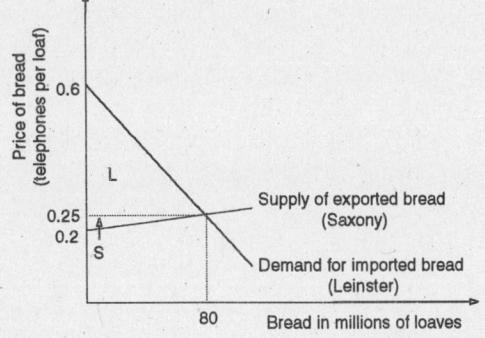

   d. The equilibrium trade price must be the same in both countries (that's why it is the price at which they trade with each other): it is 0.25 telephones per loaf. Notice that this is the price where import demand from Leinster equals export supply from Saxony.

   e. At the trade price of 0.25 telephones per loaf, excess demand for bread in Leinster equals 80 million loaves — exactly the amount of excess supply in Saxony at the trade price.

   f. Looking at Figure 2.1, consumer gain in Leinster = a + b + c; producer loss in Leinster = a; consumer loss in Saxony = d; producer gain in Saxony = d + e.

   g. Bread consumers in Leinster and bread producers in Saxony will be happy about the opening of free trade. However, Leinster bread producers will not be happy (they are undercut by cheaper imported bread from Saxony) nor will Saxon bread consumers (they used to pay a lower price before the people in Leinster became able to buy the bread).

   h. The net gain to Leinster is the area labelled "L"; this is equal in magnitude to the net gain b + c from the domestic graph. The net gain to Saxony is the shaded area labelled "S"; this is equal in magnitude to the net gain e from the domestic graph.

   i. The country with the less elastic trade curve (usually the result of less elastic domestic supply and demand curves) will gain the most from trade. In our case, this is Leinster. It has been able to "drive" the price it pays for bread far below the price it had to pay for domestic bread.

   j. The losses from closing trade would just be the net gain the countries had obtained from free trade: "L" in Leinster, and "S" in Saxony.

3. They would lose 5 cents per board-foot on the 48 million board-feet they continue to sell at home *plus* the revenue impact of selling four million less board-feet in total. This sums to a loss of $2.5 billion.

Chapter 3

True/False
1. True: that was David Ricardo's point.
2. False!
3. False: it is the *relative* abundance that matters.
4. True
5. True

Multiple Choice
1. d
2. d
3. a
4. a
5. b

Problems
1. a. Leinster has an absolute advantage in both goods since it takes less labor to make bread *and* less labor to make telephones than in Saxory.

   b. Leinster has a comparative advantage in telephones: in Leinster, the price of one telephone is 5/3 loaf of bread; in Saxony, the price of one telephone is 5 loaves of bread. At the same time, Saxony has a comparative advantage in bread: in Saxony, the price of one loaf of bread is 1/5 telephone; in Leinster the price of one loaf of bread is 3/5 telephone.

   c. With free trade, the international price will fall somewhere between the two pre-trade prices. Thus, 5/3 loaf ≤ one telephone ≤ 5 loaves and 1/5 telephone ≤ one loaf ≤ 3/5 telephone. (You might look back to Problem 2.1: the trade price turned out to be 1/4 telephone per loaf of bread.)

   d. If trade is stopped, the prices in each country revert to their pre-trade levels.

3. Look at Figure S3.3 below:

Figure S3.3

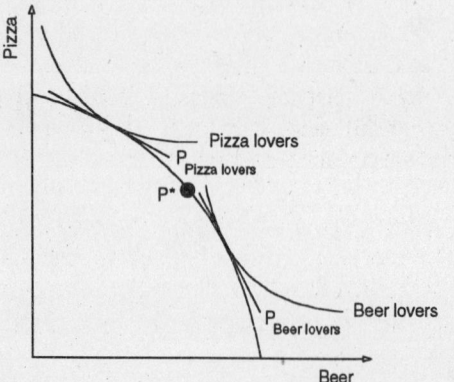

The PPCs of the two countries can be represented by the one drawn. The country with tastes skewed toward pizza will have a higher pre-trade price for pizza (in terms of beer) than the country that has tastes skewed toward beer. The two countries should trade: the pizza-loving country will produce more beer and export it in exchange for pizza; the beer-loving country will produce more pizza and export it in exchange for beer. We get the interesting result that trade causes each country to specialize *less* in production — at some middle point like P* — and trade for the preferred good.

Chapter 4

True/False
1. True
2. False: just the reverse is the case, with owners of scarce factors seeing their incomes fall.
3. True: that's why Joan Robinson will never receive the prize for her work on imperfect competition. Proof that it is an imperfect world.
4. True
5. True: unskilled labor is used relatively more in the import-competing industries in the United States.

Multiple Choice
1. c
2. a
3. b
4. a
5. d

Problems
1. When trade opens up, the price of bread falls in Leinster and rises in Saxony. At the same time, the price of telephones rises in Leinster and falls in Saxony.

   a. In the short run, Leinster's bread workers see their wages fall, while telephone workers see their wages rise. In the long run, *all* workers see their wages rise as labor moves out of the declining bread industry and into the labor-intensive telephone industry.

   b. In the short run, Saxony's bread workers see their wages rise, while telephone workers see their wages fall. In the long run, *all* workers see their wages fall as labor is released from the labor-intensive telephone industry but is not needed in great amounts in the land-intensive bread industry.

c. If the factor price equalization theorem holds, the wages of the abundant workers in Leinster should rise to meet the falling wages of the scarce workers in Saxony. (Similarly, the scarce land in Leinster will earn less than before, and the abundant land in Saxony will earn more than before — and they should equal each other if FPE holds.)

3. a. If a factor is immobile between sectors, its income is a function of whether it is employed in the price-rising industry or in the price-falling industry. So capital owners, landowners, and laborers in the computer sector would gain; capital owners, landowners and laborers in the wheat sector would lose.

b. If a factor is mobile between sectors, its income is a function of whether it is the country's relatively scarce factor or relatively abundant factor. So all capital owners would gain and all landowners would lose. Labor would migrate from the losing sector to the gaining sector.

5. a. Bread is more labor-intensive than wine: 4/9 of the cost of making bread is labor cost whereas only 1/3 of the cost of making wine is labor cost. Conversely, wine is capital-intensive.

b. If inputs cannot compete between sectors, everybody in the wine sector is likely to gain and everybody employed in the bread sector is likely to lose. Since the price of bread is being pushed down, consumers of bread will celebrate the opening of trade. But since the price of wine rose, consumers of wine will commiserate with the breadmakers.

Chapter 5
True/False
1. True: this would be a reverse of immiserizing growth.
2. True
3. True! Ask the people who raised you.
4. False: export-biased growth tends to raise trade volumes.
5. True

Multiple Choice

1. c
2. c
3. a
4. d
5. b

Problems

1.

Figure S5.1

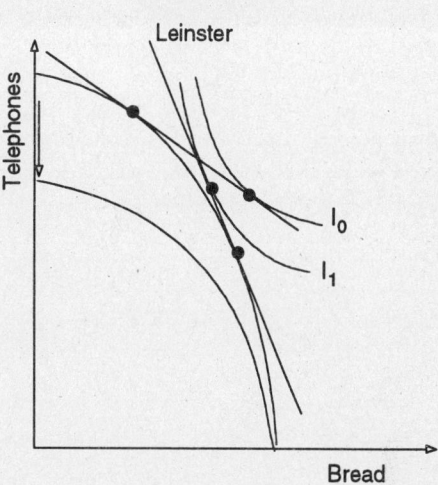

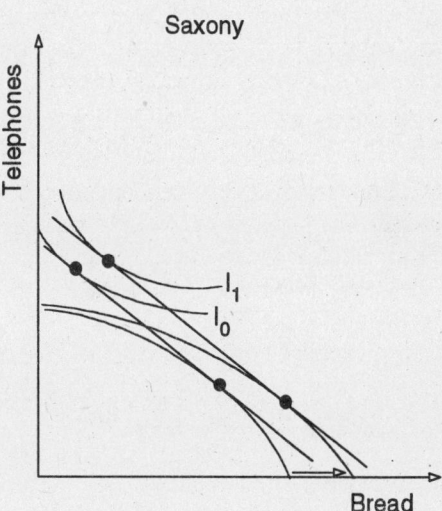

a. Saxony is experiencing export-biased growth. We would expect that the volume of trade between Saxony and Leinster would increase — the Saxon telephone industry will decline (Rybczynski) and they will import more telephones from Leinster instead.

b. Since Saxony is a "small country" we would not expect the trade price of bread to change. Consequently, Saxony will be able to reach a higher level of utility as the new indifference curve suggests.

c. Leinster is experiencing "export-biased decline." We would expect that the volume of trade between Leinster and Saxony would fall. In a reverse of immiserizing growth, the level of economic welfare in "large country" Leinster *could* rise: the terms of trade would move in its favor as the supply of telephones (and, likely, demand for bread) fell.

This is a good example of how economic analysis can miss the broader picture: although "economic welfare" in Leinster rises, it is the result of a human catastrophe.

3. a. According to H-O, Peru will export land-intensive and unskilled-labor intensive goods; it will import capital-intensive and skilled-labor intensive goods.

b. To achieve import-biased growth (to replace imports with domestically-produced substitutes), Peru would need to have an increase in its endowments of capital and skilled labor. If Peru were a large country, this would turn the terms of trade in its favor: the price of imports in particular would fall as the demand for them from Peru declines. As you might have guessed, however, there are few (if any) such goods for which Peru could have an impact on the price.

Chapter 6

True/False
1. True
2. False: IIT is more prevalent in imperfectly competitive industries.
3. False: economies of scale reduce average costs.
4. True
5. True: at least in athletic footwear!

Multiple Choice
1. b
2. b
3. b
4. b
5. b

Problems
1. Under a situation of identical tastes and production possibilities, we could not turn to standard theory for why countries would trade (ie., differences in pre-trade price ratios arising from different factor endowments or different tastes).

Instead, countries could gain by trading with each other if the goods that they produce and buy are subject to economies of scale. For example: Suppose that both the United States and Germany can produce ships or airplanes under the same conditions of increasing returns to scale in both ships and airplanes. Suppose that they both had the same tastes, causing each country to "consume" ships and airplanes. The countries could gain from trade if one country specialized in ships and the other specialized in planes. With all conditions identical, they could even flip a coin to see who specializes in ships.

Figure S6.1

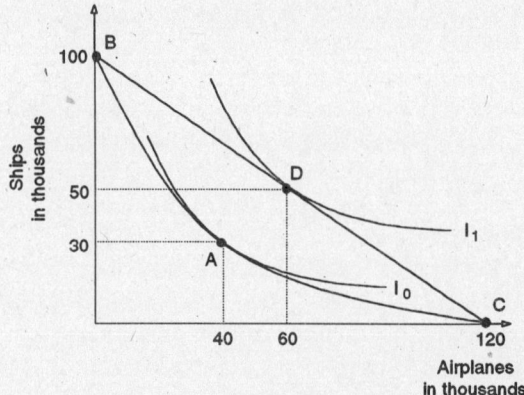

In Figure S6.1, both countries could gain as they move from the common production point A to point B for the ship specialist and point C for the airplane specialist. The two countries could then consume at point D. (Notice that this case is somewhat like the situation in problem 3.3.)

3. If there are internal or external economies of scale, trade could be beneficial even to U.S. computer buyers. You might also think of intellectual and political justifications for the opening of trade.

5. IIT share = 1 − [sum of absolute value of (X−M)]/(sum of X+M)
   a. With Japan: IIT = 1 − (|75−60| + |70 − 150|)/(145 + 210); IIT = 0.817.
   With Sudan: IIT = 1 − (|50−55| + |70 − 0|)/(115 + 55); IIT = 0.559.
   b. The IIT with Japan is higher than the IIT with Sudan. This is likely to be true "in the real world" because IIT is largely based on a rising demand for knowledge-intensive luxuries. The

higher are the incomes of consumers, the greater the proliferation of near-substitute varieties of goods and services. Higher incomes make it possible to value variety for its own sake. Thus, since the United States and Japan have higher income levels, they are buying each other's version of similar products (e.g., cars, entertainment equipment).

Chapter 7
True/False
1. False: a tariff may be welfare-increasing for a large country, but such a tariff reduces world welfare.
2. False: that is a characteristic of an *ad valorem* tariff.
3. True, until chapters 9 and 10 explore some counter-examples.
4. False: but you may think so at the end of the sections on tariffs.
5. True

Multiple Choice
1. a
2. d
3. c
4. d
5. d

Problems
1. In Figure 7.1, the tariff that reduces imports from 80 million loaves to 40 million loaves raises the price in Leinster to 0.44 telephones per loaf, and reduces the price in Saxony (the "world price") to 0.23 telephones per loaf.

   a. Consumer surplus in Leinster falls by a+b+c+d; consumer surplus in Saxony rises by e+f.

   b. Producer surplus in Leinster rises by a; producer surplus in Saxony falls by e+f+g+h+j.

   c. In Leinster, to get the net change in welfare, you must take into account that the government collects tariff revenues equal to c+h. So, the net change in welfare is (producer gain+government revenue) − (consumer loss) = h−(b+d). Notice that since the part of the government revenues coming from abroad (h) do *not* exceed the deadweight losses (b+d), this tariff is not optimal for Leinster.

   In Saxony, the tariff is a clear loss. The loss of producer surplus e+f+g+h+j far outweighs the gain in consumer surplus e+f.

   d. "World" welfare is reduced by the sum of the deadweights. On Figure S7.1, this shows up as the triangles, b+d and g+j.

Figure S7.1

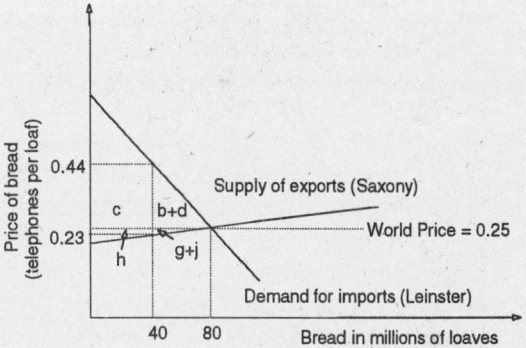

3. a. The net U.S. national gain = the rectangle of foreign-price markdown [(3.00−2.50) x 300 million] − the triangle of deadweight loss [1/2 x (4.00−3.00) x (1200m−300m)] for a total net loss of $300 million in this case.

   b. Unit value added with the tariff = $4.00−$2.00 = $2.00.
   Unit value added without the tariff = $3.00−$2.00 = $1.00. The effective rate of protection for the beer industry, then, is (2.00−1.00)/1.00 = 100%.

5. If the effective rate of protection on clothing is less than zero, this indicates that Pakistan's trade policies *reduce* the value added per unit of clothing. This can occur if tariffs on the inputs to clothing (ie, textiles) are higher than the tariffs on imports of clothing. To afford the clothing industry a higher rate of protection, either tariffs on imported textiles should be reduced, or tariffs on imported clothing should be raised.

Chapter 8
True/False
1. True
2. False
3. True: the U.S. government collected much of its revenues from tariffs for the first 50 to 100 years of its history.
4. True: as long as they auction the quota licenses.
5. True!

Multiple Choice
1. c
2. b
3. c
4. b
5. a

Problems
1. You should refer back to figures 7.1 and S7.1. The illustration of a tariff that reduced imports to 40 million loaves is the same as a quota or VER that reduced imports to 40 million loaves.

   a. A quota can be a very effective way of reducing imports; it puts strict limits on quantities whereas tariffs do not. The quota licenses can be auctioned to the highest bidders (thus gaining revenues of c+h) or can be passed out as political favors — buying votes or "good behavior." The Leinster government should be aware that a domestic bread monopolist may arise under the protection of the quota, and this will be a welfare-reducing event.

   b. Leinster could try to force a VER of 40 million loaves on Saxony. In this case, either the first-at-the-dock Saxon exporters will get the windfall from the higher price paid for their bread in Leinster, or the Saxon government could auction licenses to export and capture the revenues (c+h) for itself. In either case, the Leinster government doesn't get any revenues when it implements a VER, but it gets to *appear* as if it still promotes free trade!

3.
Figure S8.3

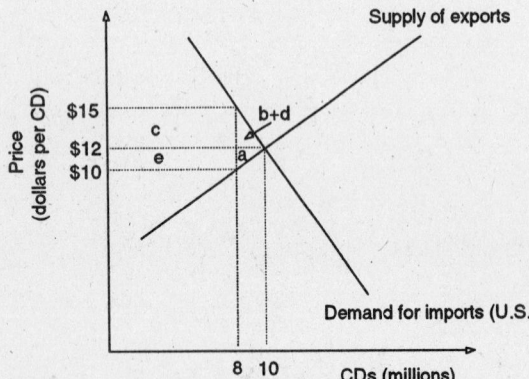

   a. With the import quota, the United States gains (e−b−d) = 13, assuming quota rents are kept in the United States. With the VER, the United States gains (−c−b−d) = −27. From a "one-dollar, one-vote" point of view, the import quota is better for the United States.

   b. With the import quota, the exporting firms (or countries) gain (−e−a) = −18. With the VER, the exporting firms (or countries) gain (c−a) = 22. So an exporter would prefer a VER to an import quota.

Chapter 9
True/False
1. True
2. True: though they are "first" in the hearts of die-hard patriots.
3. False: the tariff may be better than nothing, but some other subsidy related to the learning is better than the tariff.
4. True!
5. True

Multiple Choice
1. d
2. c
3. d
4. a
5. b

Problems
1. There would definitely be a national welfare loss for Saxony from a telephone tariff: there would be both a production effect and a consumption effect which would not be offset by any terms-of-trade effect.

   To justify incurring that welfare loss, the Saxon government could make an infant industry argument. Or, it could point to the telephone industry as somehow strategic or important in national defense (the ability to communicate is crucial to a country). There are also important spillover benefits from light industry (that would not occur in agricultural processing) such as electronic innovation. Of course, the national pride issue might come up (as it has in the electronics sector in the United States).

   If Saxony did not want to place a tariff on imported telephones (perhaps because it might fear retaliation from Leinster), it could subsidize the domestic telephone industry or provide funds for research and development in telecommunications. This, of course, will mean that the Saxon government will have to come up with funds rather than collecting revenues as in a tariff.

3. The import tariff might be better than doing nothing. That depends on how high the tariff barrier is, among other things. But the specificity rule warns that something else is probably better than the tariff in this case. Since the problem is that firms lacked the capital to see themselves through to the later high efficiency situation, then lend funds to them. Alternatively, a temporary production subsidy is virtually as good as a loan, although raising the tax rates to get revenue for the subsidy might have negative incentives elsewhere in the economy.

Chapter 10
True/False
1. True
2. True
3. False: except insofar as countries go to war over trade!
4. True, but decreasingly so.
5. True: we only get a transfer of revenues from the subsidizing country to the dutying country.

Multiple Choice
1. c
2. b
3. a
4. d
5. c

Problems

1.

Figure S10.1

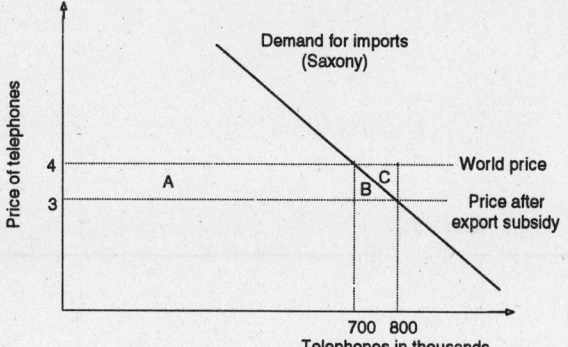

If Leinster subsidizes exports of telephones, it will reduce the "world" price from 4 loaves per telephone to 3 loaves per telephone. Leinster will lose area A+B+C; Saxony will gain area A+B. The world as a whole will lose area C: this represents wasted resources as Saxony buys "too many" telephones at a price less than the cost of production.

3. Assuming that the domestic price in the exporting country is the price at which TVs left the factory destined for domestic distribution, then both Phillips and Sharp are guilty of dumping: 250>200 for Phillips; 325>310 for Sharp. RCA is not guilty of dumping because 300 = 300.

   Alternatively, if you interpret "average unit cost" as the price at which TVs leave the factory for domestic distribution, then only Phillips is guilty (250>200), while Sharp is not (300<310) and RCA is not (295<300).

Chapter 11
True/False
1. True
2. False: there may be welfare-decreasing trade diversion.
3. False: gains would be smaller.
4. True
5. True

Multiple Choice
1. c
2. b
3. c
4. b
5. b

Problems
1. With no tariffs between them, Leinster and Saxony could be considered a free trade area. To be a customs union, however, they would have to have a common tariff against other countries of the world — and you haven't been told that any countries exist in this "world" *except* Leinster and Saxony!

   Leaving aside the issue of the external tariff, Leinster and Saxony could be a common market *if* they allow the factors of production to move freely between the countries. For the two countries to comprise an economic union, however, the governments in Leinster and Saxony would have to develop joint fiscal and monetary policies.

   You might want to speculate on the possibility of an agricultural nation joining together with an industrial nation: are there factors other than economic ones that could make this problematic? beneficial?

3. For an embargo to be effective (in economic terms), we want the trade ban to reduce welfare in the target country without causing much welfare loss to the people of the embargoing country. This will be the case if import demand in the target country is low (inelastic) and export supply from the embargoing country is high (elastic). If, indeed, import demand in China is high, the embargo will be an economic failure.

You might want to think about what types of traded goods would be "useful weapons" to use for sanctions.

5. a. $P_{wheat} = 70$. This is a case of trade creation since higher cost British wheat ($P_{wheat} = 100$) is replaced by lower-cost imports from the EC.

b. This will lead to trade diversion. Britain had imported wheat from Canada at $P_{wheat} = 65$, and was able to collect a tariff of 16.25 per unit. Now, Britain will pay 70 and will be collecting no tariff revenues.

c. Canada has the lowest cost when the tariff is 25%, so Britain should import wheat from Canada.

Chapter 12

True/False
1. True
2. False: in 1911, fur seals were the objects of protection.
3. False: much of the conflict is between the "green" developed countries and the developing countries.
4. False: it doesn't matter to whom the property rights are assigned, as long as they are assigned to one of the parties.
5. True: as long as that world government assigns property rights.

Multiple Choice
1. e
2. c
3. a
4. d
5. c

Problems
1. Since this "greenhouse" problem is between only two countries, it might be resolved by some international negotiation, or by levying a tax on all bread producers (including those in Leinster) and using the proceeds to develop new filters for bakeries or new gas-free yeast strains.

If international negotiation with Saxony fails, Leinster might place a tariff on bread imports. This is a second-best solution for Leinster, and it is likely to annoy the Saxons, who might retaliate.

3. No Montreal Protocol has stepped in to address the greenhouse/CO_2 problem for a number of reasons. Among others: there are too many "producers" of carbon dioxide around the globe; the activities that release carbon dioxide are harder to do without than CFCs; and the damage done by greenhouse gases are spread unpredictably around the globe.

Chapter 13

True/False
1. False: remember that "developed" refers to variables other than simply wealth or income.
2. False: they can be quite different.
3. True
4. False: just as in the "optimal tariff", world welfare is reduced by cartels.
5. False: it appears that the income levels may be diverging.

Multiple Choice
1. b
2. b
3. d
4. d
5. b

Problems
1. a. Among other reasons, the Saxon government could talk about the strategic importance of telecommunications equipment, and the spillover benefits gained from a light industry sector. In addition, Saxony might want to reduce her reliance on trade in bread since Engel's Law suggests that food producers stand to lose in a world of increasing incomes (the income elasticity of demand for food is less than one). Arguments against industrialization include

negative externalities of urban-industrial areas; loss of traditional occupations in farming, and the possibility that the "infant industry" will never mature.

b. A subsidy to Saxon telephone manufacturers would be a better idea than a tariff or a quota since Saxony could avoid the consumption deadweight loss. A subsidy assumes, however, that the Saxon government's coffers have enough in them to fund the subsidy.

3. Given $d = -0.5$; $s_o = 1.0$; $c = 0.5$, optimal cartel markup $t^* = c / [\, |d - s_o(1-c)| \,] = 50\%$.

Chapter 14

True/False
1. False: in fact, the smaller the number of people in the group, the more effectively they may organize themselves to ask for protection.
2. False: if NPC>1, it indicates protection of producer interests.
3. True
4. False: free riding is more likely within large groups
5. False: tariff escalation.

Multiple Choice
1. a
2. d
3. a
4. b
5. d

Problems
1. Some things to consider:
    Bakers are in the minority in Leinster. They would find it easier to organize than Leinster's bread consumers, and the free rider problem would be smaller. As the minority, the bakers might engender sympathy from the rest of the population.
    Leinster is a larger country (in absolute terms) than Saxony, and might find Saxony a weak target for a bread tariff.
    Before its "industrial revolution" Leinster probably had a domestic bread industry. The remaining bakers in Leinster can appeal to this historical tradition.
    If the remaining bakers in Leinster are spread across the country (as they would be if they were the remnants of a local bakery tradition), they would be able to voice their concerns in all the electoral districts of Leinster.

3. a. e.r.p. = $[P_{producer} - P_{world} -$ (input cost markup due to gov't policies)]/(unit value added at free trade prices); e.r.p. = $(10 - 20 - 2)/15 = -0.68$;
NPC = $(P_{prod}) /(P_{world}) = 0.50$;
PSE = $[(P_{prod} - P_{world}) +$ (gov't subsidies $-$ input price markup)]/ P_{world};
PSE = $[10 - 20 + (1 - 2)]/20 = -0.55$.

b. Since NPC < 1, agricultural producers are taxed rather than subsidized.

c. Relative to the NPC, the erp has the advantage of taking into account the effects of government policy on the prices of farm inputs.

d. PSE has the advantage of its greater comprehensiveness in capturing the effects of government policy on agricultural incomes, even though it omits some important effects.

e. Since agricultural producers are taxed (NPC < 1) this country is probably a lower income country.

Chapter 15

True/False
1. False: a net debtor is a country that has had mostly negative net foreign investment in the past, not necessarily this year.
2. True
3. False
4. True: since $Y = C + I + G + (X-M)$, when G increases, $(X-M)$ must decrease.
5. True?

Multiple Choice
1. a
2. b
3. d
4. c
5. a

Problems
1. a. We know that $Y = C + I_d + G + (X-M)$ so that for Leinster, $Y = 60 + 15 + 15 + (20 - M)$. Imports (M) from Saxony into Leinster are 10 billion lira.

b. Since Leinster is running a trade surplus with Saxony (exports from Leinster exceed imports into Leinster by 10 billion lira), Leinster is "lending" to Saxony. Saxony is paying for the extra telephones it imports by sending Leinster an IOU for 10 billion lira or by giving Leinster title to assets worth 10 billion lira.

3. The only credit item for the current account is (c): the sale of weapons to the Bosnians.

5. Foreign investments in the United States = (106 − 887.5 − 33.7) which totals a U.S. liability position of $815.2 billion.

Chapter 16
True/False
1. False: to purchase the imports, we supply dollars in exchange for francs.
2. False: intervention is more prevalent under pegged rates.
3. True
4. True (unless you are Japanese and are bidding at Sotheby's!)
5. True

Multiple Choice
1. c
2. b
3. b
4. c
5. a

Problems
1. a. The equilibrium exchange rate is 100 scudos per lira, or Ss 100 / Ll.

b. Since this is a nominal "bilateral" exchange rate, just invert it (or yourself) to find that the exchange rate from Leinster's point of view is 0.01 Ll / Ss.

c. You would expect the supply of lira in exchange for scudos to increase, shifting the supply curve out to the right and so pushing the exchange rate down. Thus, it would take fewer scudos to buy a lira, or a lira would not exchange for as many scudos. This is an appreciation of the scudo and a depreciation of the lira.

d. If the minister had wanted to keep the exchange rate at Ss 100 / Ll, she would have to satisfy the excess demand for scudos that would arise when the supply of lira increased. (In fixed exchange rate terminology, the scudo would be undervalued at the old exchange rate of Ss 100 / Ll.) This would require the Saxon minister of finance to sell scudos and buy up lira.

3. a. Since the French supply of francs would fall, we would expect the $/F exchange rate to rise: the franc would appreciate and the dollar would depreciate.

b. The American demand for francs would rise, so the exchange rate would rise: the franc would appreciate and the dollar would depreciate.

c. The American demand for francs would rise, so the franc would appreciate and the dollar would depreciate.

d. The French supply of francs would rise, so the franc would depreciate and the dollar would appreciate.

e. The American demand for francs will fall (as American speculators dump the franc) and the exchange rate would fall too: the franc would depreciate, in a "self-fulfilling prophesy."

5. The "route to follow" would be:
Tokyo yen to New York dollars to Munich marks to Tokyo yen
In Tokyo: Take the million yen and trade them for dollars, receiving $10,000.
In New York: Take the $10,000 and trade them for marks, receiving DM30,000.
In Munich: Take the DM30,000 and trade them for yen, receiving Y2.1 million.
You would end up with a profit of 1.1 million yen for being so observant and taking advantage of triangular arbitrage.

Chapter 17
True/False
1. False: the forward rate *may* approximate what investors *think* the future spot rate will be, but the actual future spot rate will be what it will be. ("Que será, será.")
2. False: speculation may occur through both short and long positions.
3. True
4. False: at least insofar as you can see many flattened hedgehogs along the roads in England.
5. True

Multiple Choice
1. b
2. a
3. c
4. b
5. d

Problems

1. a. If you sell lira forward (buy scudos forward) you will receive 95 scudos for each of the 10,000 lira, for a total of Ss 950,000.

   b. If your high guess about the future spot rate (Ss 105/ Ll) turns out to be correct, when you sell your 10,000 lira you will receive a total of Ss 1.5 million instead of the guaranteed Ss 950,000 from a forward contract. *But* if the future spot rate turns out to be on the low side, you will get only Ss 850,000.

   c. How much risk do you like in your life? Will you have to work in the bakery the rest of your life to make up the Ss 100,000 you lost? Just how understanding *are* your parents?

3. a. You should sign a contract to buy lira at the forward rate of Ss 100/ Ll. If your guess is correct, you will pay Ss 100 for every lira in 180 days, then take those lira to the spot market and sell them for Ss 120 each. You would make a profit of Ss 20 for each Ss 100 you bet.

   b. You will make positive profits as long as the spot rate that prevails in 180 days is higher than Ss 100 / Ll. You will make losses if the future spot rate turns out to be less than Ss 100 / Ll.

   c. Speculators put their money where their mind is. You have bet that the scudo is going to depreciate over the next 180 days. If there are more like you, the increased demand to purchase lira will push up the forward rate on the lira until it approximates your average guess of Ss 120/ Ll. This is how the forward rate comes to reflect market participants' expectation of the future spot rate.

5. Notice first that the British pound is at a forward discount of 2.5% : $(r_f - r_s)/r_s = (1.95 - 2.00)/2.00 = 0.025$. Also, there is a 3% interest differential in favor of Britain.

   a. The interest differential (the extra you earn by putting your funds in British assets) exceeds the forward discount on the pound (the amount you lose by paying a higher dollar price for the pounds than you will ultimately redeem each of the pounds for). So, it would be a good idea (and a riskless one!) to trade your dollars for pounds today, invest in Britain, and sell the pounds forward.

   With $100, the scheme would go like this: buy 50 pounds with your $100, invest the 50 pounds at a 7% rate, and sell the 53.5 pounds you expect to get for a price of $1.95 each. Expected total return = $104.325.

   If you had "stayed at home" and bought a U.S. asset earning an interest rate of 4%, your total return on an investment of $100 would be $104.00.

   So "going through Britain" would earn you an extra 32.5 cents per dollar invested: not much on a $100 transaction, but a *whole lot* on a million dollar transaction.

   b. You will earn zero profits if the forward discount on the British pound exactly offsets the interest differential in favor of Britain (or against the United States). This is the covered interest parity condition. $(r_f - r_s)/r_s$ should equal approximately -3%.

   Since the spot price is $2.00 / £, the forward rate would have to fall to approximatly $1.94 / £.

Chapter 18

True/False
1. True
2. True
3. True
4. True
5. True

Multiple Choice
1. a
2. a
3. c
4. a
5. b

Problems

1. You would expect that inflation is higher in Saxony than in Leinster. Referring to the purchasing power parity condition, the higher inflation rate in Saxony would require the Saxon scudo to take a downward (depreciating) trend versus the lira. That way, the "cheapening" of the scudo will counterbalance the higher scudo

price tags on Saxon goods, and Saxony can remain competitive.

3. The real exchange rate is equal to $r_s \times P_f / P$. In this case, the real exchange rate is 1.5. PPP does not hold.

5. a. If "k" is smaller, the demand for money is lower.

b. Since the ratio k_f/k rises (assuming credit cards had not also proliferated in Mexico), the exchange rate r_s rises too: the dollar depreciates while the peso appreciates.

Chapter 19
True/False
1. True: this is one of many "self-fulfilling prophesies" in economics.
2. False: the home currency will appreciate.
3. False: the investors predict as accurately as possible.
4. True
5. True, for the word's major currencies.

Multiple Choice
1. d
2. c
3. a
4. d
5. a

Problems
1. a. There will be a rush to purchase scudos before they become more expensive (in terms of lira); this will cause the scudo to appreciate immediately.

b. People will expect a contractionary monetary policy in the near future. They know that this is likely to cause the scudo to appreciate, so they will purchase scudos now (or sell off their lira now) causing the scudo to appreciate now.

c. A higher interest rate in Leinster will attract funds from Saxony. As Saxons exchange scudos for lira (in order to purchase Leinster financial assets), the scudo will depreciate and the lira will appreciate.

d. A surprisingly high trade deficit usually causes the country's currency to depreciate.

e. Real income in Leinster is likely to fall in the wake of the natural disaster. (Exports of telephones will fall and imports of bread to feed the displaced might rise.) This probably will cause the lira to depreciate and the scudo to appreciate.

f. Such political disasters are not uncommon. They usually create uncertainty about the future course of a country, and the currency depreciates.

3. a. The scudo is expected to depreciate by 1%. The interest differential is 0.5% in favor of Saxony. So the expected depreciation is greater than the interest differential, and uncovered interest parity does not hold.

b. For uncovered interest parity to hold:
$(1 + i_L) r_s^e/r_s = (1 + i_S)$
Since $i_L = 0.015$; $i_S = 0.02$; and $r_s^e = $ Ss 101/Ll, the current spot rate r_s must equal Ss 100.5/Ll. That way, the expected depreciation of the scudo (0.5%) is just offset by the extra 0.5% interest earned on Saxon assets.

Chapter 20
True/False
1. True
2. False: swings will be less severe.
3. True
4. True!
5. False: factors other than a "fixed exchange rate" contributed to that stability.

Multiple Choice
1. d
2. a
3. b
4. d
5. d

Problems
1. a. As you can see from the figure, the swings in the demand for lira would cause the exchange rate to vary between a summer high of Ss 125/Ll and a winter low of Ss 75/Ll.

b. Saxony *might* be able to defend an exchange rate

of Ss 100/Ll if they bought up (BC) lira in January and then sold them off to fund the excess demand (CD) for lira in July. For this to work correctly, the Saxon government must be sure that (BC) lira purchased will be enough to satisfy (CD) lira demanded. You should notice that the government would find it very difficult to defend a rate of, for example, Ss 80/ Ll .

There are a number reasons why a country might want to peg its exchange rate. In this case, the pegged exchange rate actually could raise national welfare. In addition, a fixed rate eliminates exchange rate risk, and this may increase economic welfare. And there are national pride arguments that can be made — witness Britain's struggle to return to the earlier gold value of the pound after World War I. (Later chapters will illustrate the usefulness of a fixed exchange rate under certain macroeconomic circumstances.)

3. a. The exchange rate between the dollar and the pound is \$4/£ .

b. If there is a chance that holders of dollars will insist on converting them into gold, the maximum supply of dollars would be \$280 billion. Of course, if no one ever cashes in their dollars, there would be an incentive to increase the money supply as needed to achieve domestic objectives.

Chapter 21

True/False
1. True
2. True: as long as other domestic components of spending do not decline.
3. False: capital may flow out in the long run.
4. True
5. False: the foreign country's goods will become less competitive.

Multiple Choice
1. a
2. c
3. b
4. e
5. a

Problems
1. a. Leinster has a Ll 10.0 billion trade surplus with Saxony.

b. Equation 21.6 from the text shows that saving = domestic investment + foreign investment where foreign investment = (X−M). So saving in Leinster = Ll 25.0 billion.

Notice that this is also equal to our definition of saving as the excess of national income over consumption and government purchases of goods and services.

c. Leinster is lending the excess of its domestic saving (Ll 25 b) over domestic investment (Ll 15 b) in Saxony.

3. a. Saxony has a Ss 1 trillion trade deficit with Leinster. (Notice this is the same as Leinster's Ll 10 billion surplus, but is evaluated at an exchange rate of Ss 100/ Ll .)

b. The open economy multiplier in Saxony = $1/(m+s) = 5$

c. With a multiplier of 5, an increase in domestic investment of Ss 500 billion should lead to an increase in Saxon income of Ss 2.5 trillion.

d. With an increase in income of Ss 2.5 trillion, Saxons will increase their purchases of imports from Leinster by m x (2.5 trillion) or Ss 375 billion. If exports to Leinster are unchanged at Ss 1 trillion, Saxony's trade deficit will increase to Ss 1.375 trillion.

5. a. Figure 21.5 shows that income in this country is \$700 billion.

b. The interest rate is 4.5 % .

c. Since the intersection of the IS and LM curves is above the FE curve, this country has a balance of payments surplus. You can also remind yourself of this by noting that returning to FE would require either an increase in income (which would raise imports and reduce a CA surplus) or a decrease in the interest rate (which would cause a capital outflow and reduce a KA surplus).

d. An increase in consumption spending would shift the IS curve out to the right. The new IS-LM intersection will definitely occur at a higher income level and a higher interest rate. Depending on how far the IS curve shifts, the country could still have a payments surplus (if the IS shifts to intersect LM to the left of A), a balanced payments stance (if the IS shifts to intersect both LM and FE at point A), or a payments deficit (if the IS shifts to intersect LM to the right of point A).

e. An increase in exports would shift both the IS curve and the FE curve to the right. The new IS-LM intersection will definitely occur at a higher interest rate and a higher income level. Depending on the size of the shifts, the IS curve may now intersect LM at A, which would be to the left of the new FE curve and thus represent a payments surplus.

Chapter 22

True/False
1. True
2. True
3. True! (Well, the last part is true.)
4. True
5. True

Multiple Choice
1. a
2. b
3. b
4. c
5. d

Problems
1. a. Using the assignment rule, Saxony should employ tighter fiscal policy to ease the inflationary pressure *and* tighter monetary policy to correct the payments deficit.

   b. Since Saxony is considered a small country (facing elastic import demand and export supply curves from Leinster), a devaluation should improve the trade deficit.

3. a. The IS and FE curves both shift to the left, causing a decrease in income and a payments deficit. This is a dilemma situation for aggregate demand policy. You might consider devaluing the currency.

   b. The IS curve shifts to the right causing an increase in income and a payments deficit. There is an easy aggregate demand response here: cut spending.

   c. The IS curve again shifts to the right, increasing income and causing a payments deficit. Again,

the answer is (theoretically) simple: reduce spending.

   d. The IS and FE curves both shift to the right, causing an increase in income and a payments surplus. This is a dilemma situation for aggregate demand policy. You might consider revaluing the currency.

   e. The FE curve shifts to the right but the IS curve is stable. The country will have a payments surplus and should use expansionary fiscal policy and perhaps a revaluation of the currency.

   f. The LM curve shifts to the left, reducing income, and causing a payments surplus. The easy solution to correct both imbalances is an expansion of the money supply.

Chapter 23

True/False
1. True
2. True
3. False: the shocks would be less disruptive.
4. False
5. True

Multiple Choice
1. b
2. c
3. b
4. b
5. d

Problems
1. a. When the scudo is allowed to float, it will depreciate to correct Saxony's payments deficit.

   b. A depreciation of the scudo would cause an improvement in the trade balance, and this will increase the level of income (and the inflationary pressure) in Saxony. In other words, achieving external balance has pushed the country further away from internal balance.

   c. A contractionary monetary policy will raise interest rates and reduce the level of income in Saxony. The inflow of capital and the reduction in import spending will cause the scudo to appreciate, reducing the level of income even further as the current account worsens.

d. A contractionary fiscal policy will reduce interest rates, causing an outflow of capital. Income will also be reduced, causing a reduction in import purchases. The first effect would cause the scudo to depreciate, while the second effect would cause the scudo to appreciate. As a result, income will not fall much at first, but will eventually be pushed down.

3. a. With a floating exchange rate, a sudden capital outflow from Saxony will cause the scudo to depreciate. The improvement in the trade balance may push income levels up.

b. If the value of the scudo were fixed, however, the capital outflow will be quite disruptive. The capital outflow will put downward pressure on the scudo, and the central bank will have to intervene and buy up scudos. The reduction in the money supply in Saxony will increase the interest rate and this will cause a reduction in income.

5.

Figure S23.5

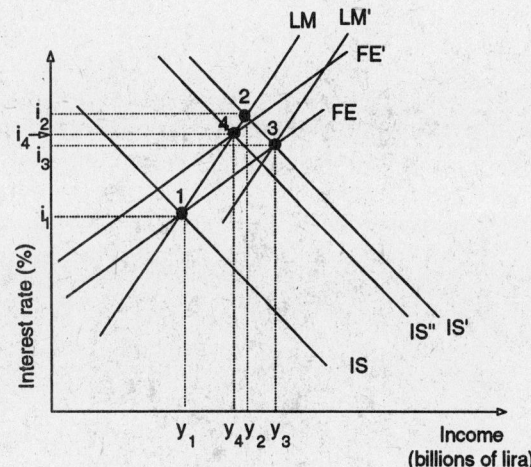

The increase in spending in Leinster pushes the IS curve to the right, causing an increase in income, an increase in interest rates, and a payments surplus at 2. (The latter is the result of high international capital mobility, as illustrated in a rather flat FE curve.)

a. There will be upward pressure on the lira as high interest rates attract funds from Saxony. To defend the exchange rate, Leinster monetary authorities will have to buy scudos and sell lira. This will push the LM curve out to intersect IS and FE at point 3. Income in Leinster will have increased dramatically to Y_3.

b. If intervention to fix the exchange rate is sterilized, Leinster monetary authorities will be conducting open market operations to soak up all the lira. The LM curve will then stay fixed and Leinster will remain at point 2 with the increased income level Y_2.

c. With floating rates, the lira is likely to appreciate and the current account will worsen. This will push the IS and FE curves to the left to intersect the LM curve at point 4. Income in Leinster will have increased only to Y_4.

In this case, with relatively high capital mobility, the Leinster economy is best protected from a spending shock by floating exchange rates. The economy has the largest income swings under fixed exchange rates without sterilization.

(You may wonder why it is disruptive to have the income level increase: If Y_1 were the full-employment level of income for Leinster, any increase in income above that would be inflationary.)

Chapter 24
True/False
1. False: the country will be less stable.
2. True
3. True
4. True
5. False!

Multiple Choice
1. c
2. c
3. c
4. a
5. d

Problems
1. a. To protect itself against international trade shocks generated by Saxony, Leinster should choose a floating exchange rate.

b. To dampen the impact of internal instability (by sending it abroad to Leinster), Saxony should choose a fixed exchange rate.

3. Things you should consider in contemplating a monetary union between the two countries: a common currency does reduce the uncertainty, risks, and transactions costs of dealing with different currencies. On the other hand, a monetary union will take away independent monetary policy in each country. It will also cause spending shocks in one country to be felt in the other country.

Can you think of political aspects of a common currency? Cultural aspects?

Chapter 25
True/False
1. True: their wages tend to rise as the domestic labor supply decreases.
2. True
3. False: the receiving country has a net gain.
4. False: it falls.
5. True!

Multiple Choice
1. b
2. b
3. c
4. c
5. a

Problems
1. a. Imagine that completely free immigration had allowed the equalization of wages between the countries, so that Leinster exported labor to Saxony and the wage in both countries was Ss 12/hour. If immigration is banned wages in Leinster fall back to Ss 10 and wages in Saxony rise back up to Ss 14.

   b. "Stay behind" workers in Leinster will lose as their wage falls with the return of the immigrants. "Stay behind" workers in Saxony will gain as immigrants leave the labor force. The immigrants themselves are clear losers—presumably the reason they immigrated was to improve their economic welfare.

   c. Leinster employers will gain as wages are bid back down again. Saxon employers will lose as wages are bid back up again. Any employers who counted on immigrant workers will definitely lose.

   d. World welfare loss would be the two small shaded triangles bounded by the curves and the Ss 12 wage line.

   Anti-immigrant factions will include Saxon workers and Leinster employers.

3. This is a bit of factor price equalization on its head. Instead of commodities moving, the factors that produce them do. Instead of equating commodity prices on the way to equating wages, we might just have labor move between countries until the wage in both countries is the same.

Chapter 26
True/False
1. True
2. True
3. True
4. False: the U.S. has been a BIG borrower since the 1980s.
5. False

Multiple Choice
1. b
2. a
3. b
4. c
5. d

Problems
1. a. There is an incentive for funds to flow out of Leinster (where the interest rate is only 6%) and into Saxony (where borrowers are offering 8%).

   b. The equilibrium interest rate with these funds flows is where the MPK schedules cross: at approximately 6.6%.

   c. Saxon borrowers will be happy to borrow at a 6.6% rate as opposed to the 8% rate they had been paying; Saxon lenders will be angry at being undercut by the new funds inflows. Saxony as a whole, however, will be better off.

   d. Leinster borrowers now will have to share the wealth of the country with Saxony; this pushes the interest rate up and hurts the Leinster borrowers. Leinster lenders, however, will be happy to get a 6.6% return. Leinster as a whole will be better off.

   e. This kind of international lending raises world welfare. In fact, this model is like a financial goods version of the standard trade model.

3. a. The Saxon debt of Ll 10 billion is initially within the "pay range" indicated on Figure 26.3. The costs of not repaying exceed the benefits of default, so the Saxon government has an incentive *not* to default.

b. When interest rates on the debt rise, Saxony has an incentive to default — at least on Ll 2 billion of the debt.

Chapter 27

True/False
1. True
2. True
3. True
4. True
5. False: DFI usually includes a large component of "human capital" such as management skills and entrepreneurship.

Multiple Choice
1. b
2. d
3. d
4. b
5. a

Problems
1. a. Since we have talked about the possibility of trade barriers between the two countries, perhaps the Leinster telephone execs want to avoid the possibility of being caught in a trade war.

b. DFI would be preferred if the execs are fed up with exchange rate risk; DFI would also be the appropriate policy if the manufacture and distribution of telephones in Saxony requires skills and assets that are unique to Leinster.

Although the Hymer view is not very applicable here (there are only two countries in this world, so who is it that Leinster is trying to preempt in Saxony?), the appropriability theory is, well, appropriate. Telecommunications equipment is typical of the goods that are produced with firm-specific advantages.

c. The Leinster government would certainly want to warn the telephone execs about the possibility of political instability in Saxony, and the resulting likelihood that a plant there could be seized and nationalized. The government might actually try to prevent DFI if the execs were moving their plant to Saxony simply to evade taxes in Leinster. And, importantly, labor in Leinster that would have been employed in the telephone industry will not be pleased about their jobs being "shipped overseas."

d. The Saxon government will actively seek the employment and tax proceeds that would come from hosting a new telephone industry, even if it is controlled by foreign owners. To the extent that there are positive spillover benefits for the Saxon economy, the DFI will also be attractive. However, insofar as the Leinster execs start to throw their weight around the Saxon political arena, the DFI could turn out to be a Trojan horse. (Or is that a Leinster horse?)

3. It's a topical question. We see this happening as capital and labor are moved to produce things like cars within a foreign country's borders and so avoid international trade barriers. Barriers to movement of goods (i.e., trade barriers) may induce factors of production to move instead. So the standard model of commodities (that embody immobile factors of production) moving between countries might be replaced with more internationally mobile factors of production.

This might make you wonder about the whole Heckscher-Ohlin concept of factor endowments. *No, the last 27 chapters were not a waste of your time!*